Scripture, Culture, and Agriculture

An Agrarian Reading of the Bible

ELLEN F. DAVIS

Duke Divinity School

Foreword by Wendell Berry

CAMBRIDGE
UNIVERSITY PRESS

CAMBRIDGE UNIVERSITY PRESS
Cambridge, New York, Melbourne, Madrid, Cape Town, Singapore, São Paulo, Delhi

Cambridge University Press
32 Avenue of the Americas, New York, NY 10013-2473, USA

www.cambridge.org
Information on this title: www.cambridge.org/9780521732239

First published 2009

Printed in the United States of America

A catalog record for this publication is available from the British Library.

Library of Congress Cataloging in Publication Data
Davis, Ellen F.
Scripture, culture, and agriculture : an agrarian reading of the Bible /
Ellen F. Davis.
p.   cm.
Includes bibliographical references and indexes.
ISBN 978-0-521-51834-5 (hardcover : alk. paper) – ISBN 978-0-521-73223-9 (pbk. : alk. paper)
1. Land use – Biblical teaching.   2. Agricultural conservation – Biblical teaching.
3. Bible. O.T. – Criticism, interpretation, etc.   I. Title.
BS1199.L28D39   2009
261.8'8–dc22   2008027119

ISBN   978-0-521-51834-5 hardback
ISBN   978-0-521-73223-9 paperback

For Dwayne, Ellie, Raphael, Luca, Ezra, Isaac, Paiter, and Nicolaas, with thanks and thanksgiving.

Contents

Foreword

This book will be welcomed gladly by readers interested in the Bible's sense of our economic life and our ecological responsibilities. Reading it is a pleasure and a help. Ellen Davis's premise is that "the message of the earliest prophetic writers of the Bible was distinctly 'agrarian.'" Her supporting argument is learned, perceptive, meticulously detailed, and, to my mind, utterly convincing. Professor Davis, moreover, offers her book as a part of the present and ongoing "agrarian conversation" among some writers, some scientists, and the multitude of patriotic citizens now working to build or rebuild local economies of food and farming.

The human situation, as understood by both biblical agrarians and contemporary ones, is about as follows. We are, howbeit only in part, earthly creatures. We have been given the earth to live, not on, but with and from, and only on the condition that we care properly for it. We did not make it, and we know little about it. In fact, we don't, and will never, know enough about it to make our survival sure or our lives carefree. Our relation to our land will always remain, to a significant extent, mysterious. Therefore, our use of it must be determined more by reverence and humility, by local memory and affection, than by the knowledge that we now call "objective" or "scientific." Above all, we must not damage it permanently or compromise its natural means of sustaining itself. The best farmers have always accepted this situation as a given, and they have honored the issues of propriety and scale that it urgently raises.

By recognizing our inescapable dependence and our finally insurmountable ignorance, we open the subject of agriculture (as, I think, all other subjects) to questions of every kind. This book seems to have begun with Professor Davis's realization that

> food production entails at every stage judgments and practices that bear
> directly on the health of the earth and living creatures, on the emotional,

ix

economic, and physical well-being of families and communities, and ultimately on their survival. Therefore, sound agricultural practice depends upon knowledge that is at one and the same time chemical and biological, economic, cultural, philosophical, and (following the understanding of most farmers in most places and times) religious. Agriculture involves questions of value and therefore of moral choice, whether or not we care to admit it.

If, on the contrary, we choose to ignore our dependence and our ignorance, as the agri-industrialists conventionally do, then we specialize the subject of agriculture and close it to all questions except those having to do with its profitability to the agri-industrial corporations.

Professor Davis assumes also the obviousness of the colonization of rural landscapes and communities everywhere by the global economy that has now replaced similarly colonializing national economies. In this she is in agreement with many contemporary agrarians all over the world. Furthermore – and this is one of the indispensable gifts of her book – she sees the similarity between this modern corporate colonialism and that of the ancient empires. She sees as well, and even more indispensably, the necessity and possibility of local resistance by means of local religion, local knowledge, and local language.

An agrarian reading of the Bible thus forces the de-specialization of one's thoughts about agriculture. With equal force it de-specializes one's thoughts about religion. It does this simply by seeing that the Bible is not a book only about "spirituality" or getting to Heaven, but is also a practical book about the good use of land and creatures as a religious practice, and about the abuse of land and creatures as a kind of blasphemy.

Any alert person will be aware that the Bible can be used as something to be seen with, a badge of social identity; or that it can be idolized as a source of complete and invariable truth, as if it were itself the very presence of God; or that it can be diminished to an import merely "spiritual"; or that it can be used fragmentarily to justify several varieties of meanness. These misuses are precisely corrected by a reading such as this one, not just because it is profusely informed by knowledge, but because it is, above all, exuberantly intelligent.

The Bible, as Professor Davis reads it, is a book about religion; it is a holy book, properly so-called. But she reads it also as a book dealing exactingly with the story of a gift. According to this story, the descendants of Israel were given, not a land, but the use of a land, along with precise instructions for its good care. They could keep the land only upon the condition of their obedience. By their disobedience they were estranged from the land and the covenant by which they received it, and were removed into exile. What we have, then, is a story and a discourse about the connection of a people to a place. This connection is at once urgently religious and urgently practical. It is urgently religous because the land is understood, never as a human "property," but as a part of an infinitely complex creation, both natural and divine, belonging to God. It is urgently practical because of the strict conditions of gratitude and care enjoined upon its users.

The Bible is not an easy book to read. It is often hard – if not, when it apparently contradicts itself, impossible – to understand. It customarily requires almost too much of us. Its estimate of human nature is hardly a comfort. And it leads us repeatedly into the temptation to use it selectively to excuse our ignorance, to justify our wishes, or to condemn people unlike ourselves.

The difficulty of reading is much helped by Professor Davis's steadfast understanding of the Israelites as a people explicitly entrusted with what we would now call ecological responsibilities and with explicit instructions for meeting them. But at the same time her clarification of the practical significance of her texts burdens and darkens the reader's sense of moral difficulty. This, I think, will be especially true for American readers.

The more an American reader thinks about the Israelite religion as a *local* practice honoring both God and the land, the more that reader will be aware of the ironies of our own religion and history, and of their present clamor for resolution. We Americans readily saw the parallel between the Israelites' entrance into the land of Canaan and our own westward expansion. We adopted the simple nationalism of the old story along with its "promised land" idea of ownership prior to settlement – we called it "manifest destiny." But we conveniently ignored the elaborate agrarianism and ecological stewardship implicit in that story's insistence upon the land's sanctity. The result, still continuing, has been desecration and destruction of the land, as well as the destruction, dispossession, and exile of the American Indians who, like the Israelites and unlike most white Americans, believed the land was holy.

Of course there are, and always have been, exceptional post-Columbian Americans who have wished for and have attempted a beneficent settlement of this country, who have tried to use the land and other creatures with care, and to be neighborly to their neighbors. But the dominant theme of our history so far has been opposite to beneficent settlement or responsible stewardship. It has been a thoughtless, heartless, greedy plunge into what apparently is still considered an inexhaustible plenty.

The irony and absurdity are not fully apparent except in the context of our claim to be a "Christian nation." What we mainly have, as Ellen Davis shows, is a "Christian religion" not rooted in any landscape, without a remnant or promise of a local ecological practice, and without any working concept of the sanctity of what it continues to call "creation." American Christians, thinking of the Holy Land as a place most of them have never seen and will never see, have made for themselves a religion that is alien to their land and therefore to their own lives.

From an ecological and agrarian point of view, the most urgent problem of agriculture, as of the human economy as a whole, is that of local adaptation – that is to say, of making a beneficent and conserving fit between work and place. As Professor Davis shows, this problem is paramount also from the point of view of the Bible. From an agrarian point of view, the Exodus was a movement from the flat, easily tillable land of Egypt to "the narrow and precariously balanced ecological niche that is the hill country of ancient Judah and Samaria." The people of Israel had to re-make their economic life to conform to a landscape that allowed "only the slightest margin for negligence, ignorance, or error."

Local adaptation, then, is authentically a scriptural issue and so an issue of religion. It is also the issue most catastrophically ignored in the economic colonization of American landscapes and in the industrialization of agriculture. Now in the presence of much destruction, we must ask the questions that this book makes obvious: Was not the original and originating catastrophe the reduction of religion to spirituality, and to various schemes designed exclusively to save the (disembodied) soul? Could we have destroyed so much of the material creation without first learning to see it as an economic "resource" devoid of religious significance? Could we have developed a reductionist science subserving economic violence without first developing a reductionist religion? What would America be now if we white people had managed to bring with us, not just a Holy Land spirituality, but also the elaborate land ethic, land reverence, and agrarian practice meant to safeguard the holiness of the land?

The poet Kathleen Raine, who is quoted twice in this book, first helped me to think of the damage inherent in the Christian attribution of holiness exclusively to the Holy Land. In 1993 she wrote in a letter that, as the Irish poets Yeats and Æ (George William Russell) had seen, "the holy places of the Bible . . . to the Jews are real places on earth" whereas "to the Christians the Holy Land is remote . . . The holy land should be the place we live on . . . " And in another letter she quoted Yeats: "Have not all races had their first unity from a mythology that marries them to rock and hill?" In thinking of this, I have remembered also that Harlan Hubbard, when a local church asked him for a painting of the Jordan, made them a painting of their own river, the

Ohio. If we who live in its watershed saw that river as he saw it, would it now be so shamefully polluted? Would we be strip-mining its headwaters?

It seems that if we follow the agrarian conversation through ecology to the need for a locally adapted land economy, then we are obliged to go on to the need for locally adapted religion. This implies no violence to religion. As agrarian principles, by remaining intact, preside over the local adaptation of agriculture, so religious principles, by remaining intact, would preside over the local adaptation of religious practice. For this the Bible gives an authorization that, in turn, gives authority to Professor Davis's argument. The Holy Land did not become holy by a divine prejudice in its favor; it is holy just because it is a part of all the world, which is a divine creation.

The good work accomplished by this book is to show forcefully and persuasively that the same principle applies to every land, and to every place in every land. And thus it exposes the falsehood of the idea that our ecological destructiveness is blameable directly on the Bible. It is blameable instead, and only within limits, on a misunderstanding and misuse of the Bible. The fault, clearly, is in the way the Bible has been *applied*. Applied religion, without a local orientation and a local practice, can be as irresponsible, as dangerous, and as sloppy as modern science similarly applied.

Wendell Berry

Acknowledgments

Agrarian thinking comes out of the experience of community, and so does this book. My first thanks are to the students – at Yale Divinity School, Virginia Theological Seminary, and Duke Divinity School – who have helped me think through these matters over a period of fifteen years. With me, they have treasured Scripture as a resource for doing so; their companionship has been invaluable. Early thanks are due also to the Faculty of Divinity at the University of Cambridge, who invited me to deliver the Hulsean Lectures for 2005–06; that invitation determined not only the timeline for this book but also its character. David Ford, Robert Gordon, and Diana Lipton were especially generous in their interest, and I thank them warmly. Two people who contributed to this work by responding to the Lectures are no longer on this side of life; I remember Brevard Childs and Daniel Hardy with gratitude.

My research and writing have been greatly facilitated by Duke University and especially by my Dean, L. Gregory Jones, who granted me an extended leave and urged me to take it all. That leave was funded in large part by the Lilly Endowment, through a Christian Faith and Life Grant from the Louisville Institute and a Lilly Theological Research Grant from the Association of Theological Schools. I am very grateful not only for their funding support but also for their advancement of the project through scholarly conversation and friendship.

I am grateful also to the other educational institutions and churches that have given me opportunities to lecture and lead seminars on this topic; among them are Duke Divinity School's Continuing Education Program, the University of Oxford, the University of Edinburgh, the University of Durham, the University of Gloucestershire, Clare Hall (Cambridge), Canadian Mennonite University, the University of Calgary, The Land Institute, the Association of Indonesian Biblical Scholars, Sanata Dharma University (Yogyakarta), Satya Wacana Christian University (Salatiga), Cipanas Theological Seminary,

Virginia Theological Seminary, the School of Theology at the University of the South (Sewanee), Bangor Theological Seminary, North Park Theological Seminary, Northwestern College, the Community of the Holy Spirit, and Church Street United Methodist Church (Knoxville).

Many friends and colleagues (happily, the same people) have been generous variously with their reading and listening time, hospitality, and thoughtful comments as these ideas, lectures, and eventually the book have taken shape. Among them are Fred Bahnson, Carol Bechtel, Ellen Bernstein, Stephen Chapman, Ann Copp, Mary Eubanks, Stanley Hauerwas, Peter Hawkins, Martha Horne, Paul Joyce, Nathan MacDonald, Mark Migotti, Patrick Miller, Sarah Musser, Michael Northcott, Bruce and Peggy Parker, Mindawati Peranginangin, Simon and Nancy Rich, Barbara Rossing, Cynthia Shattuck, Mark Soutor, Daphne and Roger Symon, and Janice Virtue. Without Wendell Berry, Wes Jackson, and Norman Wirzba – their contributions and companionship both on paper and in person – this book would not have been written.

Chadwick Eggleston and Jonathan Huddleston provided able and cheerful assistance in preparing the manuscript. My editor, Andy Beck of Cambridge University Press, has been consistently patient with my concerns and questions and a wonderful support and advocate for the book. It is better for the critical attention it received from him and the readers whom he invited to review the draft manuscript.

The cover design features Diane Palley's papercut of the Tree of Life. Palley uses a traditional artistic medium to express with striking beauty the vision of a flourishing "land community" that lies at the heart of this book and of Israel's Scriptures themselves. I am grateful for her permission to use it.

To two people I owe a debt I cannot repay. My colleague Carol Shoun worked with me for more than a year to prepare the manuscript for publication, laboring at least as hard on my thinking as on my prose; without her the book would have many more faults than it does. My husband, Dwayne Huebner, has learned about this topic alongside me, coming to care about it as fully as I, uncomplaining about the extent to which the project has dominated my thinking and our common life for three years. This book is dedicated to him and our seven grandchildren.

Durham, North Carolina

Abbreviations

Scripture translations not otherwise identified are the author's own.

Bible versions quoted or referenced *

NEB   New English Bible
NJPS   *Tanakh: The Holy Scriptures: The New JPS Translation According to
       the Traditional Hebrew Text*
NRSV   New Revised Standard Version

---

* There is only one verse quoted in full from a standard translation (the NRSV).

Introduction

If you listen willingly,
the good of the land you shall eat.

(Isa. 1:19)

And God will turn no one away
who knows how to eat.

(Raewynne Whiteley)

Agrarianism is a way of thinking and ordering life in community that is based on the health of the land and of living creatures.[1] Often out of step with the prevailing values of wealth, technology, and political and military domination, the mind-set and practices that constitute agrarianism have been marginalized by the powerful within most "history-making" cultures across time, including that of ancient Israel. Yet, agrarianism is the way of thinking predominant among the biblical writers, who very often do not represent the interests of the powerful. The sheer pervasiveness of their appreciation and concern for the health of the land is the single most important point of this study.

This volume explores the agrarian mind-set of the biblical writers by bringing Israel's Scriptures into sustained conversation with the works of contemporary agrarian writers – most consistently, those of farmer, poet, essayist, and fiction writer Wendell Berry. Over the last three generations, agrarian thought and values have been given their fullest articulation in the nearly three millennia of agrarian writing; it is now clear that this is a comprehensive way of viewing the world and the human place in it.[2] The rapidly growing body of literature is a response to the global dominance of corporation-controlled agriculture. It discloses the illogic and danger of the practice, now routine in industrialized culture, of allowing food production – the largest and most essential of all human industries – to be managed by "specialists" and ignored by the rest of us. Yet ironically, agriculture has become more worthy of widespread attention than it ever was, and for tragic reasons. According to the 2005 United Nations–sponsored Millennium Ecosystem Assessment, agriculture as currently practiced may constitute the "largest threat to biodiversity and ecosystem function of any single human activity."[3] Worldwide, it is also a major threat to economic and political democracy; sociologist and political scientist James Scott compares the functioning of industrial agriculture to that of a "totalizing state."[4]

My interest in the global crisis of agriculture comes as a direct result of my normal professional activity of reading and interpreting the Hebrew Scriptures. Some fifteen years ago, I began using biblical interpretation as a way of informing my understanding of the ecological crisis. A confirmed urbanite, I had never been curious, let alone knowledgeable, about farming until, through my study, I first noticed and then gradually acquired something of the biblical writers' own abiding interest in land care. In contrast to ourselves, they belonged to a culture that recognized land care as the life-and-death matter it unquestionably is. Thus, they can provide a vantage point from which to view and develop a nuanced critique of our current cultural practices regarding land use and food production.

In attending to issues of *land care* in Israel's Scriptures, I am to some degree shifting the terms common to biblical scholarship and contemporary theology, which have given more attention to *possession of land* as a national territory. The biblical writers themselves consistently regard the two matters as related; land tenure is conditional upon proper use and care of land in community. However, shifting the focus to the latter brings into view aspects of well-worked texts that have previously received scant attention, such as the pronounced emphasis on seeds in Genesis 1. Things that the biblical writers must themselves have intended as important conveyors of meaning become intelligible when the Bible is read from an agrarian perspective. The range of texts treated in these chapters – selected from Torah, Former and Latter Prophets, Psalms, Proverbs, and the Song of Songs – indicates how widely agrarian concerns are shared among the various writers, strands, and periods of biblical tradition. Numerous (probably countless) other passages could be adduced to support these arguments and add new insights. The very pervasiveness of agrarian thinking in the Bible challenges the common assumption that those who composed or edited the writings were members of an urban elite whose perspectives "distort or ignore the everyday reality of [villagers'] lives."[5] If the sharp urban/rural dichotomy that now characterizes the industrialized West existed at all in Israel, it was only late, in the Hellenistic period. Certainly the Bible attests to ongoing tensions between city and countryside, but there was also deep interpenetration, as my final chapter shows. An urban world completely uninvolved in and ignorant of agriculture is a quite new phenomenon, and necessarily a transitory one.

Agrarian reading is not a distinct method but rather a *perspective* for exegesis; it is *theōria* – literally, a way of viewing our world and the texts' representation of it. Bringing to bear a perspective unfamiliar to most biblical scholars (who are themselves in most cases "members of an urban elite") means asking a question rarely posed in the scholarly literature: How do these texts view the relationship between humans (or Israelites in particular) and the material sources of life as an essential aspect of living in the presence of God? If the question is unusual, the methods used to answer it are not. On the whole, this study will follow procedures that are standard for professional exegesis: paying close attention to rhythm, diction, and the poetics of a text; reading it within the larger literary context and, to whatever extent is possible, in light of the particular historical, social, and even geographical conditions related to its composition and promulgation.

The most pertinent social condition is that from the eighth century B.C.E. on – that is, from the time when the prophetic movement was firmly established in Israel's religious tradition – the economics of food production was a matter contested between the crown and its agents, on the one hand, and the bulk of the population, on the other. The biblical writers were located at the heart of the contest, held there by a conviction and a calling that was wholly theocentric. The methodological consideration that is crucial for exegesis undertaken from an agrarian perspective is that the biblical writers were theologians, but not theological idealists. On the contrary, their theological understanding led them directly into confrontation with the economic and political systems dominant in their society.

Contemporary theological exegetes are therefore under pressure from the text to read with a similar sensitivity to the dynamics of large social systems and how these affect local communities, both ancient and contemporary. For me as a biblical scholar, engaging questions of contemporary social analysis means consciously working as an amateur, going outside my area of professional expertise for the sake of love. Augustine's famous interpretive principle of *caritas* may provide a theological warrant for such a move: reading the biblical text in a way that conduces to knowledge and love of God and neighbor is the touchstone for accurate interpretation.[6] In our present intellectual environment, Wendell Berry advocates amateurism as a corrective to the tendency toward overspecialization and abstraction that afflicts all disciplines. He suggests

> widening the context of all intellectual work and of teaching – perhaps to the width of the local landscape.... To bring local landscapes within what Wes Jackson calls "the boundary of consideration," professional people of all sorts will have to feel the emotions and take the risks of amateurism. They will have to get out of their "fields," so to speak, and into the watershed, the ecosystem, and the community; and they will have to be actuated by affection.[7]

As Berry and Jackson both acknowledge, the dimensions of the local landscape are not only physical but also economic, political, and cultural. It is just because all those dimensions were inextricably entwined with Israel's religion that the move beyond a *specialized* view of the biblical text and its bearing on our present situation does not entail a move away from its *historical* meaning. Rather, a penetrating reading of the text in its full social context should guide us both in identifying fundamental causes of inequity in our own economic and political systems and in discovering more just possibilities.[8]

Our own social world is clearly discontinuous with that of ancient Israel in multiple ways: economic organization under the domination of multinational corporations rather than under kings and empires, the extent of our technological domination of natural systems and the corresponding extent of their degradation (even though the ancients themselves experienced significant ecological degradation), the size of the human population, and the growing predominance of cities worldwide. Writing about the Bible as a resource for economic ethics, Norman Gottwald aptly observes: "So, we are left with the logically perplexing but morally empowering paradox that the Bible is both grossly irrelevant in direct application to current economic problems and incredibly relevant in *vision and principle* for grasping opportunities and obligations to make the whole earth and its bounty serve the welfare of the whole human family."[9]

What the Bible can offer us are "vision and principle," not solutions from the past. An agrarian reading of the Bible is not an exercise in nostalgia, although it is in significant part a work of memory, of imagination anchored (not mired) in the past. Agrarian *theōria* looks forward to a potentially healing future; it is informed by modern science and also by traditional patterns of thought and value, even practices that have endured through centuries and millennia – if now only among a remnant – and may yet be adapted to meet present and future exigencies.

Good biblical exegesis should yield some measure of realistic hope, however chastened, because the Bible itself consistently nourishes such hope. To compare great things to small, the prophet Ezekiel is my model for the kind of work attempted here: a style of exegesis that brings forth the full critical potential of Israel's scriptural tradition, which is part of its revelatory power, and at the same time generates fresh vision. Ezekiel was the only biblical writer to reinterpret virtually the whole religious tradition up to his time; and, significantly for us, he did it in a situation of unprecedented disaster, with the fall of Jerusalem and of the Davidic monarchy first a looming threat, and then a bitter reality. Ezekiel reread the theological tradition in order to make sense of events that were literally unthinkable, in terms of Israel's regnant theology. He charted those horrific events on the map of faith and thus opened a way forward. To him and through him, God granted a vision of life on the far side of disaster for the people and the land of Israel.

I am not a prophet and have received no such vision. Nonetheless, working on this book has given me reasons to be hopeful, if not yet optimistic. I have discovered how deep are the resources in the biblical tradition for addressing the problems we face, and further, how much good work is now being done to slow destruction, cultivate new habits of mind, and clear some paths into a wiser future. Certainly, one thing I have learned in the course of writing is that a wide-ranging conversation is indispensable, both because it is encouraging and because it yields insight. This book was conceived and advanced through many conversations, first with my students, some of whom have deep experience of land care, and later with farmers, agrarian writers, and theologians – these being different ways of naming some of the same people.

The book is intended to further such conversation, and so it is written for an audience that includes, but extends beyond, those with formal training in biblical studies. Wherever I use technical language, I try to make it plain to the nonspecialist. Those without such training should be fairly warned that the texts themselves often demand patient attention to their verbal particularities. Biblical literature is altogether complex, and some texts treated here stand at the very highest level of its complexity – namely, Leviticus, Hosea, and the Song of Songs. Yet for all their literary and theological sophistication, these books are not specialized in their concerns. Rather, they speak, obliquely at times but never abstractly, of the situations and concerns of ordinary people – that is, of people who are not rich and who have to eat.

The book is composed of a series of closely related essays; the first six of them were delivered at the University of Cambridge as the Hulsean Lectures for 2005–06. The essay format is the one I find most useful for teaching, and so

I have made the argument within each chapter relatively complete. Chapters 1 and 2 are foundational for all those that follow; the other essays build upon each other to some extent, but they need not be read in sequence. The first chapter introduces the project of reading the Bible through agrarian eyes by focusing on Isaiah's and Jeremiah's visions of the unmaking of the created order through human sinfulness. It establishes the agrarian perspective as it is now, early in the twenty-first century: a sober yet not hopeless reckoning with the present widespread destruction of the material sources of life, and therefore, a reckoning with the real possibility of disaster on a massive scale. The second chapter considers specific points of connection between biblical thought and the new agrarians – that is, precisely how and why agrarian thinking, brought to bear on biblical texts, yields exegetical fruit.

The remaining chapters are devoted to close readings of texts in both their historical context and that of contemporary situations and problems. Chapters 3 through 5 focus on single texts from the Priestly tradition, whose tradents (writer-editors) were likely responsible for giving shape to Torah in its present form. Strategically placed within the biblical story (for instance, as its opening chapter), these seminal texts confirm the centrality of the agrarian mind-set to biblical tradition. Genesis 1 shows the God-given biodiversity of the earth and the human role in maintaining it (Chapter 3). The manna story in Exodus 16, the first account of the people Israel living in political freedom, introduces the vital subject of the economics of eating (Chapter 4). The culture of eating and land care are central to the book of Leviticus, which constitutes the core of the vast body of the Priestly literature and therefore of Torah altogether (Chapter 5). Chapter 7 treats the earliest prophetic books, Amos and Hosea; not coincidentally, these first "writing prophets" may also be the first agrarian writers in history.

Each of the other chapters uses two or more texts to illumine crucial aspects of agrarian thinking as it manifests itself in both biblical and contemporary contexts: the economic centrality of the local economy, summed up in the Deuteronomic concept of *naḥălâ* (Chapter 6); the character of good work, which reflects the divine ordering of the world and contributes to the maintenance of that order, versus "sloth," the traditional term for behavior and activity (!) that fails to do so (Chapter 8); and urban agrarianism, which is the integration of the city within its geographical region, to the benefit of both (Chapter 9).

Finally, two notes on the use of these essays. First, they constitute only the opening of a conversation, a kind of mutual introduction between the biblical writers and their scholarly interpreters on the one hand, and the contemporary agrarian writers on the other. Readers who wish to continue the conversation will, according to their differing backgrounds, need to read more in one body of literature or the other. They may also wish to follow new scientific developments that bear on agriculture and food production. This is not my own area of expertise, but I point toward sources of scientific data that I judge to be responsible. I write in a North American context, as do many or most of the contemporary agrarians. Yet all the social and economic issues treated here ramify around the globe; readers on other continents can recognize their manifestations, sometimes in egregious forms. My travels (to Europe, South Asia, and East Africa) while writing this book indicate that growing numbers of people in every place are aware of these issues and are beginning to work on them.

Second, these essays treat almost exclusively the part of the Bible that Jews and Christians hold in common, and I intend them to be helpful to both communities. Although I am a Christian, I give little attention to the New Testament, for the simple reason that others are better qualified to do the detailed exegetical work required. An agrarian reading of the New Testament is possible and necessary. Granted, the theme of land care is less pronounced there, likely because many of the writers expected an imminent end of the world as we know it. Yet at the same time, they asserted the inestimable value of the "groaning" creation that God will redeem from hostile domination (Rom. 8:18–25) and powerful destroyers (Rev. 11:16–18), and will ultimately renew (Rev. 21:1, 5).[10] Any such reading of the New Testament will need to begin with an awareness of the agrarian perspective that dominates Israel's Scriptures, which are as indispensable for modern Christians as they were for the New Testament writers. Only a thorough understanding of how Israel represents the human place in the created order can enable Christians to delineate a responsible vision of what participation in the renewal of creation might mean. I hope this book may contribute to that work, the most essential theological task of this generation.

1

≈

Rupture and Re-membering

[T]he catastrophe now threatening us is unprecedented – and we often confuse the unprecedented with the improbable.

(Al Gore)[1]

OPENING OUR EYES

As an Old Testament scholar, I come naturally (at least, by second nature) to a respect for land and a concern that it be "kindly used,"[2] so that it may continue to be used from generation to generation: for the Hebrew Scriptures are land-centered in their theological perspective. Rarely does one read through two or three successive chapters without seeing some reference to the land or to Zion, the city that is ideologically speaking the source of its fertility. Beginning with the first chapter of Genesis, there is no extensive exploration of the relationship between God and humanity that does not factor the land and its fertility into that relationship. Overall, from a biblical perspective, the sustained fertility and habitability of the earth, or more particularly of the land of Israel, is the best index of the health of the covenant relationship. When humanity, or the people Israel, is disobedient, thorns and briars abound (Gen. 3:17–19); rain is withheld (Deut. 11:11–17; 28:24); the land languishes and mourns (Isa. 16:8; 33:9; Hos. 4:3). Conversely, the most extravagant poetic images of loveliness – in the Prophets, the Psalms, and the Song of Songs – all show a land lush with growth, together with a people living in (or restored to) righteousness and full intimacy with God. "Truth [or: faithfulness, *'ĕmet*] springs up from the earth [*'ereṣ,*]" (Ps. 85:12 [11 Eng.]). The Hebrew word *'ereṣ* may refer to ground, to a national territory, to the land of Israel, or to what we would call the planet Earth, and (as we shall see here) it is not always possible to be certain whether a given biblical writer intends a wider or narrower reference, or both. So our starting point is the Hebrew Scriptures' pervasive interest in land, not only as national territory, but also, and more fundamentally, its interest in land as fertile, and further, in the primary human vocation to maintain its fertility (Gen. 2:15).

In recent years, I have come to believe that anyone who wishes to understand Israel's Scripture deeply would do well to learn more about the ecological crisis, and especially about its agricultural dimensions. At the same time, Jews and Christians who wish to understand the depth of the crisis would do well to ponder it in light of Israel's Scripture. The mutually informative relation between ecological awareness and biblical study rests not only on the land-centeredness of the Bible but also on the nature of the ecological crisis, which is principally moral and theological rather than technological. That is, the problem does not stem in the first instance from technological errors or omissions that can be rectified by further technological applications. It is a moral and even theological crisis because it is occasioned in large part by our adulation and arrogant use of scientific technology, so that we make applications without rigorous critical regard for questions of compatibility with natural systems, of the integrity of the world that God has made.

Philosopher Norman Wirzba poses well the problem of our current technological practice in the information age, which, as he aptly observes, is "a technique of falsification" to the extent that it has

> *reduced* our ability to truly know the world. Information is often superficial since it appears in decontextualized, easily digestible bytes. The medium that increases our access to knowledge thus at the same time decreases our grasp of the world's significance. Moreover, on the level of consciousness we see the gradual diminishing of powers of attention....
>
> It is, perhaps, the very superficiality of our knowing that best explains the irony that today we have more information about how the natural world functions than ever before, yet also are guilty of its most widespread destruction.... Should not the effect of our knowing lead to understanding, appreciation, affection, and care? Should it not train our minds into the sympathetic faculty that better (more honestly) places itself into alignment with its object?[3]

The present generation is embroiled in a crisis that is, in material terms, the most far-reaching crisis in humanity's life with God; it concerns us precisely as *creatures* – the only terrestrial creatures, so far as we know, who are susceptible to moral failure. The crisis has its roots in our moral lives, yet it now touches and probably affects every aspect of our physical existence and possibly that of every creature in the biosphere. Such an understanding of the current crisis is congruent with the biblical understanding of the world, in which the physical, moral, and spiritual orders fully interpenetrate one another – in contrast to the modern superstition that these are separable categories.

Yet because communities of Jews, Christians, and also Muslims remain slow to reckon on such terms with the now far-advanced mistreatment of the fertile earth, I begin by considering how the Bible may open our eyes to recognize that land care is an area in which theologically informed moral discernment is needed. To anticipate my argument, I shall treat our lack of recognition as a failure of the religious imagination, an inability to imagine that this world could be significantly different, for better or for much worse, than we and every human generation before us have experienced it. It should concern us that "secular" intellectuals and activists are on the whole ahead of religious leaders, including theologians, in articulating the dimensions of both our unprecedented situation and our urgent responsibility. Speaking to a group of soil scientists, Stanford terrestrial ecologist Peter Vitousek recently said that now for the first time the human species as a whole must find the will to make a drastic change in our behavior – and to make it in this generation – in order that life on our planet may continue to be viable and to some degree lovely.[4] A statement that radical from a theologian is still a rarity, even though drastic reorientation of human thought and behavior would seem to be directly in our line of work. To our traditions belong the texts that perhaps in all world literature speak most directly to the human will to change. The books of the Hebrew Prophets are in my judgment the single best biblical resource for awakening us to our situation, for they consistently speak of, and to, the faculty they call *lēb*, "heart" – which is, in biblical physiology, the organ of perception and response.

The Prophets instruct our weak religious imagination by means of "visual enhancement"; they enable us to see the present moment of history in divine perspective. The oldest Hebrew word for "prophet" is *ḥōzeh*, "seer." Prophets see the world as God sees it, with a wide-angle lens, so that the whole stretch, from creation to the end of days, is visible at once. Listen to Jeremiah:

> I have seen the earth, and here, [it is] wildness and waste [*tōhû wābōhû*];
> and [I look] to the heavens – and their light is gone.
> I have seen the mountains, and here, they are wavering,
> and all the hills palpitate.
> I have seen, and here, there is no human being,
> and all the birds of the heavens have fled.
> I have seen, and here, the garden-land is now the wasteland,
> and all its cities are pulled down,
> because of YHWH,[5] because of his hot anger. (Jer. 4:23–26)

Rā'îtî – "I have seen" – is repeated four times here. Jeremiah is speaking to people who do not see, so the hammering repetition is aimed at getting them to open their blinkered eyes to the undoing of what God has made and sustained. *Rā'îtî 'et-hā'āreṣ)* – "I have seen the earth [*'ereṣ*], and here, it is wildness and waste [*tōhû wābōhû*]." That memorable language of formlessness appears uniquely here and in the first chapter of Genesis. Jeremiah exploits the ambiguity of the word *'ereṣ*, "land" or "Earth." What he has in view here is his own land of Judah, under threat of invasion, yet he represents its collapse as a global disaster. So he takes his sixth-century audience, and by extension us, back to the first moments of the world and leads us stage by stage through the unhinging of the created order.

As is fitting, the first thing to go is the primordial light. Then the mountains, the bone structure of the earth, come loose. "I have seen the mountains, and here, they are wavering [*rō'ăšîm*]" – for the exilic poets, that word *ra'aš* serves as a technical term for what happens to the solid frame of the earth when chaos reengulfs it.[6] Now the birds are gone, the creatures that God made and blessed on the fifth day with the words "Be fruitful and multiply" (Gen. 1:22). With their disappearance, it is inevitable that the creatures likewise blessed on the sixth day will also vanish: "There is no human being [*'ên hā'ādām*]." Finally, in the absence of humans, garden-land reverts to wasteland (*hakkarmel hammidbār*), and the cities collapse.

The prophets' messages are ineluctably political; they speak to the ingrained habits of a society and its leadership, then and now. The political dimension here is illumined when Jeremiah's vision is read in conjunction with Psalm 72, a royal psalm, a prayer that the king may exercise God's own justice. Intriguingly, the psalm ends with an agricultural image, and it is one that may well have been in Jeremiah's mind:

> May there be an abundance of grain in the land,
> at the top of the mountains;
> may its fruit wave [*yir'aš*] like the Lebanon. (Ps. 72:16)

Ra'aš, "wave, toss" – it is exactly the same word that Jeremiah uses of the mountains. But the coincidence of the word underscores the clash of visions. While the psalmist sees the covering of grain tossing on the mountaintops, Jeremiah sees the mountains themselves tossing (*rō'ăšîm*) and toppling before God's hot anger.

In order to understand Jeremiah's message, we must first see why the psalmist concludes a prayer for royal justice by moving from the political sphere to the agricultural, and at the very last to the cosmic, praying that "[the king's] name may be forever, his name may endure as long as the sun" (Ps. 72:17). Robert Murray considers Psalm 72 to be the clearest reflection of the ideal world order as the biblical writers conceived it, a "divine order which is exemplified in the proper functioning of both nature and human society."[7] The well-being of humans and the enduring fruitfulness of the earth are inseparable elements of a harmony sometimes imaged as a "covenant" encompassing all creatures. According to the *mythos* of Davidic kingship, the royal administration of justice was essential to maintaining that "cosmic covenant." The blessing that the king derives from God is meant to be manifested in politics, but it also manifests itself palpably in what we call the "natural" world – for the psalmist, "the work(s) of God's hands" (Pss. 8:7 [6 Eng.]; 19:2 [1 Eng.]; 102:26 [25 Eng.]). So when Jeremiah sees the fruitful land become barren, the mountains undone, the birds of heaven fled – these are sure signs of radical social failure; there is no justice in the seat of power.

It was Jeremiah's vision of the return of chaos that came to my mind in the summer of 1996, in Kentucky, when I visited a "mountaintop removal" site. That is the remarkably bland term we have devised for the process whereby coal is now mined. Since it is cheaper to remove the mountain entirely than to dig out the coal, the mountain is simply reduced to rubble, layer by layer, and each vein is extracted. The massive infertile "overburden" of rock is pushed into the nearby valleys, burying the topsoil and filling the streams.

Mountaintop removal is an emblematic act. Along with nuclear testing, this is the most dramatic rupture of the created order that North Americans have effected on our own continent. In Appalachia, the oldest part of our continent – the place where God began work on our quadrant of the globe – we are proceeding to return God's handiwork to utter formlessness and waste, *tōhû wābōhû*, stripping bare one of the most biologically diverse temperate forest regions in the world. Kentucky writer Wendell Berry's words on the strip-mining site of Hardburly remain apt (though he wrote in 1968, when the technology and the destruction were far less advanced than they are now):

> [S]tanding there in the very presence of it, one feels one's comprehension falling short of the magnitude of its immorality. One is surrounded by death and ugliness and silence as of the end of the world. After my first trip to this place I think I was most impressed by the extent of the destruction, and its speed; what most impresses me now is its permanence.... Standing and looking down on that mangled land, one feels aching in one's bones the sense that it will be in a place such as this – a place of titanic disorder and violence, which the rhetoric of political fantasy has obstructed from official eyesight – that the balance will finally be overcast and the world tilted irrevocably toward its death.... Since I left Hardburly I have been unable to escape the

sense that I have been to the top of the mountain, and that I have looked over and seen, not the promised land vouchsafed to a chosen people, but a land of violence and sterility prepared and set aside for the damned.[8]

DESTROYING THE HEARTLAND

Mountaintop removal is an emblematic act but not an isolated one, any more than Auschwitz was an isolated phenomenon. Only by degrees and over centuries is the way prepared for such an onslaught, acts that strike at some part of the created order for which God has special care, acts that change quickly and forever the face of the globe and its human history. Moreover, such aggressive, targeted actions must be abetted in the present by a myriad of smaller, casual acts of contempt for "the work of God's hands" – a term that the biblical writers apply to both human beings and the earth itself. It is only because destructive behaviors are routine for ordinary people like ourselves that the "titanic" acts can be conceived by relatively few and then rendered plausible and acceptable to so many.

What then are those destructive behaviors in which we routinely engage? Jeremiah's particular words focus my attention on another form of collapse occurring in North America, this one so undramatic that most of us are unaware of either its occurrence or our own participation in it:

> I have seen, and here, the garden-land is now the wasteland, and all its cities are pulled down.... (Jer. 4:26)

Those words evoke with astonishing accuracy the collapse of American farming communities, the most rapidly disintegrating sector of the national economy. In the Great Plains, traditionally known as the "heartland" – although, tellingly, now more often called the "fly-over states" – many rural towns that were moderately prosperous eighty years ago, and were still economically viable fifty years ago, are now ghost towns, their schools, banks, and businesses closed.[9]

The tragedy of the heartland is the conversion of a family-based farming economy to "agribusiness," the system of petrochemical-based food production that Richard Manning calls "catastrophic agriculture."[10] In this half-century it has given North Americans probably the cheapest food in human history, but at what cost? Changes in the composition of our topsoil (through heavy application of chemicals); cultivation-induced erosion;[11] drastic narrowing of our seed base (through exclusive planting of a few hybrid strains); dangerous depletion of our water sources through overpumping, as well as chemical poisoning caused by runoff. The net result has been a significant "dilution" in the nutritional value of our food, as studies of multiple crops in Britain and the United States attest.[12] Our modern agricultural practices are a long-term disaster for the land and consequently for our bodies. They also constitute an immediate disaster for farming families, who are unable to compete in an economic system that deposits the bulk of agricultural revenues in the hands of a few multinational corporations. Many farmers who have lost their farms, or work them as employees of the corporations, now consciously claim for themselves the biblical identity of "exiles." Jeremiah, the prophet who watched his people go into exile in Babylon and Egypt, speaks for those modern exiles also: "I have seen, and here, the garden-land is now the wasteland, and all its cities are pulled down."

My point is not that Jeremiah "prophesied" (in the narrow sense) mountaintop removal and industrial agriculture, those peculiar forms of collapse that would be invented on the North American continent some 2,600 years after his own time. What Jeremiah immediately envisioned was the catastrophic invasion of Judah and Jerusalem – threatened several times (and probably by more than one great power) during Jeremiah's long career, and finally accomplished by the Babylonians in 587–586 B.C.E. Yet, in George Caird's words, "The prophets looked to the future with bifocal vision. With their near sight they foresaw imminent historical events which would be brought about by familiar human causes.... With their long sight they saw the day of the Lord" (a day of final reckoning); and they frequently "impose[d] the one image on the other," using the same language for both.[13] We are located now somewhere between the events the prophets immediately anticipated or confronted and the day of the Lord, and it is impossible to judge just where we are on that continuum. Nonetheless, from the prophets we may take words that enable us to comprehend the nature and magnitude of the evil we face, which we ourselves have brought about. If we can hear it, Jeremiah's shattering language will break through what Walter Brueggemann incisively terms "our achieved satiation,"[14] the numbness carefully wrought by industrial culture and especially by its political and economic spokesmen. Prophetic speech is the antidote to the illness from which we are not eager to recover, namely, apathy – the inability to feel shock, horror, and remorse for our actions.

THE PAIN OF SEEING

For the notion that prophetic speech is fundamentally a condemnation of apathy, I am indebted to Abraham Heschel's great study of the Prophets, undertaken in the wake of the Holocaust and dedicated "To the martyrs of 1940–45." Heschel sought to (re)discover the "intellectual relevance of the prophets," because he saw "the tragic failure of the modern mind, incapable of preventing its own destruction." The relevance of the prophets is that they saw the moral failing of their own people, and moreover, felt what Heschel calls the "pathos of God."[15] The Prophets disclose "a *divine pathos*, not just a divine judgment. The pages of the prophetic writings are filled with echoes of divine love and disappointment, mercy and indignation. The God of Israel is never impersonal."[16] Heschel's study exposes the inadequacy and folly of the modern "scholarly" project of reading the Prophets from a purely historical and sociological perspective, or alternatively, a psychological one – in either case, reading them without risking the pain of insight.[17]

For Heschel, "insight" is a precise term. In contrast to "conventional seeing," it denotes an experience of vision that is always accompanied by surprise.[18] So the prophetic attack on apathy strikes at our strange and dangerous inability to be surprised. Yet we are regularly and increasingly confronted with news that is by any measure astonishing. It is "news" in the strong sense; no previous generation has heard or seen reports like those we encounter: for instance, the United Nations–administered Millennium Ecosystem Assessment warning that "nearly two-thirds of the natural machinery that supports life on Earth is being degraded by human pressure."[19] It is a moment of grace when, despite the newscaster's even tone, or the modestly sized type of the headline, we are staggered. The first such moment I recall was a front-page photo in the *New York Times* on August 19, 2000, taken from the deck of an icebreaker at the North Pole, showing clear, open water. James McCarthy, a Harvard oceanographer on the icebreaker, set aside his professional cool and admitted frankly: "It was totally unexpected."[20]

Even more than the photo, what impressed me was Professor McCarthy's admission of astonishment and (if I read it correctly) pain – the pain of seeing that is not blunted by what we think we know. For normally "[o]ur sight is suffused with knowing, instead of feeling painfully the lack of knowing what we see."[21] That is the pain the prophets express. For Jeremiah, the most transparent of them, it throws heart and guts into turmoil (Jer. 4:19); he weeps and would do nothing else:

> O that my head were water
> and my eyes a fountain of tears,
> so I could weep day and night
> for the slain of my beloved people![22] (Jer. 8:23 [9:1 Eng.])

The open distress of the prophet, or God (their two voices often being indistinguishable), contrasts sharply with the unnatural composure of the people of Judah. The whole land/*'ereṣ*/earth is bound to be devastated, and yet the people are not aggrieved. The earth itself goes into mourning, and the heavens don black (Jer. 4:28), but there is no indication that the people respond to the prophetic summons to put on sackcloth and wail (4:8).

And what about us? If we as citizens of the industrialized world are not yet stricken to the heart, then why not? The prophetically informed answer is that we lack the healthy imagination to see and feel as we should. I began by saying that the prophets speak to the heart, and Garrett Green aptly suggests that in contemporary idiom, "imagination" may be the single best concept by which to express all that the Hebrew word *lēb* implies.[23] Jeremiah and other prophets speak *of* and *to* the diseased imagination: "The heart is more perverse than anything, and it is sick... " (Jer. 17:9). They seek to restore to the heart its proper function, which is often to assess the depth, scope, and causes of the tragedies that grip our world. In a word, the prophets aim to restore the tragic imagination, which, paradoxically, is essential to the health and ultimately the survival of any community, precisely because it is the faculty whereby we reckon with devastating loss. The tragic imagination is the faculty that, as Wendell Berry observes, "through communal form or ceremony, permits great loss to be recognized, suffered, and borne, and that makes possible some sort of consolation and renewal." In the end, then, after and through suffering, the tragic imagination enables "the return to the beloved community, or to the possibility of one."[24]

The tragic imagination reaches back into memory, in order to recall the beloved community to itself. Imagination is the means whereby writers with diverse gifts may enable their communities literally to "re-member," to work toward their own wholeness, a goal that can be achieved only by claiming a "membership" (a favorite word of Berry's) in "the wholeness and the Holiness of the creation."[25] Surely biblical scholars, theologians, teachers, and preachers have a special role to play in the work of cultural re-membering, because we live in close contact with the most powerful expressions of the tragic imagination ever to be captured in words. But to sharpen our insight, we must depend in part on the work of contemporary writers – speaking for myself, of farmers, poets, a historian who is sensitive to geography (J. R. McNeill[26]), scientists who are sensitive to history (Daniel Hillel[27] and Jared Diamond[28]). But especially I would highlight the whole body of Wendell Berry's work. His agrarian essays, poetry, and fiction, produced over forty years, may be altogether the most extensive and subtle re-membering of a way of life – once culturally dominant and now mostly eclipsed – that is fundamentally attuned to the wholeness of creation. Philosopher David Orr well describes its significance:

Agrarianism, as described by Wendell Berry, is no small, whittled-down philosophy for rural folks. It is, rather, a full-blown philosophy rooted in the realities of soil and nature as "the standard" by which we also come to judge much more. It is grounded in farming, but is larger still. The logic of agrarianism, in Berry's work, unfolds like a fractal through the divisions and incoherence of the modern world.[29]

Orr treats Berry's work under the category of "prophecy," in the nontechnical sense, and indeed there are important points of connection between the perspective and the message of the biblical prophets and those of Berry and his fellow agrarians.[30] Perhaps the most salient point of connection – one on which the contemporary agrarians at least are often misunderstood – is that for none of them does a keen awareness of the past devolve into nostalgia, simple idealization of the past. Rather, as Orr notes: "Prophets are poised between the past and a better future."[31] They look backward, noting both failures and successes, so as to imagine new possibilities better than those offered by the dominant culture of the age, be it theirs or ours. Maybe it is because they self-consciously occupy the liminal space between past and future that these "seers," both ancient and modern, so often express their visions in the form of poetry. For poetry may be, along with music, the most direct means for touching the shared memory of a people. As Wendell Berry has observed: "A poem . . . has the power to remind poet and reader alike of things they have read and heard. . . . Thus the art, so private in execution, is also communal and filial. It can only exist as a common ground between the poet and other poets and other people, living and dead"[32] – and, one might add, people yet to be born.

AN EVERLASTING COVENANT

The prophetic corpus of the Bible includes a second poem that shows the undoing of the world. Like the vision of Jeremiah, Isaiah 24 goes back to Genesis in order to place that horror within the context of God's early intention for creation.

Here, YHWH empties the earth and devastates it,
. . . and he distorts its face and scatters its inhabitants. . . .
The earth wails, it wastes;
the world weakens, lies waste ['ābĕlâ nābĕlâ hā'āreṣ 'umlĕlâ nābĕlâ tēbēl].[33]
They weaken, the exalted of the earth's people.
And the earth is polluted beneath its inhabitants,
for they have transgressed teachings, altered decrees.
They have violated an everlasting covenant.
Therefore a curse devours the earth,

and those who live on it are held in guilt.
Therefore the inhabitants of the earth are seared[34]
and few humans are left. (Isa. 24:1, 4–6)

As in the Jeremiah passage, the prophetic vision goes on to encompass the
desolation of towns and the devastation of crops, and responsibility for all of
this is brought to rest with the highest earthly powers:

And on that day YHWH will visit judgment . . .
on the rulers of the fertile soil on the soil (*'al-malĕkê hā'ădāmâ 'al-hā'ădāmâ*).

(24:21)[35]

The language points to fundamental distortion in the order of creation:
"They have transgressed [divine] teachings [*tôrōt*], altered decrees [*ḥōq*]. /
They have violated *bĕrît 'ôlām* [an everlasting covenant]" (24:5). That last
phrase clarifies the prophetic poet's intention. It appears more than a dozen
times in the Bible to characterize the unbreakable covenant between God and
Israel – and indeed, the several words highlighted in v. 5 all carry overtones of
Sinai.[36] Yet in a poem that seems to depict the whole world (*tēbēl*, 24:4) coming
apart, we should hear also a pronounced echo of the very first occurrence of
the phrase in the ninth chapter of Genesis, when God sets a bow in the heavens
as a reminder that a unilateral disarmament treaty ("an everlasting covenant")
has been established between God "and every living being, among all flesh
that is on the earth" (Gen. 9:16). So when now Isaiah says, "They have violated
an everlasting covenant," he is making the stunning claim that humans *from
their side* have broken God's unilateral treaty that dates back almost to the
beginning of the world. Against all logic and self-interest, they – the most
powerful of us, "the rulers of the fertile soil on the soil" – have thrown back
into God's face the postdiluvian promise never again to bring destruction
upon the earth:

And YHWH breathed in the savory scent [of Noah's sacrifice], and YHWH
said, "I will not again curse the fertile soil on account of the human
being . . . and I will not again strike down every living being as I have done.

> All the remaining days of the earth,
>   seed and harvest
>   and cold and heat
>   and summer and winter
>   and day and night –
> they will cease no more." (Gen. 8:21–22)

Those poetic lines sum up all that we humans have for millennia taken for granted about the stability of our climate. At the same time, the ancient poet informs us that what we have heretofore assumed to be a "built-in" feature of the world is rather, in a world disordered by human sin, a mark of divine forbearance, an expression of God's covenantal faithfulness. If we are now experiencing significant disruption of climatic patterns, then the divine promise itself condemns us, for it exposes the hollowness of claims that this is nothing more than natural fluctuation.[37] (Some "Bible-believing Christians" still make those claims, although their numbers are shrinking.) A discerning reading of the Bible – of the Genesis tradition as it is reinterpreted through Isaiah – leads us to apply to ourselves the prophet's telling diagnosis: "They have violated an everlasting covenant."

Our situation, then, is revealed to be one of complete vulnerability. We, "the rulers of the fertile soil on the soil" – have brought that vulnerability upon ourselves through our persistent refusal to heed the limits that God did indeed build into the created order, a refusal that, according to the Bible, dates back to the first human couple and escalates from there. "They have transgressed [divine] teachings"; our willful violation has returned the earth to its condition *before* God's covenant with Noah, a condition that Genesis describes in a single word: *ḥāmās*, "violence" (Gen. 6:11, 13). So the end of Isaiah's oracle portrays the sluice gates of heaven opening again, as they did in Noah's time. The foundations of the earth "totter," then "crumble"; "it falls and does not rise again" (Isa. 24:18–20; cf. Amos 5:2). Brian Doyle comments incisively: "The author sets up a two-way image of dysfunctional relationship.... For God, earth is mortal – for God, humans are earthy, both earth and its inhabitants are mutually destructive when their relationship with God is severed."[38]

Both Jeremiah and Isaiah confront us with the reality of our creatureliness, and specifically with these two related facts: First, creation is bound into a single, covenanted unity. Each of us is connected to every other creature by the great web of life that Isaiah and other biblical writers call *běrît 'ôlām*, a reality that is comprehensive in space and time (the word *'ôlām* designates something indefinitely extended in either dimension). Therefore, our charity and commitment cannot be shortsighted, nor our sense of responsibility selective. Wendell Berry comments aptly on the Bible's "elaborate understanding of charity," as set forth in Deuteronomy through Job, and on into the New Testament: "Once begun, wherever it begins, it cannot stop until it includes all Creation, for all creatures are parts of a whole upon which each is dependent, and it is a contradiction to love your neighbor and despise the

great inheritance on which his life depends."[39] The second fact with which
the prophets confront us is this: Like every other member of this covenanted
unity, we humans occupy a place that is delimited by *tôrōt*, divine teachings,
and when we violate the prescribed limits, the consequences are inevitably
disastrous, for ourselves, for "all flesh," and for the earth, the fertile soil itself.

In her poem-prayer "A Short Testament," Anne Porter articulates the sensibility to which the prophet-poets Isaiah and Jeremiah direct us, an active
apprehension of moral failure that reaches to every corner of God's "wide
creation":

> Whatever harm I may have done
> In all my life in all your wide creation
> If I cannot repair it
> I beg you to repair it,
> . . . .
> And where there are lives I may have withered around me,
> Or lives of strangers far or near
> That I've destroyed in blind complicity,
> And if I cannot find them
> Or have no way to serve them,

Remember them. I beg you to remember them

> When winter is over
> And all your unimaginable promises
> Burst into song on death's bare branches.[40]

In this chapter, I have tried to demonstrate that the biblical writers give us
language, verbal images, to see what we are doing and the likely consequences.
The next chapter engages the modern agrarian writers more directly, with the
aim of showing how and why their sensibilities illumine the biblical text and
guide us in bringing its insights to bear on our current practices of land use.

2

⌘

Reading the Bible Through Agrarian Eyes

Rabbi 'Aḥai ben Josiah says:

He who purchases grain in the market place, to what may he be likened? To an infant whose mother died: although he is taken from door to door to other wet nurses, he is not satisfied.

He who buys bread in the market place, what is he like? He is as good as dead and buried.

He who eats of his own is like an infant raised at its mother's breast.[1]

At the beginning of the creation of the world, the Holy One, blessed be he, began with planting first.

For it is written:

"And the Lord God planted a garden eastward in Eden"

(Gen. 2:8)

You too when you enter the land shall engage in nothing but planting. Therefore it is written:

"And when ye shall come into the land, ye shall have planted . . . "

(Lev. 19:23).[2]

> Though he works and worries, the farmer
> never reaches down to where the seed turns
> into summer. The earth *grants*.
>
> (Rainer Maria Rilke)[3]

ETHICS AND EXEGESIS

The first essay in this volume suggests that the contemporary agrarian writers may help us re-member a way of life that honors the wholeness of creation.

Now I want to make a stronger and therefore riskier claim: Reading the work of the contemporary agrarians can make us better readers of Scripture. The exegetical project begun in these essays is developing as a conversation between critical biblical study and contemporary agrarian thinking, and the one is as indispensable to it as the other. I am learning to read the Bible through agrarian eyes, helped by the now rapidly expanding body of agrarian writings, some of them literature of the highest quality. I am helped also by my students; since we live in a region of the country that is (or has recently been) semirural, some of them have much more direct knowledge of the land and its care than I do. Yet, this is slow work. If agrarianism were a technique of literary criticism, even a hermeneutic, I might more quickly become adept. But it is a mind-set, a whole set of understandings, commitments, and practices that focus on the most basic of all cultural acts – eating – and ramify into virtually every other aspect of public and private life. Agrarianism is aptly described as "a cultural contract fashioned to work in a specific time and place."[4]

The essential understanding that informs the agrarian mind-set, in multiple cultures from ancient times to the present, is that agriculture has an ineluctably ethical dimension. Our largest and most indispensable industry, food production entails at every stage judgments and practices that bear directly on the health of the earth and living creatures, on the emotional, economic, and physical well-being of families and communities, and ultimately on their survival. Therefore, sound agricultural practice depends upon knowledge that is at one and the same time chemical and biological, economic, cultural, philosophical, and (following the understanding of most farmers in most places and times) religious. Agriculture involves questions of value and therefore of moral choice, whether or not we care to admit it.

The biblical writers share that understanding of agriculture and of eating itself, as the essays that follow demonstrate. To use contemporary religious language, they have a "theological ethic" that embraces those crucial areas of cultural activity. Precisely for that reason, their mind-set differs from that of most contemporary readers of the Bible, although there are a few noteworthy exceptions. Orthodox Jews have a theological ethic of eating, and in some quarters that has come to include ecologically responsible eating. The Amish, many of whom earn their livelihood from farming, might constitute the fullest exception: As a community, they have retained a recognition, once widespread, of the ethical and theological significance of agriculture.

Growing into an agrarian mind-set or ethic is challenging, not only for me personally, but also for our society as a whole, including many or most of our agricultural "professionals." Currently, there are active in our culture two opposing agricultural ethics, and the one dominant among scientists and industrial-scale food producers is what botanist and plant pathologist Robert Zimdahl calls the "productionist ethic." He identifies its sole imperative thus:

> . . . to produce as much as possible, regardless of the ecological costs and perhaps even if it is not profitable to the producer. . . . The experts who conduct agricultural research and those who apply the resultant technology to produce food have not paid much attention to the long-term ecological and social effects of the enterprise because the immediate utilitarian benefit of production has been so apparent.[5]

The chief value operative in our industrial food system is monetary, and it is measured by the profit margins of large corporations. The productionist ethic has prevailed thus far with the North American public because its short-term benefit is food that is cheap at the supermarket. However, that food is purchased at the high cost of enormous ecological damage. Zimdahl details various interrelated forms of damage that can be traced substantially, if not wholly, to agriculture.[6] They include:

- *Depletion of water resources* by irrigation, along with *waterlogging and salinization of soil* through overirrigation. Agriculture consumes 70 percent of the water used by humans, yet the millennia-long history of agriculture shows that irrigation practices eventually result in irretrievable damage: "No irrigation dependent society, with the possible exception of Egypt, has survived."
- *Desertification* and *soil erosion*, both results of the removal of forest and moisture- and soil-retaining plant cover. Seventy percent of the world's drylands may now be threatened by desertification. Perhaps one-third of all topsoil in the United States has already been lost, and erosion rates greatly outpace the soil replacement rate – under agricultural conditions, about one inch every 500 years.
- *Fertilizer and pesticide contamination* of water sources (from local streams to the Gulf of Mexico), food, and animal feed; atmospheric contamination by ammonia and methane. Most of the 220,000 deaths that result from pesticide pollution each year occur in the developing world.

Ecological damage is correlated with and compounded by social costs: the steady and widespread deterioration of rural communities around the world, and the unsustainable swelling of cities, especially in South Asia and Africa, due to the influx of farmers who have lost their land and livelihood. The productionist ethic assumes that humans, armed with technology, can control natural systems and direct them to our ends. In other words, it assumes that science and technology are both limitlessly powerful and benign – although ordinary reason would judge that combination to be unlikely.

The productionist ethic is a way of thinking aimed solely at maximizing short-term profit for the relative few. It contrasts completely with the "land ethic" set forth by Aldo Leopold in an essay, written in the mid-twentieth century, that remains seminal for ecological and agrarian thinking. The land ethic expresses itself in patterns of thought and life directed toward the long-term health (sustainability) of the "land community." *Homo sapiens* belongs, as "plain member and citizen,"[7] to a community consisting of soil, water, air, and animate creatures ranging from the microbial to the mammal; the lives of all these are intertwined in countless complex ways, most of them still unknown. Leopold identifies the one great change we must make in order to be responsible citizens: "[Q]uit thinking about decent land-use as solely an economic problem. Examine each question in terms of what is ethically and esthetically right, as well as what is economically expedient. A thing is right when it tends to preserve the integrity, stability, and beauty of the biotic community. It is wrong when it tends otherwise."[8]

Leopold, a forester and professor of agricultural economics and game management (University of Wisconsin), has the sensibility of a naturalist; he combines the scientist's precise awareness of the operation of natural systems with the poet's esthetic sensitivity to wholeness and beauty, including beauty that is being lost or (more commonly now) actively destroyed. "We are remodeling the Alhambra with a steam-shovel, and we are proud of our yardage. We shall hardly relinquish the shovel, which after all has many good points, but we are in need of gentler and more objective criteria for its successful use."[9] Such a sensibility and voice is even more indispensable to the ethical conversation now than it was sixty years ago. Leopold himself was a naturalist utterly unlike the (eighteenth-century) stereotype of an assiduous hobbyist writing for the edification of the "gentle" class. The contemporary naturalist, Barry Lopez suggests, serves as "a kind of emissary..., working to reestablish good relations with all the biological components humanity has excluded from its moral universe." Therefore, she cannot afford to be economically naïve or politically apathetic; "a politics with no biology, or a politics without field biology... is a vision of the gates of Hell."[10]

Neither Lopez nor Leopold expresses a religious sensibility, and certainly not a biblical one. Leopold objects to what he takes to be the Bible's view of unlimited human privilege,[11] and Lopez seeks "to keep the issue of spirituality free of religious commentary."[12] Yet their understanding that humans are bound to the earth in an integrity that is biological, moral, and "spiritual," as well as political and economic, is not so alien to the biblical worldview as they themselves might suppose. Evidence of such an awareness appears with particular density in the poetic writings of the Bible. Psalm 85, a liturgical poem that modern readers might otherwise take to be merely fanciful, offers an example:

> You showed favor, YHWH, to your land;
> you turned the fortune of Jacob.
> You forgave the iniquity of your people;
> you covered all their sin.
> . . . .
> Show us, YHWH, your faithful action [*hesed*];
> and grant us your salvation.
> I will listen for what God might say –
> YHWH, for he speaks *shalom*
> to his people and to his faithful ones,
> that they may not return to folly.
> Yes, [YHWH's] salvation is close to those who fear him,
> so glory may dwell in our land.
> Faithful action [*hesed*] and truth meet each other;
> righteousness and *shalom* kiss.
> Truth springs up from the earth
> and righteousness peers down from heaven.
> Indeed, YHWH will give what is good
> and our land will give its yield.
> Righteousness goes before him,
> that he may set his steps on the way. (Ps. 85:2–3, 8–14 (1–2, 7–13 Eng.))

This poem-prayer seems to reflect some disruption in the social and also the natural order. "[God's] people" have endured severe but unspecified suffering: likely military defeat followed by exile and vassalage. Another possibility is prolonged drought, the most common form of "natural" disaster in Israel – although to the biblical writers it represents a rupture in Israel's relationship with God (see 1 Kgs. 17:1; Jeremiah 14). In any case, the poet seeks and envisions healing, on terms that have certain points of connection with the kind of contemporary land ethic we have considered. What Leopold calls "the land community," the biblical writers call "heaven and earth." Here they appear in perfect harmony; the original wholeness (*shalom*) of creation is reestablished within the historical order. Underlying this picture are several related assumptions: that humans and land exist in a biotic unity before God, that their unity has identifiable moral dimensions (faithful action, truth, righteousness), that the moral restoration of God's people elicits God's gracious response in the form of agricultural productivity, and further (as suggested by the final purpose clause), that human righteousness is the one condition that invites and even makes possible God's continued presence in the land. Those might be identified as the basic elements of the Bible's distinctly *theological* land ethic.

Every writer who has a land ethic – Leopold, Lopez, and the psalmist included – also has a specific territory. Writing that is genuinely agrarian can come only from a relationship with a place deep enough to shape the minds of writer and readers. My own mind and habits of biblical interpretation are being reshaped as I learn to take account of the biblical writers' abiding awareness of their place; I now see things I previously read past, even in very familiar texts. The effect is to make my readings more *material*. I notice how carefully the biblical writers attend to the physical means of human existence, the chief of those being arable land. I notice also how often the text – in its narrative detail or legal prescriptions, in the metaphors chosen by its poets – reflects the particularities of place. "All enduring literature is local," says the American Midwestern writer Scott Russell Sanders – "rooted in place, in landscape or cityscape, in particular ways of speech and climates of mind."[13]

Certainly the Scriptures of ancient Israel know where they come from. They reflect the narrow and precariously balanced ecological niche that is the hill country of ancient Judah and Samaria – "a strip of land between two seas," as they say, with water to the west and relatively barren wilderness to the east. The Israelite farmers knew that they survived in that steep and semiarid land by the grace of God and their own wise practices. And it was no small part of Israelite wisdom to recognize that, unlike their neighbors – the Philistines on the fertile plain of Sharon, the Egyptians and Babylonians ranged along the banks and canals of their great rivers – they had only the slightest margin for negligence, ignorance, or error. The Bible as we have it could not have been written beside the irrigation canals of Babylon, or the perennially flooding Nile, any more than it could have emerged from the vast fertile plains of the North American continent. For revelation addresses the necessities of a place as well as a people. Therefore, ancient Israel's Scripture bespeaks throughout an awareness of belonging to a place that is at once extremely fragile and infinitely precious. Fragility belongs essentially to the character of this land and may even contribute to its value. Seasonal aridity and periodic drought, a thin layer of topsoil, susceptibility to erosion – these mark the land of Canaan as a place under the immediate, particular care of God. Thus Moses instructs the Israelites in the wilderness:

> For the land into which you are entering to take possession of it – it is not like the land of Egypt from which you have come out, where you would sow your seed and water with your foot, like a vegetable garden. The land to which you are passing over [the Jordan] to possess it is a land of mountains and valleys. By the measure of the rain from the heavens it drinks water [or: you will drink water]. It is a land which YHWH your God looks after; always the eyes of YHWH your God are on it, from the beginning of the year to the end of the year (Deut. 11:10–12).

This is a brilliant piece of agrarian rhetoric. The authorial voice of Deuteronomy is that of a skilled preacher, here urging the Israelites to reimagine their land as blessed precisely in the fragility that necessitates and therefore guarantees God's unwavering attention. Thus indirectly the Deuteronomic preacher commands the people's caring attention to their land, and that is the basic aim of all agrarian writing. Scott Sanders observes: "What most needs our attention now ... is the great community of land – air and water and soil and rock, along with all the creatures, human and otherwise, that share the place. We need to imagine the country anew ... as our present and future home, a dwelling place to be cared for on behalf of all beings for all time."[14] I believe that the Bible is much more able to promote that sort of imagining than we in this generation have recognized, for the simple reason that agrarianism is the mind-set native to many if not most of the biblical writers themselves. At the same time, if we who read the Bible, each in our own place, stretch our minds to reimagine the land we know as a home to be cherished, that effort will make us better readers of Scripture.

For ethics informs exegesis, at least as much as the other way around. In his study of New Testament ethics, Richard Hays distinguishes four "critical operations" that overlap and interpenetrate one another: (1) exegesis, (2) reading in canonical context, (3) drawing the connection with the contemporary situation, and (4) "living the text." "The first thing we must do," he says, " ... is to explicate in detail the messages of the individual writings in the canon. ... "[15] But my point here is that it is not always possible to do good exegesis as a first step. Sometimes important aspects of the text are not visible to an interpreter – or a whole generation of interpreters – until there has been a reordering of our minds and even our lives, until certain gaps have been supplied in the sphere of our "active apprehension."[16] To put that in theological language, sin – lack of proper knowledge and love of God and neighbor – impedes exegesis.

These essays explore how multiple strands of the Hebrew Scriptures articulate a clear message about respect and care for the land and conversely about
its destruction, and further, how that message, heard in our present context,
may be crucial to ensuring the continued habitability of the earth. No generation before us needed to hear it as much as we do, because ours is the
first society that has presumed to style itself as "post-agricultural." At the
end of the millennium, Steven Blank, an economist in the Department of
Agricultural and Resource Economics at the University of California, Davis,
announced – in a publication called *The Futurist* – that "American agriculture
is heading for the last roundup," and that Americans must learn to let go
of a "lifestyle choice" that is becoming prohibitively expensive. "In the long
run, this means becoming citizens of the world, dependent on others for food
commodities while Americans produce the marvels and the know-how for
the future."[17] Blank's blithe assumption that food can be grown anywhere –
"The whole world can do it"[18] – and transported long distances to wherever
(wealthy) people wish to eat it suggests a lack of prescience about peak oil, not
to mention terrorist and climatic threats to regional food security. It is now
becoming evident to many that our current practices of moving food around
the world have a short future; that lifestyle choice will soon be prohibitively
expensive. Moreover, it should be sobering for readers of the Bible to recognize
that the tacitly accepted cultural presumption that agriculture has no essential
place in the American "portfolio" separates us completely from the agrarian
mind-set of the biblical writers and thus renders us incapable of seeking their
guidance with respect to a matter that is vital to human health and survival
in every place. That incapacity is a moral failing for which future generations
will surely hold us accountable.

THE PRIMACY OF THE LAND

In the rest of this essay, I highlight four aspects of contemporary agrarian
thinking that touch and illumine central elements of biblical thought about
land care. The first of these is the principle that "the land comes first,"[19] in
a sense that is more than geological. About a dozen years ago, early in my
attempts to teach on the subject of biblical theology and land use, I was reading
the shelves in the soil science section of Yale's undergraduate library, hoping
to get a broad and manageably shallow overview of how scientists view land
and its fertility. One title in particular caught my eye: *Meeting the Expectations
of the Land*. Thinking, "Whoever came up with that title understands how
the Bible thinks about land," I pulled it off the shelf. That collection of
agrarian essays, edited by Wes Jackson, Wendell Berry, and Bruce Colman,

was my first introduction to a fundamentally different way of viewing land in contemporary settings.

"Meeting the expectations of the land" – agrarians know the land, not as an inert object, but as a fellow creature that can justly expect something from us whose lives depend on it. If my instinctive response to this notion was one of recognition, that is because a fundament of biblical anthropology, as set forth in the first chapters of Genesis, is that there is a kinship between humans and the earth: "And YHWH God formed the human being ['ādām], dust from the fertile soil ['ădāmâ]" (Gen. 2:7). Although the wordplay is captured surprisingly well by the English pun "human from humus," the Hebrew is more fully descriptive of their family resemblance. Both words are related to 'ādōm, "ruddy"; in the Levant, brownish red is the skin tone of both the people and the earth. *Terra rossa*, "red earth," is the geological term for the thin but rich loam covering the hill country where the early Israelites settled. Thus 'ādām from 'ădāmâ is localized language; it evokes the specific relationship between a people and their particular place.

To my mind, the most suggestive expression of the primacy of the earth appears a few verses after that pun, in the first Yahwistic statement about human vocation: "And YHWH God took the human and set him in the garden of Eden *lĕʿobĕdāh ûlĕšomĕrāh*" (Gen. 2:15). I leave those words untranslated for a moment, because any translation dissolves the meaningful ambiguity in both verbal phrases. A common translation is "to till it and tend it" (NJPS), but that implies that the terms are horticultural and agricultural, and they are not. ʿ-b-d is the ordinary verb equivalent to English "work," and it normally means to *work for* someone, divine or human, as a servant, slave, or worshiper. Much less frequently, ʿ-b-d denotes *work* done *on* or *with* some material, and in all cases but one, that material is soil (e.g., Gen. 2:5; 3:23; 4:2). In view of those nearby references to working the soil, one may certainly translate here "to work it." But the wider usage of the verb suggests that it is legitimate also to view the human task as *working for* the garden soil, serving its needs. Even the connotation of worship (cautiously applied) may inform our understanding. While biblical religion clearly forbids divinization of the earth, one might recall that the English word "worship" originally meant "to acknowledge worth." In that sense, the Hebrew wordplay translates well into English. The soil is worthy of our service.

In a study of Genesis 2–11 – perhaps the first full study of a biblical text to have been undertaken from an agrarian perspective – Theodore Hiebert often translates the verb ʿ-b-d thus, as "serve." Extrapolating from that understanding, however, he goes too far in asserting that for the Yahwistic writer, "the land is a sovereign to be served."[20] As is clear from the rest of the Primeval

History, including and especially the account of the flood, the creator God alone is sovereign in heaven and on earth. Although there is some truth to Hiebert's claim that "[c]ultivation was an act of service to that which held absolute power over one's survival and destiny,"[21] the early history of humankind acknowledges power, potential for doing good and inflicting harm, on both sides of the relationship between humans and the fertile soil. When humans violate the terms of what is in fact a three-way relationship – among themselves, the fertile earth, and God – then the soil suffers degradation; it is "accursed on [their] behalf" (Gen. 3:17). The fertile earth withholds its strength (4:12), and farmers, beginning with Cain, suffer the consequences. A contemporary prayer delineates accurately the biblical understanding that our intended service to the land is a holy obligation precisely because it is part of our service to God: "Give us all a reverence for the earth as your own creation, that we may use its resources rightly in the service of others and to your honor and glory. . . ."[22]

Since the first of the two verbs in Genesis 2:15 *can* be applied to working the soil, it is the second verb that confirms the ambiguity of the whole phrase; *š-m-r* does not elsewhere refer to land care.[23] A common translation is "keep" – for example, a flock (1 Sam. 17:20), or a household (2 Sam. 15:16), or a brother (Gen. 4:9). But frequently the verb translates "observe," with a variety of nuances, several of which may be apt here: to acquire wisdom by observation of the workings of the world (Ps. 107:43; Isa. 42:20), to abide by moral guidelines or the dictates of justice (Hos. 12:7 [6 Eng.]; Isa. 56:1) or even the rhythms of nature (Jer. 8:7), and – the sense that applies in the majority of instances of the verb – to observe the ordinances of God: "Yes, my Sabbaths you shall keep!" (Exod. 31:13).

So it may be that the human is charged to "keep" the garden and at the same time to "observe" it, to learn from it and respect the limits that pertain to it. Indeed, keeping the ordinances of God is the sole condition on which Israel may retain its hold on the God-given – or better, God-entrusted – land of Canaan. Thus Moses instructs the Israelites just on the eve of their entry into the land: "And you shall keep [*wĕšāmartā*] his statutes and his commandments which I am commanding you this day, so it may be good for you and for your children after you, in order that you may live a long time on the fertile soil [*'ădāmâ*] that YHWH your God is giving to you, for all time" (Deut. 4:40). This instruction to keep the garden might then point toward the obligation to keep *torah*, the totality of divine teaching that directs Israel's life with God, in and on the land.

"And YHWH God took the human and set him in the garden of Eden to work and serve it, to preserve and observe it." Even in this (fleeting) narrative moment of life under ideal conditions, the human does not take priority over the land. Adam comes to Eden as a protector, answerable for the well-being of the precious thing that he did not make; he is to be an observer, mindful of limits that are built into the created order as both inescapable and fitting. The biblical writer does not subscribe to the fantasy that our society has embraced as an ideal – that human ingenuity runs up against physical limits only in order to overcome them. Rather, the ambiguous verbs suggest a different orientation to reality. The land instantiates limits that God has set; we encounter it as a fellow creature to be respected and even revered.

Notably, the Yahwistic writer begins the second part of the composite creation account[24] by establishing the fact that the land's existence as an integrated "natural system" predated humankind: "On the day that YHWH God made earth and heaven, and before there was any shrub of the field on the earth, or any grain of the field had sprouted (for YHWH had not yet brought rain upon the earth, and there was no human to work/serve the fertile soil), then a mist would rise up from the earth and water the whole surface of the fertile soil" (Gen. 2:4b–6). This look back to the beginning is recognizably that of an Israelite, whose social world was dominated and indeed made possible by a mixed agricultural economy of rain-fed crops ("the grain of the field") and small animal husbandry, sheep and goats pastured on the "shrub of the field."[25] The effect is that hearers of the creation story were reminded not so much of how things might have been in a bygone age, but of the particular features of their distinctive social and ecological niche and of the blessings and responsibilities that pertained to it. (A different account of the time before humans and culture indeed was told in Mesopotamia, where great rivers and irrigation canals, not rain, enabled the rise of agricultural empires.)[26] Natural systems may have been transformed by human presence and agency, but that does not mean that humans could (or ever can) control these systems. Rather, we are included within them; our life depends entirely upon their continued integrity. If we are wise, then, we will recognize that the land rightly "expects something from us." Wendell Berry's fictional character Wheeler Catlett makes that assertion and continues the thought: "The line of succession, the true line, is the membership of people who know it does."[27] Wheeler, the lawyer for the farming community in Berry's (semiautobiographical) world of Hargrave and Port William, Kentucky, is speaking of the line of those who properly belong to the land, whose care of the land makes them worthy to inherit it – that is, to hold it in trust for the next generation.

The Bible has a story that exemplifies the line of succession that can be secured by land care. It is the story of Noah, that "righteous man [who] was distinguished for integrity in his age" (*'îš ṣaddîq tāmîm hāyâ bĕdōrōtāyw*, Gen. 6:9; cf. 7:1). At his birth, Noah's father Lamekh declares: "This one will bring us relief" from the long-accursed condition of the soil (5:29; cf. 3:17). That destiny is fulfilled, but only after the flood has washed away the human-initiated "ruination" of the earth (6:11–13), when God has restored the steady cycle of "seedtime and harvest" (8:22) and through Noah initiated the covenant "with all flesh on the earth" (9:17). At that point, Noah the righteous man receives a new "heroic epithet," complementary to the first: "And Noah got started [as] *'îš hā'ădāmâ* [a man of the fertile soil], and he planted a vineyard" (9:20).[28] Norman Wirzba aptly comments:

> There is an integrity to creation that depends on humans seeing themselves as properly placed within a network of creation and God. The drama shows us that neither God nor the creation itself can tolerate violence, manipulation, or shame. Instead of the hubris that characterized Adam and his descendents, Noah stands out as a beacon of the humbled *adam* who is faithful to the needs of *adamah*.[29]

The verbs *'-b-d* and *š-m-r* imply a humble recognition of the land's primacy and its needs. The latter suggests also an element of vulnerability; anything that humans are charged to preserve, they are also capable of neglecting or violating. So the two elements of the human vocation stand in some tension as well as in complementary relation; each verb leads us back to the other. In order to live, we are obliged to "work" the land (*lĕ'obĕdāh*) – manage it and take from it. In order to "live a long time" on it, we are equally obliged to "preserve it" (*lĕšomĕrāh*). Limiting our take, we must submit our minds, our skills, and our strength to serving its needs – the second sense of *'-b-d*. Of the tension inherent in the biblical statement, Evan Eisenberg observes:

> There is no escaping the need to manage nature. The best we can do is to observe the following rule: So manage nature as to minimize the need to manage nature. . . .

> We are destined to work our way across the globe, turning Eden into something else. And we are destined – in our better moments – to protect Eden against our own work. The command to protect puts upper limits on the scope of our work and lower limits on its quality. In other words, we must not try to manage too much of the world, but what we do manage – our cities, our factories, our farms – we must manage well.[30]

Wes Jackson's Natural Systems Agriculture epitomizes a style of management that begins with recognition of the land's primacy. An evolutionary biologist and plant breeder, Jackson and his colleagues at The Land Institute in Salina, Kansas, look to nature as "model, measure, and mentor,"[31] allowing imagination and action to be limited and guided by the way the world itself works. While most farmers and scientists take contemporary problems and achievements as their starting point, Jackson began thirty years ago to reorient his thinking, to focus on the problem *of* agriculture, rather than problems *in* agriculture. In effect, he went behind ten thousand years of farming practice based on the domestication and cultivation of annuals. He is creating a new model based on what he observed in the tall-grass prairie: Perennial grasses and flowers, growing in mixtures, reproduce abundantly year after year, even as they build and maintain rich soils without erosion and fend off pests and disease. By contrast, annual crops grown nearby – maize, sorghum, wheat, sunflowers, and soy – require inputs of pesticides, herbicides, or fertilizers. Thus they make heavy use of fossil fuels, both directly (for farm machinery) and indirectly (for processing of the chemical inputs).

Living on and learning from the tall-grass prairie, the researchers at The Land Institute are developing a new agriculture based on perennial grains grown in polyculture. "With their roots commonly exceeding depths of two meters, perennial plant communities are critical regulators of ecosystem functions, such as water management and carbon and nitrogen cycling." In addition to requiring less fossil fuel inputs, perennial crops sequester 50 percent more carbon than do annuals. Thus they "lower the amount of carbon dioxide in the air while improving the soil's fertility."[32] The Land Institute scientists do not imagine that the particular agricultural practices suited to the North American prairie could be utilized everywhere. The importance of the model they offer to agriculturalists lies in their twin principles of local adaptation and learning from natural systems. To biblical interpreters, they may provide the best exemplar currently available of what it might mean for this generation to work the garden and serve it, to observe and thus to preserve it.

WISDOM AND INFORMED IGNORANCE

A second element of contemporary agrarianism that may be correlated with a biblical mind-set is the forthright embrace of ignorance: "Since we're billions of times more ignorant than knowledgeable, why not go with our long suit and have an ignorance-based worldview?"[33] Wes Jackson has long asserted that the ecological crisis is the result of "a knowledge-based worldview founded on the assumption that we can accumulate enough knowledge to bend nature pliantly and to run the world." The alternative he proposes is "regarding informed ignorance as an apt description of the human condition and the appropriate result of a good education."[34]

Likewise, botanist and plant pathologist Robert Zimdahl describes his own professional education as growth into an appropriate ignorance:

> I recall learning as a student that metaphorically speaking science was able to shine light on human problems and solve them. . . . However, we also learned that as the area of light grew, the area of darkness surrounding it grew more. It seemed incongruous, but as our knowledge grew, our ignorance grew even more. But, that is how the world works. We learn through education what we don't know.[35]

Jackson and Zimdahl have both devoted a lifetime to scientific study, and they share a concern to "expand the realm of enquiry about agriculture."[36] If they share also the understanding that ignorance is not finally a fixable problem, or even a problem at all, that is not because they repudiate the value of scientific knowledge. What they do reject is the modern conceit that human behavior is invariably ameliorated by more knowledge: If we knew for certain that some of our behaviors were wrong, we would stop them. Thus, they share the biblical writers' view that what underlies moral failure is not simple ignorance but rather sin (a word that Jackson at least is willing to use): a culpable pride, a destructive lack of humility.

The idea that moral and spiritual health begins with the willingness to be "void of self-wisdom"[37] is especially strong in the thought of the biblical sages:

> Trust to YHWH with your whole heart
> and do not rely on your own understanding.
> In all your ways know him;
> it is he who will keep your paths straight.
> Do not be wise in your own eyes;
> fear YHWH and turn away from evil. (Prov. 3:5–7)

As with the agrarians, the biblical writers' willingness to accept and even highlight ignorance as basic to the human condition reflects, not laziness or despair, but their confidence that there is a wisdom worked into the very fabric of things:

> YHWH by wisdom founded the earth;
> he established the heavens with understanding.
> By his knowledge the deeps were cleaved,
> and the clouds dripped dew.

> My child, do not let these depart from your eyes;
> hold onto discernment and astuteness,
> and they will be life to your soul
> and grace to your neck.
> Then you will walk safely on your way,
> And your foot will not stumble. (Prov. 3:19–23)

The willingness to be ignorant in this deepest sense is what the biblical writers call "the fear of YHWH." It is "the beginning of wisdom" (Prov. 1:7), for its essence is the rejection of arrogance and intellectual dishonesty:

> The fear of YHWH is hatred of evil:
> pride and arrogance and an evil way,
> and a mouth [speaking] inversions I hate. (Prov. 8:13)

The fear of YHWH leads to a critical appreciation of both the world and ourselves; it is the necessary condition for reading the world accurately, speaking truthfully about it, and acting out of humility. Something of the practical content of the fear of YHWH is expressed in this characterization of wisdom, written by contemporary theologians: "[W]isdom is about trying to integrate knowledge, understanding, critical questioning and good judgement with a view to *the flourishing of human life and the whole of creation.* Theological wisdom attempts all that before God, alert to God, and in line with the purposes of God."[38]

For an agrarian reading of the Bible, it is instructive that the sages treat agriculture as a primary realm in which God's wisdom is needed and utilized by humanity. Proverbs includes various instructions for farmers (e.g., 24:27; 27:23–27); moreover, the bad farmer is for the sages the epitome of *'aṣlût*, "sloth," the destructive quality that constitutes the antithesis of wisdom (24:30–34).[39] However, the most direct picture of the good farmer drawing upon God's wisdom comes from Isaiah:

> Does the plowman plow all day in order to seed,
> open and harrow his soil?
> Does he not, if he has leveled its surface,
> then scatter black cumin and broadcast cumin,
> and put wheat in rows,
> barley in strips,[40]
> and spelt in its own section?
> He instructs him in the right way;
> his God teaches him. (Isa. 28:24–26, cf. v. 29)

A wise farmer varies his work, observing the different moments of the agricultural task. These lines may also imply that the farmer matches his actions to the particular features of his own land – a necessity for all good farming, and particularly in the highly diverse uplands of Canaan, which can be worked successfully only in patches and small lots. A concern for scale in all uses of technology, for choosing a scale small enough so that the work matches the place, is for the contemporary agrarians one of the marks of wisdom. Conversely, "[w]e identify arrogant ignorance by its willingness to work on too big a scale, and thus to put too much at risk."[41]

If we can see God's wise foundational work shaping our world, then we are ready to dispense with the false distinction between "practical work" on the one hand and "spiritual work" or "religious service" on the other, and likewise with the separation between scientific knowledge and practical wisdom. All our mental and physical activity should be directed toward shaping human life and (inescapably) the earth we must manage in order to survive, in accordance with the divine wisdom manifested in natural systems. With a poetic concision and a perspective that align his thought with that of the biblical sages, poet and farmer Wendell Berry confesses a wise ignorance and, at the same time, a clear sense of our common human vocation to serve the earth:

> . . . I am slowly falling
> into the fund of things. And yet to serve the earth,
> not knowing what I serve, gives a wideness
> and a delight to the air, and my days
> do not wholly pass. It is the mind's service. . . . [42]

A MODEST MATERIALISM

A third point of connection between modern agrarianism and biblical thinking is so pervasive and fundamental to both that it might seem hardly necessary to mention – namely, their exacting concern with the *materiality* of human existence. The agrarians pose the question overtly: How can we meet our material needs, in the present and for the indefinite future, without inflicting damage? The biblical writers are likewise concerned with ordering material existence in ways that are consonant with God's will and the design of the world. So they are all in a sense materialists: They prefer to write in concrete and specific terms rather than abstractions.[43] But they are *modest* materialists. They do not claim that what we humans can (or theoretically, ever could) see or touch or make is exhaustive of what *is*, nor even that it constitutes the larger or more important part of what is. They simply insist, and model by example, that we "owe a certain courtesy to Reality, and that this courtesy can be enacted only by humility, reverence, propriety of scale, and good workmanship."[44]

Yet if it sounds altogether odd to call the biblical writers and the new agrarians "materialists," that is because our society is characterized by materialism of a very different sort. Our materialism extends beyond our addiction to the acquisition and eventual disposal of vast quantities of unnecessary stuff. We are materialistic in a second, more abstract sense. A generation ago, E. F. Schumacher spoke of industrial society's unquestioning acceptance of the presuppositions and illusions of "materialistic scientism."[45] Among the most powerful and probably the most dangerous of its illusions is the idea that "science can solve all problems" – even though it is common experience that the efficient solution of an individual problem generates a host of new ones.[46] That sort of trust in the omnipotence of science is of course a kind of faith stance, albeit a wobbly one.[47] If it were to be found in a premodern society, we would unhesitatingly label as "magical" a kind of thinking that presumes to guarantee certain physical results and yet bears such a tenuous relation to empirical reality. For, despite its ostensible grounding in science, this form of materialism is strangely oblivious to what may be the most readily observable and nonnegotiable characteristic of our material world, namely, finitude. Those who work consciously and intelligently within material reality (as though we could work elsewhere!) are continually confronted with limits of time, space, matter, and energy. Writing some thirty years after Schumacher, Barbara Kingsolver gives an updated report on the status of the illusion:

> Most of our populace and all our leaders are participating in a mass hallucinatory fantasy in which the megatons of waste we dump in our rivers and bays are not poisoning the water, the hydrocarbons we pump into the air are not changing the climate, overfishing is not depleting the oceans, fossil fuels will never run out, wars that kill masses of civilians are an appropriate way to keep our hands on what's left, we are not desperately overdrawn at the environmental bank, and *really*, the kids are all right.[48]

Within the first few pages of the Bible, we find a mocking exposé of an attitude very similar to our scientific materialism: the ambition and perverse confidence that led the people "on the plain of Shinar" (central Mesopotamia) to build "a city, and a tower with its head in the sky." "Let's make a name for ourselves, so we won't be scattered over the face of the earth!" (Gen. 11:4). City-builders all clumped together, resisting dispersion, with their inflated imaginations in the clouds – this is a caricature of what the Israelites saw in the technologically dominant culture of their age, the great riparian civilization to the east. Beginning already in the fourth millennium B.C.E., aggressive channeling of the Tigris and the Euphrates produced an agricultural system of unprecedented productivity, which in turn produced a burst of population. The surplus of food and labor enabled the construction of immense walled cities – most notably, in biblical times, Nineveh and Babylon – each with a ziggurat dominating the skyline. Yet centuries of heavy irrigation exacted their environmental price, in the form of a rising water table, salinization of the soil, erosion, and silting. As Aldo Leopold observes, the violence of humanly induced land transformation varies in proportion to population density; "a dense population requires a more violent conversion."[49] The Israelite caricature perhaps reflects the historical fact that over the millennia, the cities in the lower part of the plain suffered eclipse. Gradually and repeatedly, when the "breadbasket" for each city became unproductive, the center of power moved upstream to a less damaged region.[50] A large section of the once-Fertile Crescent remains salt fields to this day.

The Israelites, in contrast to their materially more fortunate neighbors, never had enough water or arable land to waste. They managed to establish themselves in the steep, rocky hill country because it was the only part of the land of Canaan that nobody else wanted. They survived as farmers by becoming intimate with their land, by learning to meet its expectations and its needs, and by passing on their knowledge, with each generation serving as the human "seed stock" indispensable for the well-being of the next. Probably that is why they developed agrarian insight, and therefore they could see that the Babel-onians' folly lay in taking their minds off the ground, neglecting the well-being of the soil. Laboring on a city with its sky-scraping tower, they fancied that they could avoid "scattering over the face of the whole earth" (Gen. 11:4). The Tower of Babel story captures what may be the essence of all technologically induced disaster: the illusion that our cleverness will somehow deliver us from the need to observe the normative form of materialism that sustains life.

> The heavens are YHWH's heavens,
> but the earth he has given to human beings. (Ps. 115:16)

The tower builders aspire to be exceptional – "Let's make a name for ourselves" – by pursuing an alternative "lifestyle" disconnected from the earth. In the story, God shatters that illusion with one quick divine visitation, although in real time it may take generations, centuries, even millennia for the disaster to complete itself. By the grace of God, the biblical story might yet enable us to recognize ourselves in that tragic historical process somewhere short of the end. Thus it gives us a reason and a chance to do justice in the ordering of our material lives, to practice the "elaborate courtesy," as Berry calls it, that the well-being of all creatures, ourselves included, demands.[51]

VALUE BEYOND PRICE

A fourth and final point of congruence between the contemporary agrarians and the biblical writers concerns the way they assign value to land. As a native Californian, I am acutely aware that real estate has a price, and it is a high one. To be overly dramatic, I am an exile; I could never afford to own property on the small island in the San Francisco Bay on which I grew up. So the agrarian principle most deeply challenging of my personal experience is this: In any economy with a long-term future, the price of land is not an essential matter. Indeed, any culture or people with a long-term future must understand that the value of land is not monetary; as Berry's character Wheeler Catlett observes: "[W]hen you quit living in the price and start living in the place, you're in a different line of succession."[52]

It is noteworthy (if too little noted) that in ancient Israel agricultural land seems to have been literally invaluable. There is no record, biblical or inscriptional, of an Israelite voluntarily selling land on the open market,[53] because – in contrast to their neighbors in Egypt and Mesopotamia – Israelites seem to have had no concept of arable land (*'ădāmâ*) as a commodity, to be bought and sold freely. Whereas Leviticus (25:29–30) allows for sale of houses within the city wall (these would have been essentially landless houses, jammed one against the other), the fertile soil cannot be handled thus, as "private property." Rather, a piece of land is the possession of a family, to be held as a trust and transmitted from generation to generation.[54] Although the rights to land use may temporarily be sold to pay off debts, the land reverts to the original family unit every fiftieth year (Lev. 25:31). There is to be no permanently landless underclass in Israel.

Where does a people – any people, ancient or modern – find the courage to resist the cultural norm to value land as a source of ready cash? Wendell Berry's answer, though not made with reference to the Bible, is strikingly apt to that context:

> Agrarians value land because somewhere back in the history of their consciousness is the memory of being landless.... If you have no land you have nothing: no food, no shelter, no warmth, no freedom, no life. If we

remember this, we know that all economies begin to lie as soon as they assign a fixed value to land. People who have been landless know that the land is invaluable; it is worth everything.... Whatever the market may say, the worth of the land is what it always was: It is worth what food, clothing, shelter, and freedom are worth; it is worth what life is worth.[55]

The memory of being landless is central to the biblical story and therefore should be common to every Israelite. The Deuteronomic preacher's rhetoric makes the experience of land deprivation immediate and personal, as each Israelite farmer recites "before YHWH": "My father was a stray Aramean, and he went down to Egypt and sojourned there . . . , and the Egyptians treated *us* badly . . . , and *we* cried out to YHWH . . . and he brought *us* to this place, . . . a land oozing[56] with milk and honey. And now, here, I have brought the first fruit of the fertile soil [*'ădāmâ*] that you gave to *me*, YHWH . . . " (Deut. 26:5–10). The voices we hear in the Old Testament bespeak throughout an agrarian mindfulness that land – this particular land, my land, our land – is inseparable from self "before God." Land is the earnest of the covenant, the tangible sign and consequence of God's commitment to the people Israel.

Implicit in that recitation is a claim on both God and land that is intensely personal yet not private. In his indispensable study of Israel's land theology, Christopher Wright suggests that the covenant is properly conceived as a triangulated relationship among Israel, the land, and YHWH, "all three having the family as the basic focal point at which the conjunction of the three realms issued in ethical responsibilities and imperatives. . . . "[57] That sentence could almost come from one of Wendell Berry's essays, in which the claims of family, community, land, and human decency are treated as the ordinary and, therefore, essential manifestations of God's claim in human life. Unless that whole indissoluble web of relationships is kept in view, even a text as familiar as the Fifth Commandment is enigmatic precisely in its specificity: "Honor your father and your mother, *so that your days may be long on the fertile soil* [*'ădāmâ*] that YHWH your God is giving you" (Exod. 20:12, cf. Deut. 5:16). Wright observes: "Because of its explicit links with the land traditions, the relationship between God and Israel was thoroughly 'earthed' in the socio-economic facts of life – shaping and being shaped by them, and at times threatened by developments in that realm."[58] He is speaking of the Iron Age, of course. But Berry and the other new agrarians might well say that the manifold crises of contemporary agriculture and industrial culture realize such threats in our own socioeconomic situation; they show us what the unraveling of the web of covenant relationships looks like "on the ground." The chapters that follow offer an agrarian (re)reading of foundational biblical texts, with the aim of discovering in them clues as to how we may contribute to the reweaving of that fragile web.

3

⁂

Seeing with God: Israel's Poem of Creation

God's seeing protects the world from falling back into the void, protects it from total destruction. God sees the world as good, as created – even where it is the fallen world – and because of the way God sees his work and embraces it and does not forsake it, we live.

(Dietrich Bonhoeffer)[1]

To preserve our places and to be at home in them, it is necessary to fill them with imagination. To imagine as well as see what is in them. Not to fill them with the junk of fantasy and unconsciousness, for that is no more than the industrial economy would do, but to see them first clearly with the eyes, and then to see them with the imagination in their sanctity, as belonging to the Creation.

(Wendell Berry)[2]

READING GENESIS 1 AS A POEM

The first chapter of Genesis would seem to present an initial and perhaps insurmountable challenge to my thesis that the dominant mind-set expressed in the Hebrew Scriptures is agrarian. Ecologically sensitive readers, both professional and lay, generally take offense at the notion that God commands humans to exercise dominion over the earth. The attitude of Genesis 1 is "arrogant and narcissistic," according to soil scientist Daniel Hillel, in contrast to the "more responsible role assigned to humanity in the second creation story."[3] Similarly, Theodore Hiebert, perhaps the only biblical scholar to have offered a thorough agrarian reading of one section of the Bible (Genesis 2–11), contrasts the so-called Priestly ("P," Genesis 1) and Yahwistic ("J," Genesis 2) accounts of creation of the human in this way: "Two opposite views of the relationship between humanity and the earth are present here: for P the human is the land's master, coercing it into service, while for J the human is the land's servant, performing the duties demanded by its powers and processes."[4] Norman Habel, who has devoted some years to reading the Bible "from the perspective of Earth," attempts to salvage most of the first chapter by suggesting that the account of the human is inserted as an interruption and contradiction within the "story of the unified cosmos,"[5] although he does not explain how this supposed interruption occurred within a passage that bears such strong marks of comprehensive unity.

My own view is that there is coherence not only within the first chapter but also between that chapter and the succeeding chapters, which are well described by Norman Wirzba as "the drama of soil."[6] Moreover, the first chapter provides a perspective that is essential for reading the subsequent Yahwistic account with full insight. The Priestly tradition offers a highly articulated picture of the order of creation into which we as readers are initiated on terms that are at once encouraging and deeply sobering.

The coherence and importance of Genesis 1 are best appreciated when it is read as a liturgical poem. More than twenty years have passed since Walter Brueggemann described it thus,[7] but we have not yet gained the full benefit of his insight. Carol Newsom points out that any genre represents a distinctive mode of perception; it is a "means of grasping and perceiving reality, quite literally a *form of thought*."[8] As a liturgical poem, Genesis 1 is giving form to a certain way of seeing the world, and accurate perception provides an entrée to active participation in the order of creation. Moreover, like all good liturgy, this poem is sensitive both to the reality of God and to the concrete experience of the people who may use it to enter more deeply into relationship with God. Reading the text as a poem means following its orderly presentation and highlighting the elements that suggest an aesthetic intention[9] – which is to say, noting how the text speaks to and for the imagination.

Looking for an aesthetic intention within the Priestly tradition implies a view of it very different from Gerhard von Rad's influential characterization of the Priestly "document" (in contrast to the Yahwist "narrative"): "It contains *doctrine* throughout. It is the result of intensive, theologically ordering thought. Consequently ... [t]he language is succinct and ponderous, pedantic and lacking artistry."[10] But if, as I suppose, Genesis 1 conveys meaning aesthetically, then we may begin to discern its intention by following Wendell Berry's suggestion that through the use of form, a poet "affirms and collaborates in the formality of the Creation."

> By its formal integrity a poem reminds us of the formal integrity of other works, creatures, and structures of the world. The form of a good poem is,

in a way perhaps not altogether explainable or demonstrable, an analogue of the forms of other things. By its form it alludes to other forms, evokes them, resonates with them, and so becomes a part of the system of analogies or harmonies by which we live. . . . This, I think, is a matter of supreme, and mostly unacknowledged, importance.[11]

The art of the poet, Berry suggests, is to bring words into conformity with the God-given facts of material reality, thus making their harmonies perceptible. If by the ordering of language a poem can participate in the formality of creation, then the Bible's first great poem of creation, with its highly formalized structure and language, would seem to be the ideal place to witness that participation.

Once we recognize what we are reading as poetry, then there come into play certain literary axioms suited to that form of thought. At least four such axioms bear on this reading of Genesis 1 and enable us to make sense of what is there. First, form and wording are to be taken with full seriousness. It is difficult to make too much of the words a good poet employs, although one might read them badly – for instance, by confusing poetic language with dogmatic or scientific statements. This poem then should be read with the presumption that every word is deliberately chosen and therefore important. If a word seems out of place, that is all the more reason to assume we are meant to be slowed down or arrested by it. Where repetition occurs and is pronounced (as it is here), then it must be purposeful.

Second, every poem draws upon older works, more or less consciously. Probably no good poet, and certainly no good liturgist, creates *ex nihilo*. The poetic art, observes Wendell Berry, is "communal and filial. It can only exist as a common ground between the poet and other poets and other people, living and dead. . . . Poetry can be written only because it has been written."[12] The Priestly writer is a traditionalist – is indeed so steeped in a tradition that it is hard to think of this poet as an "individual" in the modern sense. With the vast majority of biblical scholars, I assume that the Priestly writer worked within a long, multicultural tradition of creation stories and that at many points this present telling of the *mythos*, the sacred story, echoes that multicultural tradition. At the same time, the Priestly account of creation is a distinctly Israelite one, and further, this first poem of the Bible is at points innovative even within Israelite tradition. It is unlikely that the Priestly writer valued "originality" as such; the aim, presumably, was to give an account that was whole and true, albeit schematic. Nonetheless, tradition can be – in this case, is – the environment in which a great poet receives the inspiration to say something substantially new. Because our own culture's bias against tradition may blind us to its innovative aspect, it is especially crucial to listen carefully for how the poet uses words that evoke particular cultural memories and at the same time yield fresh insight.

Third, poetry, like other forms of crafted language, is a work of the imagination that reflects concrete experience, including the experience of place. The contemporary agrarian writers frequently note that literature that seeks to engage the imagination characteristically takes shape in response to a known place, the place where the writer's own imagination is rooted.[13] "Writing is to living as grass is to soil," says Scott Russell Sanders, sounding like who he is: a writer from the Great Plains of North America.[14] This is no less true of poetry that serves a liturgical function, for its aim is in large measure to enable us to discern the presence and action of God in our particular circumstances, to seek and become receptive to the gifts of God befitting this place and this situation. Methodist ranchers in San Angelo, Texas, pray for rain on a weekly basis; their coreligionists in Seattle or Suffolk are less likely to do so.

Fourth, a poem holds a "surplus of meaning"; it may mean more than one thing at any given time. Further, it can speak to different audiences in varying ways through the centuries.[15] In that sense, all of Scripture is poetry, and surely its inexhaustible potential to say something new and stunningly apt is a large part of what we mean when we call the Bible the word of the living God. My own reading suggests that Genesis 1 speaks about the human project from the standpoint of a fresh beginning, *the* beginning. And yet it already shows awareness of the possibility – indeed, the reality – of eventual failure, specifically, humanity's failure to claim its proper role in the created order. If that is so, then this text may speak to us more sharply than to any previous generation of hearers.

CATCHING THE RHYTHM

We begin to respond to a poem *as* a poem when we catch its rhythm. The rhythms of biblical Hebrew poetry are set primarily by structured repetition, verbal and thematic repetition-with-variation. In the fourth verse of Genesis 1, the baseline of the rhythm appears: "And God saw the light, that it was good [or: how good it was]." The affirmation of goodness is repeated (with variation) a total of seven times, culminating in the vivid evocation of God's experience on the sixth day:

> And God saw all that he had made,
> and here! It was very good. (Gen. 1:31)

Theological interpreters generally focus on the fact of creation's goodness. Yet the goodness of the world is presented not as simple fact, nor even as an authoritative pronouncement, but as a divine perception. Indeed, the rhetoric, especially in this climactic affirmation, conveys the immediacy of fresh response.[16]

The focus on God's experience of seeing is noteworthy, because biblical narrative usually confines itself to externals; it tells us what a character (including God) said or did. Only occasionally does it move inside the eyes, to tell us what and how someone saw, and when it does so, the specific perception is important. As the biblical narrative unfolds, it records three moments of human perception that echo this first report of God's seeing the world in its goodness: one when Eve, having listened to the snake, suddenly "saw *how good was* the tree [of knowledge of good and evil] for eating, and . . . she took some of its fruit" (Gen. 3:6); another when the "sons of God [*běnê-hā'ĕlōhîm*] saw the daughters of humanity [*běnôt hā'ādām*], *how good they were*, and they took wives for themselves" (Gen. 6:2);[17] and the third when Moses' mother first "saw him, *how good he was*," and determined that this baby boy would not be thrown into the Nile (Exod. 2:2). In each case we are invited to see how a moment of perception, human or divine, has lasting consequences for the characters in the narrative, and also for us who share their story.

Philosopher Erazim Kohák observes that the post-Enlightenment "disenchantment" of the world, which many see as the root of the ecological crisis, is chiefly a failure in perceiving what is good: "The painful flaws in our conception of value . . . call less for a new conception of the good than for a new way of *seeing* the good."[18] Kohák makes the suggestion, surprising not just for a philosopher but for anyone in the (post-)modern period, that what is most needed is a "contemplative strategy," whose purpose is to enable us to stand "in mute awe before the wonder of being."[19] I suggest that Genesis 1 is a banner instance of such a contemplative strategy, demonstrating the goodness of the world, and further, making that goodness perceptible from the vantage point of Israel's particular place in the world.

Kohák retreats somewhat from his own call for a contemplative strategy when he concedes that it is vulnerable to naïve romanticism and "poetic impotence" and therefore must be balanced and corrected by the "practical strategy" of taking active and selfless care of others.[20] However, the poet of Genesis 1 might well say that Kohák was right in the first place, for deep contemplation issues in a renewal of mind and therefore necessarily in new patterns of action. With the ordered elegance typical of the Priestly tradition, the poet is inducting us into the practice of what the theologians of the early

Greek church called "natural contemplation": looking at the world with a view to discerning "the inner principles in accordance with which things were created and are organized."[21] Such contemplation is an essential stage of the spiritual life. It enables the transition from uncomprehending action to *theology* – the latter being genuine understanding of the creative will of God in Trinity, which makes it possible to use each created thing "wisely, in accordance with nature and with the proper science."[22] True contemplation can be achieved only by those who accept *metanoia*, a profound change of mind – what English speakers call (somewhat inadequately) "repentance" – "as a path and way of life."[23]

Metanoia, like poetry, is largely a work of the insightful memory. In a poetic prayer based on the first chapter of the Bible, the fourth-century theologian Basil the Great expresses the pain of remembering that attends the experience of seeing the world differently, while at the same time he prays for renewal of mind and heart:

O God, enlarge within us the sense of fellowship
with all living things, our brothers the animals
to whom thou gavest the earth as their home in common with us.

We remember with shame that in the past
we have exercised the high dominion of [humankind] with ruthless cruelty
so that the voice of the earth, which should have gone up to thee in song,
has been a groan of travail.

May we realize that they live not for us alone
but for themselves and for thee,
and that they love the sweetness of life.[24]

The understanding of the Greek theologians opens up the biblical text more fully than can Kohák's view of contemplation, precisely because the former shares the theocentric focus of Genesis. While Kohák focuses on exemplary human action *in se*, the biblical and theological tradition holds up God's action and perception as the model for our own. Moreover, as we shall see, the structure of the text implies that seeing the world with God entails taking a critical stance toward ourselves. Contemplation and action are not separate strategies, nor is the latter a corrective to the former. They are part of a single complex process: accurate perception leading to *metanoia*, and that in turn leading to more reflective behavior. "To change one's mind . . . is to change the way one works,"[25] says Wendell Berry. Perhaps it is his dual work of writing poetry and farming that enables him to recognize the indivisibility between contemplation, a renewal of the mind, and appropriate modes of action, including our interaction with the nonhuman creatures. There is good evidence that the poet of Genesis 1 also recognizes it; the description of the "dry land" seems designed to elicit responsible action as a result of seeing the world afresh through God's eyes.

SEEDS

The base rhythm in this poem that opens the Bible is established through the first two days of creation, and it is spare. With as few words as possible, and no details, the poet traces the pattern of divine summons, or making – of light, of a firmament – followed immediately by a notice of fulfillment ("and it was so," v. 7; cf. v. 3). There is, however, a pronounced shift in rhythm on the third day, just when the dry land has been "seen" (*wĕtērā'eh*) and pronounced good (vv. 9–10). The narrative pace slows as the earth is first furnished for living – with a carpet of vegetation, with fruit trees (vv. 11–12) and "lights" (vv. 14, 15, 16)[26]–and then inhabited by "every animal being" (v. 21). Each stage of the process is more detailed than the last. The divine work on the dry land culminates in the creation, blessing, and (uniquely) the commissioning and instruction of the human creature (vv. 26–28).

Moreover, the poetic device of bracketing accentuates the significance of this portion of the narrative. The whole description of the dry land is marked off by lengthy notices about plants: at the beginning, concerning their variety and self-perpetuating fruitfulness (vv. 11–12); and at the end, concerning their distribution on the food chain: plants with cultivatable seed for humans, all other "greenery" (*yereq*) for the animals (vv. 29–30).

Those bracketing passages should attract attention by both their length and the sudden awkwardness of their language. The strict verbal economy that characterizes the rest of the chapter breaks down completely in lines such as these:

> "Let the earth sprout-out sprouts [*tadĕšē' hā'āreṣ deše'*], plants seeding seed [*mazrî'a zera'*],
> fruit trees making fruit, each of its own kind – with their seed in them – on the earth,"
> and it was so.
> And the earth brought forth sprouts, plants seeding seed each of its own kind,
> and trees making fruit with its seed in it, each of its own kind....
> (vv. 11–12)

The first phrase of the opening bracket is an ostentatious neologism: "sprout-out sprouts."[27] Its effect is magnified by the proliferation of "seed" that follows immediately here and appears again in the closing bracket:

> Here, I give you every plant seeding seed
> that is on the face of all the earth,
> and every tree that has on it tree-fruit seeding seed;
> for you it shall be, for eating. (v. 29)

When a writer as disciplined as this one sacrifices concision and elegance, there must be a good reason. It is curious, then, that biblical scholars have given scant attention to the literary character and function of these passages that bracket the whole description of the dry land.

Claus Westermann sees the first notice as an indication of how far the Priestly writer has departed from older mythic traditions of the Near East. Mesopotamian stories of origins, he argues, treat only those plants that are useful to humans for food or medicine, whereas the Priestly writer moves toward a properly scientific view of the world, by means of "processes of systemization or abstraction":[28]

> Just as creation is a subdivided and circumscribed whole, so too are the plants that cover the earth. As long as the earth exists, every single one of the millions of plants must belong to its species as part of the organized whole. The most unprepossessing piece of grass or strip of moss is part of God's coordinated world; each in its own species fits into the ordered whole.[29]

Westermann rightly perceives a comprehensive interest that might be called systematic and even scientific; the poet observes the plant world as an intricate, self-perpetuating system. But there is no "abstraction" here, if (as Westermann infers) that means that the writer is not centrally concerned with how plants and humans fit together, along with the animals, in a single system of perpetual fruitfulness. Rather, I shall argue that Genesis 1 represents in specific terms the plant world as it was known to those who occupied the highlands of the Levant, and that that view of the world has a direct bearing on the poet's understanding of the human place in the created order.

With its emphasis on seed-bearing plants in their variety and fruitfulness, Genesis 1 could not have been written just anywhere. In its very awkwardness, it points with startling clarity to the most important botanical fact about the land Israel occupied: In terms of genetic heritage, this is one of the nutritional centers of the whole earth, both for human beings and for animals. Historians and biblicists frequently observe that Canaan's location – contiguous, or nearly so, with three continents – left it wide open to passage by both trade caravans and armies. It is equally true, but less obvious to those who think history can be written entirely in terms of political and military events, that Canaan's liminal location gave that small corridor of land a gene flow with few parallels worldwide. Evan Eisenberg observes: "Even today its genetic diversity is dazzling, with flora and fauna of Europe, Africa, and Asia mingling in sometimes unsettling ways. A few thousand years ago, when the region was less bruised by human use, the mix was more dazzling still."[30]

That botanical fact eventually became cultural fact, one of the most widely consequential of all time. Ten to twelve thousand years ago, the first permanent human settlements appeared in the uplands and foothills bordering the Fertile Crescent. The hunter-gatherers known to us as Natufians built stone houses and storage facilities for the wild grains they collected: emmer wheat, einkorn wheat, and barley. The Natufians were succeeded in a millennium or so by the world's first farmers, their wild harvests by domesticated crops of wheat and barley, along with leguminous grains such as lentils, peas, chickpeas, and vetch. The single factor that most effectively conduced first to food storage and then to the invention of cultivation was the very thing that Genesis 1 celebrates: seed – specifically, readily harvestable, nutritious seed. A notable characteristic of the native plant distribution in the hill country of the Fertile Crescent is the abundance of cereals and legumes. Among these originally wild grasses was a genotype with non-shattering seed heads (in contrast to the majority of plants, whose seed scatters as soon as the heads reach maturity). Agriculture apparently originated with the selection and progressive dominance of the non-shattering type.[31] It seems likely that the phenomenon of seed-retaining, life-sustaining grains is above all what moved the poet to write of "plants seeding seed." In addition, permanent settlement allowed the domestication and improvement of the native fruits that grew in variety and abundance within the microclimates afforded by the region's hilly terrain: grapes, figs, olives, dates, pomegranates – "fruit trees making fruit . . . with their seed in them." In view of this natural and cultural history, it is evident that the seemingly otiose repetitions of the root z-r-‛, "seed," in Genesis 1 are purposeful: They bespeak a poet's alertness to the world. Far from abstract analysis, this is liturgical celebration of the familiar yet inexhaustible mystery of fruitfulness as it was experienced by the Israelites and other agrarian peoples of the Near Eastern uplands.

Read in this way, the Priestly account of creation seems not far removed from the overtly agrarian character of the Yahwist's "drama of soil." Westermann's judgment that "a scientific . . . objective interest has taken the place of a purely functional interest in plants as nourishment for humans"[32] reflects our own culture's objectivizing view of land and its products more than any attitude we could reasonably ascribe to ancient Israel. Indeed, the closing bracket of the chapter specifically mentions that the food is "for eating," by both humans (v. 29) and the other creatures (v. 30). This should not be overlooked, especially in a poem belonging to the Priestly tradition, which transmitted most of Israel's dietary regulations (Gen. 9:1–4; Lev. 11:1–46; 17:10–16).

If, however, most contemporary readers of Genesis 1 do overlook its concern for eating, that is because we belong to a culture characterized by unprecedented ignorance about where food comes from – our own food, let alone that of the other creatures. Concerning the dominant consumption patterns in our industrialized food system, Norman Wirzba observes that they

> suggest a profound disengagement from the vitality of creation. Rather than seeing eating as the most intimate engagement with the life forms all around us, a sharing in the well-being and flow of all life, we have instead turned eating into the purchasing of commodities that we can manipulate, control, and use according to convenience. . . .
>
> In the past, often because of scarcity, but also because of its inherent spiritual significance, food was central to a culture's attempt to define itself and what it held dear. It carried immense symbolic power since food consumption was the concrete act in terms of which social relations, work life, *geographical identity*, and religious ritual came together. . . . [W]hether we are intentional about it or not, the act of eating, perhaps more honestly than our public piety, expresses our moral and religious sensibilities.[33]

For most poetry – and certainly for biblical poetry – a significant aspect of a poem's "surplus of meaning" tends to be confrontational. In its original context, this poem about a world of self-perpetuating fruitfulness must have served to counter the religious ideologies of Israel's pagan neighbors. Likely the verbal sword cut in more than one direction. On the one hand, it challenged the power of the Canaanite *ba'alim*, the fertility gods thought to inseminate the earth; against that ideology, it asserted that fruitfulness, activated by seed, is a built-in feature of the design created by the one Maker of heaven and earth. On the other hand, it countered the religio-political ideology of Mesopotamia, which maintained that humans were created to provide food for the gods – a divine commission that was fulfilled through an integrated and state-sponsored food system of irrigated agriculture and cultic sacrifice.[34] The Genesis account claims the reverse: the Creator of heaven and earth is the generous One who provides food for every living creature. Further, the poem has the capacity to counter the principles of our own culture as they are expressed in our dominant system of food production. Currently, those principles would seem to be the exact opposite of the ones upheld by the Priestly tradition.

If the Priestly poem celebrates the region's amazing variety of seed as God's beneficent gift, our present agricultural system has effected a drastic reduction in plant diversity worldwide. Over two-thirds of the world's cropland is planted with monocultures of annual crops: cereal grains, food legumes, and oilseeds.[35] Moreover, the "efficiency" of industrial-scale agriculture depends upon limiting the variety for each crop. While there are in existence some 50,000 varieties of corn grouped in 200 to 300 landraces, U.S. commercial production "relies almost exclusively on the cultivation of a handful of hybrid varieties from two of these races."[36] As plant geneticist Wes Jackson points out, this is about the same amount of genetic information as is found in one human couple. The situation is similar with wheat and rice varieties. The National Center for Genetic Resources Preservation in Fort Collins, Colorado, "the putative Fort Knox of seed diversity," stores only 3 percent of the vegetable varieties that were available from seed houses at the turn of the nineteenth century.[37] The vulnerability of such a food system was evidenced when, in 1996, the fungus Karnal Bunt destroyed half the U.S. wheat crop for the year.[38]

In the industrialized food system, the biblical vision of self-perpetuating fruitfulness collides with the profit strategies of corporations aiming to control the global seed market. Just ten corporations sell an astonishing 55 percent of the seeds that produce the world's food crops.[39] It was reported in 2005 that seed giant Syngenta had applied for a multi-genome patent in 115 countries that would have given it "monopoly power over the flowering sequences of some 40 plants," until pressure from NGOs forced withdrawal of the application.[40] Had the patent gone through, it would have been illegal for farmers to save seed from the previous year's crops – a practice that dates back to the beginning of agriculture and remains indispensable to economic survival for many, especially in the Southern Hemisphere. An alternative strategy, the biological control mechanism known as the "Terminator" technology, renders sterile the second generation of seed – again forcing farmers to buy new seed each year.[41]

Sterile seed was first developed by the U.S. government, working with the seed industry, and patented in 1998. It and other genetic use restriction technologies (GURTs) have provoked heated controversy worldwide.[42] The seed industry's case is that protection of intellectual property rights encourages research and development by breeders and that farmers and the poor will, in the long term, profit from improved plant varieties.[43] In complete contrast, Pat Roy Mooney, executive director of the ETC group (formerly

Rural Advancement Foundation International [RAFI]) calls Terminator and other trait control technologies "an offensive biological weapon.... In the final analysis, trait sanctions are war on farmers and on the hungry."[44] An intermediate position is staked out by the important Consultative Group on International Agricultural Research (CGIAR), which supports fifteen independent agricultural research centers around the globe. The majority of their research focuses on "traditional breeding techniques made more efficient by new information about genes and new technologies." Although CGIAR has rejected Terminator technology and asserts its commitment to seed-saving, it states: "Where enhanced traditional breeding techniques have not been able to solve a specific problem, such as improving the vitamin content in rice, CGIAR-supported crop scientists consider that genetically modifying organisms through genetic transformation can be a valuable option." This policy may reflect the growing influence of industry on agricultural science in and for the developing world; the multinational seed corporation Syngenta is the major funding partner the CGIAR-affiliated Insect Resistant Maize for Africa program.[45]

The new realities of corporate agriculture create unprecedented and deeply disturbing possibilities for human action, specifically concerning plant production and distribution along the food chain[46] – that is, the matters treated in the framing notices around the Priestly account of the furnishing of dry land with plants and "all animate life." The closing frame immediately follows, and thus highlights, the event to which the whole section points: the creation of humans in (or as[47]) the image of God, with the charge to exercise dominion (vv. 26–28). So the question to be considered now is, how do these notices about the food supply bear on our understanding of human dominion and the command to subjugate the earth? Under the present circumstances, is there such a thing as faithful dominion, and if so, what form might it take?

THE FORM OF DOMINION

That humans now dominate the planet, and do so in a way that would have been unimaginable to any inhabitant of the ancient world, is a fact beyond dispute. Since the Priestly writer calls our attention to plant growth and other events on the dry land, I begin with the plain observation of a team of Stanford terrestrial ecologists that "between one-third and one-half of the [earth's] land surface has been transformed by human action."[48] The earth's total primary plant growth (the annual output as it would be sustained by natural ecosystems) is reduced by 40 percent through human activity, both direct consumption (for food, building, etc.) and activities that inhibit plant growth (such as paving of roads and parking lots).[49] Worldwide, about the same proportion of arable soils – a resource renewable only in geological time – are degraded to some degree.[50] The proportion is much higher for genetic "hot spots" (such as the Levant), the several regions around the globe that are richest in species variety. In these, "our activities have destroyed closer to four-fifths of the natural ecosystems.... We have high-graded the planet, taking the best bits."[51]

More than sixteen centuries ago, St. Basil cited as already long-established fact the "ruthless cruelty" of humans that prevented "the voice of the earth" from rising to God in song. Sadly, the reports of these contemporary ecologists corroborate his confession of shame and indicate that our ancient style of domination continues unabated, and with accelerated effect, so that, in our time, land transformation is the chief cause of extinction for plant and animal species. Rates are "now on the order of 100 to 1000 times those before humanity's dominance of Earth.... [A]s many as one-quarter of Earth's bird species have been driven to extinction by human activities over the past two millennia."[52] In Britain, a 1998 report to the Government's Joint Nature Conservation Committee revealed that in twenty-five years habitat loss and agricultural biocides had drastically reduced the populations of several of the (formerly) most common birds – for example, tree sparrows, by 95 percent; grey partridges, by 86 percent; and turtle doves, by 69 percent.[53] With 75 percent of marine fisheries either fished to capacity or overfished, perhaps 30 percent of fish species are threatened.[54] Our record makes an eerily exact mockery of God's commandment to the living creatures on the fifth day: "Be fruitful and multiply, and fill the waters in the seas – and the birds, let them multiply on the earth" (Gen. 1:22). Read in light of the current data, it would seem that the mockery begins already with the parallel commandment addressed to the humans on the sixth day:

> And God blessed them and said to them:
> "Be fruitful and multiply; fill the earth and conquer it [*věkibšūhā*]
> and exercise mastery among [*rědû b-*] the fish of the sea and among the
>   birds of the sky
> and among every animal that creeps on the earth." (1:28)

So the contemporary data and the biblical text together demand that we press the question, does the human "exercise [of] mastery among" the creatures necessarily make it impossible for the nonhuman creatures to thrive?

Notably, and perhaps surprisingly to the layperson, the professional ecologists' answer is "no." A Stanford team of terrestrial ecologists concludes its survey of grievous and even disastrous conditions with the paradoxical statement that precisely because our activities are causing "rapid, novel, and substantial changes" in ecosystems, "maintaining the diversity of 'wild' species and the functioning of 'wild' ecosystems will require increasing human involvement."[55] The ecologists have run into a paradox worthy of theological investigation: The extent of our interference obligates humans to exercise what they call "active management" – in the language of this biblical poem, "mastery among" the creatures. This translation is in several respects preferable to the standard "exercise dominion *over....* " The Hebrew preposition can mean "among," and the verbal phrase as a whole may denote rule that is characterized by firmness rather than harshness (see Ps. 72:8). Koehler and Baumgartner observe concerning *r-d-h* that "the basic meaning of the verb is not to rule; the word actually denotes the travelling around of the shepherd with his flock."[56] Thus, the language of Genesis 1 acknowledges the unique power of *Homo sapiens,* yet without separating us from the other creatures. J. Richard Middleton arrives at a similar conclusion when he observes concerning this verse that "the characteristic human task or role vis-à-vis both the animal kingdom and the earth *requires a significant exercise of communal power....* "[57]

The rest of this essay examines the terms with which the Priestly writer spells out a theological vision of the exercise of "mastery." That vision is conveyed in two memorable terms – *bĕṣelem 'ĕlōhîm,* "image of God" (Gen. 1:27), and *vĕkibšūhā,* "conquer it" (1:28) – both so startling that they beg for theological reflection. In fact, each term calls forth distinctive memories and associations within the historical experience of the people Israel. Their resonance is important for the function that this remarkable poem now serves: to induct its hearers into the vision of life set forth by Torah and the Bible as a whole, and further, to guide members of the community that identifies with Israel through situations that are unprecedented and even appalling.

It would seem that conformity to the image of God is the single enabling condition for the exercise of "mastery" among the creatures:

> Let us make humankind as our image, after our likeness,
> that they may exercise mastery among the fish of the sea, etc. (1:26)

The concept of *imago Dei* is so frequently evoked in postbiblical tradition[58] that it is easy to overlook its rarity in the Bible. The divine image is mentioned only five times within Hebrew Scripture – all in the Primeval History, three of them right here (Gen. 1:26–27).[59] After that, the concept recedes, not to reemerge until the Apostle Paul speaks of Jesus Christ as "the image of (the invisible) God" (2 Cor. 4:4, cf. Col. 1:15 and 3:10). Its usage suggests that the notion of *imago Dei* is inherently both powerful and open ended; its meaning cannot be fully grasped within the first chapter of the Bible, even by the most thorough exegete. Rather, one must keep reading, and living in biblical faith, in order to know what our creation in the image of God yet might mean. Middleton is surely right that Genesis 1 is meant to be read in continuity with Genesis 2, not as an alternative to it; it serves as "a prelude to the rest of the Genesis narrative, setting up the normative conditions for what follows."[60] Yet "what follows" is not Genesis alone but the whole Bible. So, the central metaphor of this poem is eventually read through a series of literary contexts – Genesis, the larger Priestly work, Torah, Hebrew Scripture, and even the entire Christian Bible – with an understanding that deepens as the context of reading expands. The present essay only begins to demonstrate the implications of such a reading.[61]

Before anything else, creation in the image of God indicates that human life has both value and form: inestimable value, and a form that is uniquely and richly expressive of divine intentions. It is widely asserted that the background of the notion of divine "image" is the ancient Near Eastern rhetoric and ideology of kingship; it denoted the Egyptian and Assyrian king's capacity and right to represent the divine will in political, social, and cultic matters.[62] The Priestly poet takes the bold step of democratizing the concept, so that humankind as a whole may be involved in "representing and perhaps extending in some way God's rule on earth through the ordinary communal practices of human sociocultural life."[63] Every ancient would have known that there is no communal practice more essential than agriculture, and we shall see how the poem registers this awareness in its representation of the human role in the cosmos.

As the Priestly vision unfolds through Torah, it becomes evident that if that ideal form of human life is to be realized anywhere, it will be in Israel, and the form of life intended for Israel is specified as holiness: "You shall be holy, for I am holy" (Lev. 11:44, 45; 19:2; 20:7, 26; cf. 21:6). Holiness in Leviticus is not primarily a quality of individuals ("you" is a grammatical plural here); holiness is the character of a community observing a comprehensive pattern of life that is healthful. As we shall see, the Priestly vision of holiness emphatically includes the land, the covenanted community of creatures who prosper along with a people living in accordance with the design of creation – or, alternatively, who suffer when the intended pattern is violated.[64]

Yet, already in the first chapter of the Priestly work, one can discern that the form of human life is fundamentally *ecological* – understanding "ecology," with Aldo Leopold, as "the science of relationships."[65] The result of conforming ourselves to the pattern given is that we are enmeshed in a harmonious web of relationships, infinitely complex in their intersections, that have in God their origin and their point of cohesion. "For with you [God] is the source of life [or: fountain of life, *měqôr ḥayyîm*]" (Ps. 36:10 [9 Eng.]). The understanding that the world is ordered as a comprehensive series of interconnected and interdependent structures is of fundamental importance for the agrarian writers, for those complex entanglements are best known as "food chains." Seminal to the agrarian discussion is Leopold's notion of land as "a fountain of energy flowing through a circuit of soils, plants, and animals. Food chains are the living channels which conduct energy upward; death and decay return it to the soil."[66]

Rereading the whole Priestly poem of creation in light of Leopold's metaphor, one sees that the Bible begins with a picture of life flowing from a twofold center – or, as the psalmist puts it, a fountain that is *with* God. Genesis 1 represents the earth as the primary acting subject, second only to God, as has been noted by readers as diverse as Norman Habel and Dietrich Bonhoeffer. Through God's action on the third day, "there comes into being the life whose true nature it is to create further life."[67] That picture is exactly in line with Berry's description of the "universal order" as it is portrayed in the traditional poetry of cultures still living in healthy relationship with their land: "The old idea of universal order was earth centered, but it does not follow . . . that it was [hu]man-centered. The structure of *meaning* was God-centered. One structure exactly reverses the other. . . . The earth and God, then, are *both* centers, and the axis connecting them is the Chain of Being."[68]

Genesis 1 is a poem in the transcultural tradition of the Chain of Being. That way of reading it reveals the flaw in Norman Habel's argument that the "Earth story" in Genesis 1 is ruptured by an "overtly hierarchical" human story that reduces "Earth to a force or thing that must be subjugated."[69] The millennia-long hierarchic tradition of poetry may take a "special species perspective" (to use a modern term), yet its purpose is to enable us to see that human life has a potentially exquisite form. Life created in God's image is meant to conform, with other forms of life, into a single harmonious order. Having worked thus far through the Priestly creation poem, we are in a better position to appreciate Wendell Berry's suggestion that a good poem by its form "alludes to other forms, evokes them, resonates with them, and so becomes a part of the system of analogies or harmonies by which we live."[70] This poem is characterized by an unspecialized yet developed ecological intelligence, derived from "the understanding that one lives within an order of dependence and obligation superior to oneself."[71] That vertical orientation helps us get our bearings on

the horizontal plane; we can see where we are in the world and act in ways
that fit our place.

By following this poem's carefully ordered representation of God's intention
for the world, we may discern that the most essential activity befitting humans
created in the image of God is to secure the food system that God gives to
sustain all creatures.[72] That understanding is implied by the literary technique
of juxtaposition, by which the biblical writers often suggest a significant
connection. Immediately following their creation in/as the image of God
and the charge to exercise mastery among the creatures, there comes this
concluding notice about the food supply:

> And God said,
> "Here [*hinnēh*], I give you every plant seeding seed
> that is on the face of all the earth,
> and every tree that has on it tree-fruit seeding seed;
> for you it shall be, for eating.
> And for all living creatures of the earth
> and for all fowl of the heavens
> and for all that creeps on the earth that has a living soul in it –
> all the grassy herbage [I give] for eating."
> *And it was so.* (vv. 29–30)

The final line, the seventh and final occurrence of a notice of fulfillment (see
also vv. 3, 7, 9, 11, 15, 24), refers to God's gift of food, adequate for every creature
and distributed according to their nutritional needs: non-shattering plants
"seeding seed" for the humans, forageable grasses for the other creatures.
Seven is the number of completeness in the creation story;[73] the world is
now fully viable. The juxtaposition of the divine image in humans and the
detailing of divine food provision would seem to suggest that recognizing and
perpetuating the sufficiency God has provided is an important element of
how we humans are to live out our unique resemblance to God and exercise
mastery among the creatures.

It should not be surprising if such a representation of the human role
emerged or achieved prominence while Israel was in exile in Mesopotamia,
a region whose power had long been based on state- and temple-controlled
agriculture. Beginning in the third millennium b.c.e., there emerged a form
of social organization in the Sumerian city-state that remained influential for
the subsequent empires. "[T]he characteristic and most significant organization was the temple-estate, in which thousands of people co-operated in
works of irrigation and agriculture in a politico-economic system centred on

the temple, with all these people thought of as the servants of the god."[74] However, the bold Israelite move of democratizing the notion of the divine image accorded power, responsibility, and potentially honor, not just to the king, but to all persons working within the agricultural system on which life depends.

In view of the regular pattern of the Priestly creation account, in which divine command or action is followed immediately by a notice of fulfillment ("and it was so"), it is striking that no such notice attaches directly to the charge to the humans to exercise mastery (v. 28). It would seem that the question of how far God's intention is fulfilled is deliberately left open. Thus the poet subtly confers upon us, the hearers, the burden of exercising moral judgment on ourselves: how are we doing? As we have seen, the twenty-first-century evidence in itself would seem to tell against us, living as we do in the "Holocene extinction event." Although it is the sixth such event in our planet's history, this one is unique in that it has been precipitated or greatly exacerbated by human activity (including reproduction). According to biologist Edward O. Wilson, "*Homo sapiens* has become a geophysical force, the first species in the history of the planet to attain that dubious distinction."[75]

The pressure to exercise moral judgment on or against ourselves is increased, I shall argue, by the second jarring term by which the poem characterizes God's intention for humanity – namely, that we are to exercise mastery of the earth by "conquer[ing] it."

"CONQUER IT"

If we judge a poem to be well crafted, then the elements that seem ill chosen are probably those most worthy of attention. Yet the majority of biblical scholars downplay the divine charge to "conquer" the earth. Most render the verb *k-b-š* here as "subdue,"[76] or sometimes "master" (NJPS), without further comment. James Barr suggests that it refers to cultivation of the soil.[77] Norbert Lohfink observes that the verb appears several times in the Priestly version of the entry into Canaan (Num. 32:22, 29; Josh. 18:1), in each case with reference to *'ereṣ*, "land," elsewhere "earth" – the same word that is the implied object of the verb in Genesis 1. Lohfink suggests translating here "as undramatically as possible . . . :'Take possession of it.'"[78] However, if Genesis 1 is a liturgical poem, then its language may not be devoid of drama. Especially is this the case where it employs a word that, on account of both its force and its infrequency, foreshadows the event that constitutes the fulfillment of all God's early promises to Israel and remains a point of reference throughout biblical history. It is better to assume that the poet intends an audience to be sufficiently startled by the command "Conquer it" to puzzle over its meaning.

Walter Brueggemann is virtually alone in arguing that the command serves an important poetic function: By echoing the conquest narrative "precisely [at] the moment of *landlessness*," it affirms that Israel in exile still has a future in the promised land.[79] While it cannot be proven that the poem, or every word of it, originated in the period of the Babylonian exile,[80] there is no question that the command to conquer would have resonated powerfully in the ears of a people for whom exile was a present reality, a vivid memory, or even a looming threat, as it was for Israelites beginning in the eighth century B.C.E. and throughout the biblical period. However, whereas Brueggemann hears in that charge pure encouragement ("Israel would again experience blessing and well-being in the new conquest"),[81] I hear it as challenging and convicting those whose religious imagination has been formed by the biblical story. This one sharp word *k-b-š* acts as a probe, touching the imagination of people no longer settled securely in their land – be it Judah or our newly vulnerable planet – and moving them (us) to a new evaluation of the situation.[82]

The use of conquest language in Genesis 1 suggests that the Priestly writer views the land of Canaan as a microcosm; what Israel is to do when the land has been "conquered" is a specific instance of the whole human project on the earth. So what does our poet know about the conquest of Canaan? Two points drawn from the larger Priestly tradition seem crucial for this evocation of the conquest. First, God is the owner of the land (Lev. 25:23). Israel is allowed to "possess" it only on the rigorous condition of obedience, and the land is forfeited when that condition is not met. Second, the Priestly tradition in particular celebrates the God-given fruitfulness of Canaan, the land of gargantuan grape clusters (Num. 13:23). This is entirely in line with the Priestly poem's emphasis on God's provision of food for all the earth's creatures. Moreover, Israel's divinely sponsored establishment in the land, the so-called conquest, is the intended means for perpetuating the productivity of the land. Leviticus draws a direct threefold connection among Israel's obedience, the "fruitfulness" of both people and earth, and the immediate presence of God to both. The verbal and thematic connections with the early chapters of Genesis are unmistakable:

> If you walk in my ordinances and keep my commandments and do them,
> then I will give you your rains in their season,
> and the earth will give her produce,
> and the tree of the field will give its fruit.
> For you, threshing will overtake vintage,

and vintage will overtake seeding. . . .
And I will turn toward you,
and I will make you fruitful, and I will multiply you,
and I will establish my covenant with you. . . . (Lev. 26:3–5a, 9)[83]

Conversely, if Israel does not obey, neither will the land fulfill its divine mandate:

> Your land will not give its produce,
> and the trees of the land will not give their fruit. (26:20)

The land's fruitfulness is the "natural" consequence of covenant faithfulness (*ḥesed*) enacted on both sides, Israel's and God's. A productive land is a gift something like a child to a healthy marriage; in each case, thriving results from and witnesses to long-sustained faithfulness between two partners. In one of his Sabbath Poems, Berry speaks of just such a fruitful partnership, as he views a clearing made

> By human work,
> Fidelity of sight and stroke,
> By rain, by water on
> The parent stone.
> We join our work to Heaven's gift,
> Our hope to what is left,
> That field and woods at last agree
> In an economy
> Of widest worth.
> High Heaven's Kingdom come on earth.[84]

The Priestly writers of Genesis and Leviticus would easily recognize the terms of Berry's vision: divine gift, manifested especially as rain; human fidelity, discernible in both "sight and stroke," perception and fitting action. Berry's poem implies the experience of loss: "we join . . . our hope to what is left." Reckoning with loss makes both fidelity and hopefulness more meaningful as the terms on which we live, and also more difficult to practice.

From first to last, the Priestly tradition reckons with the harsh realities of exile and land loss. It was a plain fact, anticipated by the prophets and probably others before 586 B.C.E. and impossible to ignore afterward, that Israel's conquest of the land of Canaan had ended in failure, in expulsion – and the failure was not sudden. The history of Judges and Kings chronicles the long and mostly steady slide into exile; the prophet Ezekiel traces Israel's disobedience all the way back to Egypt (Ezek. 20:7–8). The Priestly work corroborates the judgment that Israel's tenure in and management of the land was no better than a qualified failure, perhaps from the outset. The same chapter of Leviticus cited above includes a harrowing description of divine chastisement for disobedience, culminating in exile:

> And I myself will make the land [*'ereṣ*] desolate,
> so your *enemies* living in it will be aghast over it,
> and you, I will scatter among the nations,
> and I will unsheathe the sword after you,
> and your land will be desolate,
> and your cities will be a ruin.
> Then the land will honor her Sabbaths, all the days that she is made
>   desolate,
> while *you* are in the land of your enemies.... (Lev. 26:32–34)

The shape of the canon means that exile is a felt reality even before Israel enters the land; the end is adumbrated at the beginning. Likewise, *bĕrēšît*, "in the beginning" of the human project, the call to conquer the *'ereṣ*, "the earth," is set before exiles and ourselves as an encouragement, perhaps, but also as a sober warning. Frank Matera has made the important observation that it is a profound mistake to read Scripture as though it assumes a virtuous or successful audience.[85] "Conquer [the *'ereṣ*]" – when that charge is read with careful attention to the successively larger contexts of Genesis 1, the early history of humankind, the Priestly work, and the Bible, it is possible to hear in it, not triumphalism, but a poignant irony that calls into question the moral integrity of humankind, including and even especially the worshipers of Israel's God.

Only in recent years has irony been highlighted as a key element of biblical rhetoric and theology.[86] One of its most important functions is to issue an indirect call on listeners to exercise moral judgment. Linda Hutcheon perceptively notes that irony comes into being "through the semantic playing off of the stated against the unstated," but "it is asymmetrical, unbalanced in favor of the silent and the unsaid."[87] Irony implies an unstated judgment and, like humor, it is culture-specific; you only "get it" – that a judgment is being made – if you belong to or can identify with the community for whom the barb is relevant. I would add that irony can prompt moral reflection only in a community with a tradition of and capacity for self-criticism.

What is *stated* in Genesis 1:28 is that humans play a special role, both powerful and responsible, in maintenance of the order that God has established. The earth may be "conquered," that is, claimed for God's purposes and rendered hospitable to the whole created order. Opposition to God, from whatever quarter, can be overcome. What is left *unstated* here – but should be burned into the memory and moral understanding of those who hear – is that land, the habitable earth, can be lost in penalty for disobedience. Again, what is left unsaid, but is clarified in the third chapter of Genesis and then reinforced time and again through the rest of Scripture, is that humans are the primary source of opposition to God, the source of most if not all threats to the integrity of the created order. "In interpreting irony, we can and do oscillate very rapidly between the said and the unsaid."[88] So it is legitimate to hear this commissioning statement as simultaneously encouraging and deflating. Humans do have a special vocation within the created order. Yet hearers who share the Priestly poet's awareness of exile must at least suspect the presence of a silent judgment. *Conquer the land/'ereṣ/earth*: The human project on Earth, the macrocosm, may yet fail as dismally as did Israel's project in Canaan, the microcosm.

The suspicion of irony may be confirmed by comparing this poem to another, Psalm 104, that offers a similar picture of a complex and harmoniously differentiated created order. Unlike most other ancient Near Eastern and biblical poems that evoke the events of creation (e.g., Psalm 74), these two liturgical poems show no awareness of a primordial struggle with chaos monsters. Only in the very last verse does Psalm 104 mention any threat to the harmony God has established:

> May sinners be finished off from the earth,
> and the wicked, until they are no longer. (Ps. 104:35)

The descriptors "sinners" and "the wicked" appear in the Bible only with reference to human beings. So in each poem, hearers are invited to share God's vision for the world but are also "stung" at the end by a moral judgment, suspended perhaps for the moment. Yet, listening with full awareness, we must recognize that it is suspended over our own heads.

PERFECT PLEASURE

As we have seen, the Priestly poem concludes with no affirmation that the human responsibility to exercise mastery among the creatures has even begun to be fulfilled. The sense that humankind has not yet claimed a proper place within the created order is confirmed by the drama that unfolds just a chapter later, which shows the first *failed* human attempt to "be like God" (Gen. 3:5) – orchestrated, ironically, by one of the nonhuman creatures.[89] As I have noted, that failure derives from a moment of perception, or misperception: "And when the woman saw how good was the tree for eating, and how appealing it was to the eyes, and that the tree was desirable to contemplate, she took some of its fruit and she ate" (3:6). Thus the larger story of the beginnings of humanity and the world, traced through the first three chapters of the Bible, shows the essential connection between accurate seeing and action appropriate to our place, and it suggests that the privileged status of humans among the creatures is a divine intention still awaiting realization. Nonetheless, the Priestly poem offers some direction for its realization, namely, in the poem's concluding movement, the blessing and sanctification of the seventh day.

That the seventh day is not so much a conclusion as an opening into the future is indicated by the *toledot* formula that immediately follows the Priestly poem: "These are the generations of heaven and earth in their creation" (2:4a). The formula always marks a genealogical beginning – but what is unfolding from here? Middleton asserts that it is human dominion: now humans come "into their true power as makers of history, as representatives and emissaries of God, called to shape the world in imitation of the creator's own primordial activity on the first six days of creation."[90] Further, Middleton argues that what is sanctified through God's rest is not one particular day of the week, "the Sabbath" per se, but rather "the entirety of human history."[91] However, that claim seems excessive. If Genesis 1 is read in conjunction with what follows immediately in Genesis (not to mention the rest of the Bible), it is evident that very much, maybe most, of human history is not eligible for sanctification.[92] It seems preferable to focus on the specificity of this narrative moment. What is sanctified is not human history as a whole, not even the institution of Israel's Sabbath (important though that is, from Exodus on), but simply the seventh day of this first week. It is sanctified as a day of divine pleasure in the created world. Rather than marking the transition from divine creation to human dominion, the seventh day represents the paradigmatic exercise of God's own dominion of delight.

In one of his earliest Sabbath poems, Wendell Berry names the essential quality of "Creation's seventh sunrise" as God's "perfect pleasure" and describes it thus:

> Time when the Maker's radiant sight
> Made radiant every thing He saw,
> And every thing He saw was filled
> With perfect joy and life and light.[93]

Throughout the first chapter of the Bible, what characterizes the God in whose image we are made in relation to creation is approbation, true delight in the creatures: "And God saw how good it was." Appreciation and enjoyment of the creatures are the hallmark of God's dominion and therefore the standard by which our own attempts to exercise dominion must be judged.

This is confirmed by Psalm 92, the one biblical poem specifically associated with the Sabbath day (v. 1 [title in Eng.]). Here the poet represents the great differential between the faithful and the wicked as the capacity to delight in "the works of [God's] hands," a phrase that elsewhere (Ps. 8:7 [6 Eng.]) specifically denotes the created order:

> For you have given me to rejoice in your action;
> the works of your hands I celebrate.
> How great are your doings, YHWH!
> Your thoughts are very deep.
> A dull person does not know,
> and a fool does not comprehend this –
> while the wicked grow like plants;
> and all workers of iniquity spring forth,
> [only] for them to be destroyed forever. (Ps. 92:5–8 [4–7 Eng.])

Like so many of the psalms, this one presents two stark alternatives for human existence. The psalmist has chosen the only good portion: celebrating and wondering at "the works of [God's] hands." Tragically, many choose the destructive alternative: "workers of iniquity" sprout like weeds, "[only] for them to be destroyed forever." The final phrase is marked as a result clause – and notably, the object of destruction is ambiguous: is it the workers of iniquity or the works of God's hands that are "to be destroyed forever"? Probably it is both. The psalmist knows that those who set themselves against God and the creation will not survive their own bad choice (v. 10 [9 Eng.]); the open question is how much devastation of God's finely wrought work they may accomplish before they perish.

4

∾

Leaving Egypt Behind: Embracing the Wilderness Economy

The industrial era at climax ... has imposed on us all its ideals of cease-less pandemonium. The industrial economy, by definition, must never rest.... There is no such thing as enough. Our bellies and our wallets must become oceanic, and still they will not be full. Six workdays in a week are not enough. We need a seventh. We need an eighth.... Everybody is weary, and there is no rest.... Or there is none unless we adopt the paradoxical and radical expedient of just stopping.

(Wendell Berry)[1]

> It is vain for you, early to rise, late to sit down,
> eating the bread of the aggrieved.
> Yes, he gives to his beloved sleep.

(Ps. 127:2)

A MARGINAL CULTURE

Agrarianism is more than a set of farming practices, more than an attitude toward food production and consumption, although both of these are cen-tral to it. Agrarianism is nothing less than a comprehensive philosophy and practice – that is, a culture – of preservation. Agrarians are committed to preserving both communities and the material means of life, to cultivating practices that ensure that the essential means of life suffice for all members of the present generation and are not diminished for those who come after. Agrarianism in this sense is, and has nearly always been, a marginal culture, existing at the edge or under the domination of a larger culture whose ide-ology, social system, and economy are fundamentally different. So agrarian writers, both ancient and modern, always speak with a vivid awareness of the threat posed by the culture of the powerful. The earliest explicit articula-tion of the agrarian view comes from Hesiod, the poet farmer of Boeotia, a younger contemporary (in the eighth century) of the prophets Amos, Hosea, and Micah, who share his perspective and sense of threat.[2] It is instructive for biblical readers to hear the Greek Hesiod sounding for all the world like an Israelite prophet when he denounces those whom he calls *basileis* ("barons"):

> . . . those who by crooked decisions
> break other men, and care nothing for what the gods think of it.[3]

Because they are aware that agrarian cultures have always existed under threat, the contemporary agrarian writers are not nostalgic for some romantically reconstructed past. Historian Brian Donahue observes: "We agrarians can't be taken seriously unless we begin with the premise that life has been brutally hard for most farm people," hard not just because of the physical labor and the uncertainties of weather, but even more because "for most of human history . . . farmers have been ensnared in political and economic systems designed to extract what they produce, and leave them barely enough to survive."[4] So the new agrarians are engaged in a critique of a millennia-long past, and they are working from the margins toward a different kind of future. Within our own culture, perhaps the most crucial distinction is between genuine agrarianism and the romantic impulse that drives many people out from the city to what we call (ambiguously enough) "developments." Leo Marx terms this impulse "sentimental pastoralism," which may be summarized as "the wish to live in rural harmony by means of industrial exploitation."[5] The positive aim of the agrarian critique is not that all suburbanites should be farmers but rather that they should move beyond romanticism – a mind-set that always includes a deluded and therefore potentially destructive element – to a realistic relationship with the land on which all our lives depend, a relationship of multigenerational commitment and nurture.

Wendell Berry writes: "I believe that this contest between industrialism and agrarianism now defines the most fundamental human difference, for it divides not just two nearly opposite concepts of agriculture and land use, but also two nearly opposite ways of understanding ourselves, our fellow creatures, and our world."[6] In the narrow sense, industrialism is a modern phenomenon, but as I have already implied, it has ancient roots – and in one case at least, something like a full cultural counterpart. The focus of this chapter is the contest between agrarianism and the dominant culture that was the closest the biblical writers knew to industrialism, namely, Pharaonic Egypt. The paradigmatic account of that contest is found in the story of the giving of the manna in Exodus 16, the first extended story about Israel on the far side of the Reed Sea – that is, the first exploration of Israel's thinking when they are in a position to make their own decisions. Moreover, it is a unique moment, when Israel is temporarily outside any culture. They have left Egypt and not yet entered Canaan, where they will experience the blessings, temptations, and (as the Bible represents it) moral failures that landed life makes possible. They have not yet established even the culture of the wilderness years. So, this is a decisive moment in the formation of the mind-set of the people Israel – a new mind-set, ideally one characterized by obedience to God's commandments, that will enable them to be free of "all the sickness of Egypt" (Exod. 15:26).

I shall try to show that the manna narrative bespeaks an awareness of the general social and cultural shape of Egypt, even granted Donald Redford's judgment that "[b]iblical writers of the seventh to sixth centuries B.C. lacked precise knowledge of Egypt as recent as a few generations before their own time."[7] What is important is that the scene is drawn against the background of the dominant cultures from which Israel is meant to be fundamentally distinct, in terms of social ideology and social structure, as well as what we may more narrowly term "religion." The historical circumstances of Israel's emergence as a distinct political entity at the cusp of the Iron Age continue to be debated. Granted the new consensus that the people who came to be known as Israel shared very large elements of common culture with the Canaanites, it is reasonable to suppose (as many do) that they originated within Canaan, and therefore to ask this question: Is the memory of enslavement in Egypt genuine, and if so, did the sojourn in Egypt involve any significant portion of the ancestors? I do not intend to enter into the historical debate,[8] for what is generally agreed upon is sufficient for my purposes. Egypt was the dominant military and cultural force throughout Late Bronze Age Canaan, encompassing Palestine and Syria within a loosely controlled empire. Canaanite slaves were regularly shipped to Egyptian ports; Canaanite fields were cultivated and taxed to support Egyptian temples and the New Kingdom's administration and garrisons abroad; the Egyptian state regularly extracted forced labor from Canaanite peasants.[9] Moreover, with respect to land ownership and labor on the land, there was much similarity in the social organizations of Egypt and the Canaanite city-states. For Israel to differentiate itself from one – ideally, in the intention of the biblical writers, if not in fact – was to differentiate itself from both. These were highly stratified, strongly militarized societies in which the whole land belonged (at least in name) to the monarch. In practical terms, that meant the wealth of the land flowed upward, away from the small farmers, serfs, and slaves who composed the overwhelming majority of the population, to the large landowners, the nobility, the great temples, and the crown. Canaanite peasants would have felt a double burden, being subject to and supporting both the local "princes" and the Egyptian officials resident in Canaan.[10] And the wealth that accumulated at the very top of the economy, in Egypt, was prodigious. Egypt of the New Kingdom (ca. 1540–1075 B.C.E.) is the society that invented the "lifestyle" (the concept, though perhaps not the word), self-consciously gracious living for the few.[11] Against this social background, the wilderness narrative in Exodus traces the emergence of a people charged to cultivate a radically different way of living in community on the land.

THE COUNTERNARRATIVE OF MANNA

The Deuteronomist aptly names Egypt "the Iron Furnace" (Deut. 4:20), for it is the biblical archetype of the industrial society: burning, ceaseless in its demand for slave labor (the cheapest fuel of the ancient industrial machines), consuming until it is itself consumed in the confrontation between divinized Pharaoh and the God of the Burning Bush. Egypt consumes itself, as the royal courtiers acknowledge when, after the seventh plague, they pose the incredulous question to their hard-hearted master: "Do you not yet know that Egypt is lost?" (Exod. 10:7). Soon, Pharaoh and his army are drowned in the Reed Sea (Exod. 14:26–15:19), yet just six weeks (and a few verses) later, it becomes evident that Israel is not wholly free of the ideology and habits of Egypt. God gives them what they need and some of them take more than they need. God says there will be nothing to gather on the seventh day, and some of them go out anyway, evoking the first expression of divine exasperation with Israel: "How long will you [plural] refuse to observe my commandments and my teachings?" (16:28). The manna story reveals Israel's need for healing and shows the means by which "YHWH [the]Healer" (15:26) seeks to accomplish it, before the people get to Sinai and are initiated fully into the new practices of covenant.

"If only we had died *by the hand of YHWH* in Egypt, when we sat by the fleshpots, while we ate our fill of bread! For you have brought us out into this wilderness to kill this whole congregation with hunger" (Exod. 16:3). These words are sufficient to show that the Israelites are infected with the sickness of Egypt (cf. 15:26). They are the only words the Israelites speak, apart from the equally uncomprehending *Mān hû'* – "What is it?" (16:15). Here the phrase "by the hand of YHWH" indicates more than a wish for a natural death (*pace* Sarna[12]); rather, it shows the perverseness of Israel's imagination. "The hand of YHWH" is, in the story of the exodus, the leading image of God's mind-boggling power (14:31; cf. 15:12, 17), working salvation for Israel and destruction for Pharaoh. Pharaoh is destroyed, along with his land, because he *could* know God yet refuses to do so. Now the Israelites imagine that God's hand is the agent of their own destruction, and the memory of the fleshpots is further evidence that their mind carries Egypt's disease.

It is telling that they long for the food of Egypt – at least, the food that they imagine they might have enjoyed in Egypt. Egyptians did indeed eat a nutritious and relatively varied diet; no people would eat so well again for thousands of years. The myriad canals and swamps meant that fish was normally available even to serfs and slaves "for free," as well as leeks, onions, and other vegetables (Num. 11:5). At the end of the twelfth century B.C.E., workers on the royal tombs at Thebes called a strike because their accustomed rations were months in arrears: "We have no clothes, no oil, no fish, no vegetables."[13] Meat, however, was eaten chiefly by the wealthy. So the Israelites speak more accurately than they may themselves realize when they recall sitting *beside* the fleshpots, eating *bread*. For the poor, the staple was grain, consumed as gruel and groats, bread and beer.[14]

Even if there be some measure of fantasy in the complaint, God's answer is simple and generous: "Here, I am about to make it rain down for you bread from the sky" (Exod. 16:4). God responds to their sick hunger by initiating a different mode of food production. In proverbial speech, "manna from heaven" refers to an unqualified boon for which it is easy to be grateful, but in fact this story makes it clear that manna is both gift and test, like the land of Canaan itself. It is given on certain conditions and thus is meant to reveal whether Israel "will walk by [God's] teaching or not" (16:4). The fact that food constitutes the litmus test of Israel's separation from the culture and mind-set of Egypt confirms the insight that is the starting point for all the agrarian writers: Eating is the most basic of all cultural and economic acts.[15] Therefore, at this liminal moment in the wilderness, the formation of Israel as a counterculture to Egypt begins with a negotiation between God and Israel that clarifies the principles and restrictions pertinent to the moral economy of eating.

The story gets its edge from the fact that here both God and Moses become angry with the people for the first time: God, because some ignore the Sabbath rest; and Moses, when they fail to get rid of the excess manna, which then rots in the course of a single night. On the face of it, the intensity of their response to Israel's error is hard to understand. Sabbath is a new and hitherto unexplained concept, while manna is a preternaturally perishable substance; moreover, one might expect some sympathy for wilderness travelers (and former slaves) who try to exercise some moderate control over the food supply. God and Moses patiently endured the Israelites' whining and even the insult about God's malevolent intent in bringing them out "into this wilderness."

So, exasperation at this point would make sense only if the stakes governing the manna economy are higher than is obvious, and I believe that this is the case: The economic principles adumbrated here are meant to separate Israel definitively from Egypt. Just two verses before the beginning of this story, God promises to avert the diseases of Egypt if Israel proves obedient (Exod. 15:26), and Norbert Lohfink argues that the narrator thus establishes the absolute contrast between the "sick society" that is Egypt and the healthful society that the people Israel is intended to be.[16] It is apt to see the present story as amplifying the contrast between those two societies, viewed now in their economic aspect. My intention here is to show how the manna story serves as a counternarrative, sketching a compelling alternative to the agricultural economy Israel claims to remember from Egypt, which the first chapter of Exodus sums up thus: "They, Egypt, ruthlessly put the Israelites to slave labor. They embittered their lives with hard labor at mortar and bricks and with every kind of labor *in the field* – all their labors that they imposed on them ruthlessly" (1:13–14).

The Egyptians, perhaps the only ancient people as fascinated with themselves as we with ourselves, left a clear picture – literally, through their tomb paintings – of what field work was like for the laborers who found themselves at the bottom of the social pyramid by the Nile. At harvest time, the landowner or his agent went out to the fields with the peasant laborers and a host of surveyors and scribes. Every centralized economy requires its bean counters, and in the ancient world, Egypt's was, over centuries, the most stable and most intensely centralized government in existence; Jacquetta Hawkes describes it as "an essentially totalitarian regime."[17] In theory, the land and all its produce belonged to Pharaoh; and in fact, a significant percentage of the grain crop – for large estates, up to half the total yield – was appropriated for the royal granaries, to be disbursed for both food and seed.[18] The first tasks were to measure the field and then the number of grains per bushel, in order to calculate precisely the tax owed to the state or perhaps the temple authorities. Lionel Casson describes the harvest scene thus:

> While the scribes set out their inkpots, pens, and scrolls in shaded comfort under a tree, the line of reapers got to work, . . . and women with baskets followed behind to gather up what had been cut. In their wake came the gleaners, women, children, old men. One tomb painting shows a woman gleaner pathetically holding out her hand and saying, "Give me just a handful. I came last evening. Don't make my luck as bad today as it was yesterday." Another picture, in a lighter vein [?], shows two girls pulling each other's hair in a fight over the gleanings while the reapers unconcernedly carry on their work.[19]

I believe that in the manna story, the Priestly writer[20] is working consciously against this cultural background – working against it in the strong sense. That is, the biblical storyteller is imaginatively recreating social reality, painting a new picture of work in the field for those who have left Egypt behind. Taking my clues from the tomb painting, I read the manna story as a counternarrative that outlines a new moral economy of food production and distribution.[21] This does not of course mean that the Priestly writer functioned as an Egyptologist, with access to detailed information about a period hundreds of years before his time. Nonetheless, a comparison with Egypt is likely implied in Exodus 16, as is the case elsewhere in the Priestly corpus.[22] Exploitative agricultural economies were for millennia a fixed feature of various Near Eastern societies, including that of Israel and Judah in the period of the divided monarchy. By the time the book of Exodus was composed (possibly in several stages during the monarchic period), Israel bore at least some resemblance to New Kingdom Egypt and also its own contemporary, the Neo-Assyrian Empire, in terms of the economic dominance of centralized agriculture under state control. All had some form of a "redistributing" agricultural economy, with the wealth concentrated within a very small upper class. There is doubtless considerable truth to Diana Lipton's suggestion that "when the biblical writers say 'Egypt,' they mean the kings of Israel."[23] We can surmise, then, that the Priestly narrator knew enough to counter and subvert on several significant points the economic reality they associated with Egypt. Moreover, comparing the divinely instituted economy of Exodus 16 with Egypt of the New Kingdom highlights aspects of our own context of reading. For we now read the Bible within an industrial economy that exploits both "natural resources" (itself an entrepreneurial term) and human beings on a wider scale than any economy the world has ever known. An agrarian reading of the manna story may point us toward the way out of such an industrial economy.

FOOD AS REVELATION

The most dramatic point of contrast between the Egyptian harvest and manna collection lies in the intention and character of their respective masters: on the one hand, an acquisitive overlord who takes the gifts of the earth and the Nile for his own profit, for the gain of the state and its religious establishment; on the other, the One who generously gives bread from heaven. The tomb paintings show the Egyptian master driving his chariot into the field with an attitude of command. He arrives, smartly attired in pleated linen skirt with leggings (to protect his soft shins), wig, and necklace, holding staff and scepter. Barefoot servants lay out a picnic and even a toilet set, so the master may sit at ease while the business of surveyors, harvesters, and scribes goes on around him.[24] The picture that emerges from the tomb paintings conforms in every detail to the basic claim of industrial agriculture in our own time: Food is business.

The immediate goal of the business is consistent through the millennia: to produce a surplus for trade, often on an international scale. The Pharaohs often asserted, "I fed the hungry in the years of distress";[25] and indeed, since Egypt could produce only one harvest each year, centralized collection and disbursement of grain could be an important hedge against hunger in bad years. Genesis 47:13–26 is the biblical account of how, in a time of severe famine, "Joseph gained possession of all the arable land of Egypt for Pharaoh" (v. 20) and, in return, provided food and seed rations for the people. Further, centralized oversight of the system of canals and dikes was a critical element in controlling the Nile floodwaters, whose height bore directly on the extent of cultivation and the size of the harvest. In addition to feeding the local populace, however, Egypt's grain was widely traded on the international market, and (there being no merchant class) the income went directly into Pharaoh's treasury.[26] In the ancient world as in the modern one, the grain trade was the source of what a former U.S. assistant secretary of agriculture called "agripower,"[27] an indispensable key to personal wealth and international power. For wherever food production is concentrated in the hands of a few, as in New Kingdom Egypt and our industrialized world, food is very big business, and often enough, as was observed by Earl Butz, secretary of agriculture under Presidents Nixon and Ford, "Food is a weapon."[28]

In complete contrast to agribusiness in both ancient and contemporary cultures, the first story of Israel out of Egypt shows that food is, more than anything else, an expression of God's sovereignty over creation and generosity toward humankind. It is, moreover, a clear sign of God's immediate Presence, a sign that Israel must recognize and comprehend. *Hinĕnî mamṭîr lākem leḥem min-haššāmāyim*, "Here, I am about to make it rain down for you bread from the sky" (Exod. 16:4). Notably, God's very first words to the Israelites echo an earlier speech to Pharaoh, when God says, *Hinĕnî mamṭîr . . . bārād*, "Here, I am about to make it rain down . . . hail, exceedingly heavy, such as there has never been in Egypt from the day it was founded until now" (9:18). The plagues are signature actions of the Creator God, and they bespeak an intent that is "retributive, coercive, and educative," as Nahum Sarna aptly says.[29] God's educative intention becomes explicit in the announcement of this seventh plague: "Now this time I am directing all my plagues at your heart and to your servants and to your people, in order that you may know that there is no one like me on all the earth" (9:14). It was Pharaoh's sickness not to secure that healthful knowledge of God in long-term memory (9:27–35). But Israel must do so. That is why manna collection assumes the form of a test; Israel is now being held responsible for what it has seen and should now know of the Creator God. "So Moses and Aaron said to all the Israelites, 'Evening – and you shall know that YHWH brought you out from the land of Egypt, and morning – you shall see the Presence of YHWH . . .'" (16:6–7). "Evening, morning" – those words point far back beyond Egypt to the beginning of the world; they recall the rhythm of God's first creative work as God now initiates a new act of creation here at the edge of the wilderness. Similarly, a few verses later, there is an allusion to God's redemption of Israel: "At twilight you shall eat meat . . . " (16:12) – *bên hā'arbayim*, a phrase that previously appeared only in the instruction for slaughtering the Passover sacrifice (12:6).[30] Eating is a primary occasion for knowing the work of YHWH.

Accordingly, as in the first chapter of the Bible, all the action proceeds from God's luminous Presence, signaled by the characteristically Priestly term *kĕbôd YHWH* (traditionally, "the glory of the LORD"), which occurs here for the first time in the Bible (16:7,–10). The narrator paints God's arrival as a scene no less ritualized than the arrival of the Egyptian master at the harvest. Several elements of the language here are used elsewhere in the Priestly corpus with reference to cultic encounter: "Then Moses said to Aaron, Say to *the whole congregation of Israelites* [kol-'ădat bĕnê yiśrā'ēl], '*Draw near before YHWH* [qirĕbû lipnê YHWH (a phrase for ritual approach)]'[31] . . . ; and as Aaron spoke to *the whole congregation of Israelites*, they turned to the wilderness, and here, *the Presence of YHWH appeared in a cloud* [wĕhinnēh kĕbôd YHWH nir'â be 'ānān]." Then God makes that promise: "At twilight you shall eat meat, and in the morning you will have your fill of bread; *and you shall know that I, YHWH, am your God* [wîda'tem kî 'ănî YHWH 'ĕlōhêkem]" (16:9–12). The "recognition formula" is familiar to those who have followed the Exodus narrative thus far. God's repeated threat and promise for Pharaoh and the Egyptians is that they should ultimately know YHWH, albeit in their own demise.[32] But here the recognition formula functions in the opposite way, to point toward new life, specifically, the new food economy of the wilderness. For those who draw near and offer themselves before God, satisfaction of hunger is neither an end in itself nor a wholly "secular" event. In this economy, eating is worshipful, even revelatory; it engenders a healthful knowledge of God.

Such knowledge of God is essential if the Israelites are indeed to experience satisfaction in the wilderness, for the simple reason that there they remain in a situation of dependence as real as the one they knew in Egypt. For the narrative clearly identifies their work in the wilderness as "gleaning" (*l-q-ṭ*).

As is evident from the Egyptian tomb paintings, gleaners were the most vulnerable and often the most desperate participants in the ancient food economy. In this one chapter of Exodus, the verb occurs nine times (16:4, 5, 16, 17, 18, 21, 22, 26, 27) – more than all its other occurrences in Torah combined. Within the context of the larger narrative, that repetition serves to identify the Israelites with the vulnerable, namely the sojourners and the other poor whose interests are elsewhere protected by the injunction against making a clean sweep with the harvest: "When you harvest the harvest of your land, you shall not finish harvesting the corner of your field, nor shall you glean the gleaning of your harvest" (Lev. 19:9 and 23:22).[33] Even as the Israelites begin their journey to the land they will possess, they are put in the position of the most dependent members of the society they themselves will form. Healthful formation of the community – "the whole congregation" (*'ēdâ/qāhāl*) as they are repeatedly called here (Exod. 16:1, 2, 3, 9, 10) – is based upon certain trust in God as the One who provides a sufficiency for all. Only thus can the Israelites find joy and contentment in the wilderness, recognizing that their dependency on YHWH is not oppressive or tragic, but sustaining.

RESTRAINT, THE PROOF OF KNOWLEDGE

The experience of manna fall and collection might seem to be wholly exceptional, with no clear analogue and, therefore, little to teach us about creating (or re-creating) a "normal" agricultural economy, where we humans produce our own food – or so we think. And here we have arrived at the central question about the food economy: Are we food producers in any genuine sense? The agrarian writers insist that this is the fundamental delusion of the agricultural industrialists, that we make the food. Norman Wirzba, reflecting on the manna story, asserts that those who see food as a concrete sign of God's care understand that it "is not a 'product' but a gift that we must nurture. Ultimately, as every good farmer and gardener knows, whether or not we will have food is beyond our control. The best that we can do is practice patience and trust, attention and responsibility, before the processes of life and growth."[34] In the manna economy, Israel is called upon to engage in two concrete practices of restraint, namely, eschewing excess and keeping Sabbath. These practices might be viewed as the earnest of patience and trust in God; they are the evidence that Israel knows the power of the God who brought them out of Egypt, and further, that Israel is ready to live out of that knowledge.

Each household is limited to what it can use in a day: an omer "per capita" (*laggulgōlet*, Exod. 16:16). It is intriguing to juxtapose the Exodus account, which describes in some detail the measuring of the intake, with the depiction of the precise measuring that was such an important part of the activity in the Egyptian fields. There, anyone who came up short had to answer for it; the paintings on the tomb of Menna, "scribe of the fields" in the Eighteenth Dynasty, depict a field worker being beaten with a rod.[35] In God's field, however, the amounts miraculously adjust themselves, so that "the one with a lot had no extra, and the one with a little had no lack" (16:18). In this new Master's harvest, the goal is to ensure that everyone has enough to eat, and no one has a surplus, not even for a single night. From one perspective, the total ban on short-term leftovers seems an illogical exaggeration of that goal, but the Priestly writer is an associative thinker, not a narrowly rationalistic one.[36] So the prohibition works analogically to epitomize the difference between the wilderness economy and the economy of Egypt.

Exodus identifies two forms of work that the Egyptians imposed on the Israelites: field work and the equally "hard labor in mortar and bricks." And what were they building? "Storage cities for Pharaoh, Pithom and Ramses" (1:11) – whole cities of silos to store the agricultural surplus that accrued to Pharaoh as the titular owner of all the land and ensured his absolute control over the lives of his people. Egypt's towering silos were important enough to figure in the iconography of power that is the tomb paintings. Pierre Montet describes them thus: "The interior walls of these sugar-loaf buildings were carefully plastered, the outer walls whitewashed. A ladder led up to the opening through which the bushel measures were successively emptied. The grain could afterwards be drawn as required through a small door at ground level."[37] To the symbolic imagination of the Priestly writer, the strict prohibition on saving food means that no Israelite tent can be a silo; the Israelite camp cannot be a storage city. The Israelites are to remain dependent on and therefore mindful of God as the One who provides food daily. No wonder Moses was angry when some violated the ban (16:20).

The ban on hoarding and manna that spoils overnight are symbols that touch us closely, living as we do in a culture of unprecedented hoarding, consumption, and waste. Our take is unlimited – the destruction already accomplished is staggering. Within the last century, a third or more of the earth's original forest cover has been cleared, much of it converted to agriculture; the conversion is driven in large part by the need to replace depleted agricultural land.[38] In addition, half the wetlands on the planet have been drained and filled or otherwise destroyed. In California, fully 90 percent of the wetlands have disappeared; 60 percent of native fish species are either threatened or already extinct. In the dry season, rivers such as the Colorado, the Ganges, and the Nile no longer reach their mouths. Forty percent of the world's population lives in countries suffering from serious freshwater short-ages, and irrigated agriculture accounts for a staggering 70 percent of water usage.[39] These and other factors, including climate change, are already caus-ing "biotic impoverishment . . . on a global scale"[40] and thus endangering the food supply over the long term. At the present time in North America and Europe, the food surplus is huge. Yet, even that is destructive – not only for the overloaded bodies of individuals (obesity being the single greatest threat to health in the United States and a rising threat in Britain) but also for national economies less robust than our own.[41] Below-cost food exports work against farmers in the "Two-Thirds World," driving down food prices and forcing them off the farms, with the result that agricultural production in countries such as India, South Korea, and Colombia has plummeted, and poverty and malnutrition has risen. As Douglas Boucher observes:

> We now see that [combating world hunger] is not simply a matter of whether food is available in the market; people must have the money to buy it. In a world economy in which food is a commodity, poverty will lead to starva-tion no matter how productive agriculture becomes. The basic problem for hungry people is not a scarcity of food, but a scarcity of income.[42]

With its strict ban on hoarding – or better, its strict emphasis on contem-poraneous eating – the manna story points obliquely to another dimension of the divide between rich and poor: the impoverishment of future generations that is the likely result of our present failure to practice "the economics of futurity." Echoing another biblical story about an excess of foodstuffs, Luke's parable of the rich fool whose barns will not hold all he has taken from the land, Wendell Berry comments: "By laying up 'much goods' [Luke 12:19] in the present – and, in the process, *using up* such goods as topsoil, fossil fuel, and fossil water – we incur a debt to the future that we cannot repay. That is, we diminish the future by deeds that we call 'use' but that the future will call 'theft.'"[43]

We have incurred damage on a scale that bewilders us, that we cannot repair, and even worse, our currently dominant economies implicitly mandate that the damage continue. The manna story attests to the inherent difficulty of living with restrictions we do not wholly understand. Yet we must do so, if we are to live at all, for every human economy is embedded within and subordinate to the larger economy of creation, which Wendell Berry calls "the Great Economy." It encompasses all creatures and the order in which they are interconnected. We humans can neither comprehend nor control that Economy, just because we are comprehended by it. Therefore, "humans can live in the Great Economy only with great uneasiness, subject to powers and laws that they can understand only in part."[44] Our challenge is to conform our small local and temporal economies to the Great Economy that is creation itself. Because food procurement and consumption constitute the most essential economic act within every culture, they may be seen as the first and best test of such a healthful conformity; that is the logic underlying this first story of the people Israel in freedom. Accordingly, "bread from heaven" is the test of whether or not Israel can live by God's teaching (Exod. 16:4).

This wilderness story might fruitfully be read in light of the first, paradigmatic account of a divinely imposed eating restriction and its violation, namely, the story of the first humans taking fruit from the tree of knowledge of good and evil, contrary to the sole divine prohibition that obtains in Eden. For a moment we are taken into the woman's mind as she begins to deceive herself: "And when the woman saw how good was the tree for eating, and how appealing it was to the eyes, and that the tree was desirable to contemplate,[45] she took some of its fruit and she ate; and she gave [it] also to her husband, [who was] with her, and he ate" (Gen. 3:6). God's incredulity at their action is palpable in his question to the man: "From the tree – that I commanded you not to eat from it – you ate!?" (3:11).[46] With that act they begin to separate human culture, our corporate way of knowing the world and acting upon it, from obedience to God. When the two stories are read together, it is evident that if an adequate and even generous food supply may provide the occasion to know God (Exod. 16:12), then *accurate* knowledge of God, the world, and our place in it – in short, wisdom – is available only to those who eat with restraint.

Both forms of restraint enjoined here, not hoarding and Sabbath observance, are meant to heal Israel through daily and weekly acts of recognition that YHWH is God, whose "hand" is steadily manifested for their good. This first mention of Israel's Sabbath anticipates Sinai, where Sabbath observance is commanded explicitly as the weekly memorial of creation. At this point, Israel is learning Sabbath by the inductive method, yet this first instruction already implies that Sabbath is meant to enable Israel to see the world as God's creation – in the vision of the Priestly tradition (Genesis 1), a complex harmony orchestrated by God, where every creature, including humans, can rest in the goodness of the whole. Jürgen Moltmann observes that Sabbath "distinguishes the view of the world as creation from the view of the world as nature; for nature is unremittingly fruitful and, though it has seasons and rhythms, knows no sabbath."[47] Sabbath blessing is the realization in our lives of the distinction between creation and nature, a distinction that must be observed in our economies, if it is to be meaningful at all.

In an insightful study of Sabbath living as the "most important and all-encompassing goal,"[48] for Christians as well as Jews, Norman Wirzba recalls his upbringing in a farming community in Southern Alberta, where all work stopped on Sundays – even during harvest time, when time was at a premium. He comments:

> One would think that Sabbath rest would thus be the occasion for considerable anxiety, especially in an agricultural economy. . . . My experience of farmers at that time, however, is that they experienced daily multiple examples of God's goodness and power, most basically in the germination and growth of crops and the birth and health of livestock. To be sure, crop failure and disease, as well as painful death, were perennial possibilities, but the experience of farming overwhelmingly taught the beneficence of grace. (It is no accident that as farming has turned into agribusiness, the practice of Sabbath rest for farmers, animals, and the land has come to an end.) If the farmer is honest, and thus appropriately humble, he or she will recognize that there is much more to be grateful for than there is to fear. Authentic rest becomes possible, even in the midst of harvest time, because it is informed by the palpable, concrete understanding that God provides. The means of divine care, whether in plant and animal cycles of birth, growth, decay, and death or in the kindnesses of kin and community, are ample and clear for those who care to notice.[49]

It is hard to live that way; as Wirzba and Scripture imply, it takes courage and accurate memory, a memory that stretches back to the creation of the world. These stories point to elements of human character and experience that often make memory unreliable: intellectual pride (Genesis 3) and lack of trust in God (Exodus 16). Accordingly, the manna account ends with the creation of a visible reminder: a jar with an omerful of manna to be set "before YHWH as a keepsake for [the] generations . . . before the covenant [ark]" (Exod. 16:33–34). This note is often seen as an anachronistic appendix; the Priestly writer is thought to be retrojecting something belonging to settled life and temple worship back to the first weeks in the wilderness. It is more apt to say that the manna jar implies that there is an essential integrity to Israel's experience both in the wilderness and in the land of Canaan.[50] The next two chapters focus on Israel's foundational vision for living by God's word in the land it has received as a trust from God.

A Wholesome Materiality: Reading Leviticus[1]

For you love all things that exist,
and detest none of the things that you have made,
for you would not have made anything if you had hated it.

(Wisdom of Solomon 11:24 NRSV)

In law is rest
if you love the law,
if you enter, singing, into it
as water in its descent.

(Wendell Berry)[2]

The ultimate goal of farming is not the growing of crops, but the cultivation and perfection of human beings.

(Masanobu Fukukoa)[3]

THE LAND COMMUNITY

A generation ago, economist E. F. Schumacher described the mind-set and economic practice dominant in our time as "the forward stampede";[4] those committed to it are bent on ignoring the limits inherent in human existence, their watchwords being "more, further, quicker, richer."[5] In their view, the crises we face are to be handled, not by reconsidering the course of our technological "progress," but rather by completing it. Schumacher contrasted the people of the forward stampede with those he called "home-comers." The latter recognize that the beauty and dignity of human life depends upon living within certain limits that are necessary and therefore becoming. As Schumacher famously observed: "Man is small, and therefore small is beautiful. To go for giantism is to go for self-destruction." In his view, the Christian gospel provides the basic text for the home-comer mentality: "How blessed are those who know that they are poor. . . . "[6] Accordingly, insightful and pre-scient though he was, even Schumacher might be surprised at the ingenuity with which, a few decades later, the gospel has been appropriated by advocates of the forward stampede. For instance, a few years ago one of my students had a job interview at a Christian school in California, where staff members cited the lack of recycling bins as an expression of their faith; by using up "resources" as quickly as possible, they were hastening the coming of the Lord and the New Creation.

There is a strange alliance between their worldview and, at the far end of the religious spectrum, the scientism of the late Carl Sagan. While dismissing philosophy and conventional religion as false "palliatives," Sagan's *Pale Blue Dot* gives his own vision of the "sacred project," the "new *telos*" that lies immediately before us.[7] His vision of homesteading the Universe is evangelical religion in a variant mode:

> I think that, after some debugging, the settlement of the Solar System presages an open-ended era of dazzling advances in science and technol-ogy; cultural flowering; and wide-ranging experiments, up there in the sky, in government and social organization. In more than one respect, exploring the Solar System and homesteading other worlds constitutes the beginning, much more than the end, of history.[8]

In that happy future, after "the Great Demotions" of both God and this terrestrial ball are well behind us, then our much-altered descendants[9] will be eligible to participate in the kind of "true religion" that Sagan envisions, a possibility realizable only "when we are acclimatized to other worlds and they to us, when we are spreading outward to the stars."[10]

What that Christian school in California and Sagan share is a willingness to consign this world to its inevitable destruction, or even to help it along, on the supposition that by their efforts humans can enter into some better world. That attitude is directly opposed to the biblical view of the projected destruction of the world. It is telling that the book of Revelation, upon which this particular brand of Christianity draws heavily, shows the twenty-four elders who are enthroned in heaven greeting God's judgment thus:

> The nations raged,
>> but your wrath has come,
>> and the time when the dead are to be judged
> and to give the reward to your servants the prophets
>> and to the saints and those who fear your name,
>> to the little and the great,
> *and to destroy those who are destroying the earth.* (Rev. 11:18)

Although contempt for God's creation can convincingly be shown to be a bad interpretation of biblical faith, it has always come too easily to Christians. Already widespread in the second century was the Gnostic conceit that the spiritual elite could by means of their knowledge (*gnosis*) transcend the ordinary limitations of material existence in this world. Heresy thrives on the neglect of important texts.It is surely no coincidence that the biblical texts that most fully express regard for the material being of all creatures, including ourselves, are nearly all in the Old Testament, which seemed contemptible to the Gnostics and their spiritualizing kin, the Marcionites.[11] To exacerbate a bad situation, the most detailed scriptural witness regarding how we might live within the intended harmony of God's creation is to be found especially in that part of the Bible that Christians to this day dismiss most readily, and even on principle: namely, the legal codes of Exodus, Leviticus, and Deuteronomy.

Here in the heart of Torah lies a vision of what I am calling a "wholesome materiality," a value and practice that is central to the agrarian view of life. Wendell Berry criticizes the pious high-mindedness that neglects "the commonplace issues of livelihood" and observes:

> The Devil's work is abstraction – not the love of material things, but the love of their quantities. . . . It is not the lover of material things but the abstractionist who defends long-term damage for short-term gain, or who calculates the "acceptability" of industrial damage to ecological or human health, or who counts dead bodies on the battlefield. The true lover of material things does not think in this way, but is answerable instead to the paradox of the parable of the lost sheep: that each is more precious than all.[12]

Taken as a whole, biblical law seeks to inculcate a precise awareness of physical being: of human life in a particular place, the land of Canaan, shared with other creatures – trees (Deut. 20:19) and birds and animals (Deut. 22:4, 6–7; 25:4) – whose own lives are precious and vulnerable.[13] The legal codes view the world, and especially a particular part of it, as well designed for habitation (cf. Isa. 45:18); they offer guidance for how the people Israel may order its life – including its work, its eating practices, and its worship – in conformity with the larger design of that place. I suggest that this part of the Bible is then especially worth reconsideration by home-comers, or those who are at least trying to come home – as Wes Jackson puts it, to become "native to our places in a coherent community that is in turn embedded in the ecological realities of its surrounding landscape."[14]

The law codes of Torah envision the people Israel becoming native in that sense; their aim is that people and land together should thrive in the presence or sight of the God who allows Israel to dwell in the highlands of Canaan. When the biblical codes are reread in light of the contemporary agrarian writers, it is evident that Torah is setting human life in the larger context that Aldo Leopold once termed the "land community," arguing that we may understand our situation differently, and more realistically, by extending the boundaries of ethical consideration "to include soils, waters, plants, and animals, or collectively: the land."[15]

The law codes, and especially the Priestly tradition in Leviticus, are crucial resources for enlarging our ethical vision in just this sense, yet the bulk of this material is usually regarded by all but orthodox Jews as the most time-conditioned portion of the Bible and therefore the least relevant to our own situation. To counter that prejudice hermeneutically, the insight of H. H. Schmid is important. He observes that in ancient Israel, as generally in the ancient Near East, "creation faith did not deal only, indeed not even primarily, with the origin of the world. Rather, it was concerned above all with the present world and the natural environment of humanity now."[16] Throughout the region, including Israel, "[l]aw, nature, and politics are only aspects of one comprehensive order of creation."[17] Schmid's comprehensive notion of creation faith may explain why the legal codes draw no clear distinctions between categories that in our culture are considered wholly discrete: agricultural, sexual, and economic practices; cultic regulation; ways of cooking, eating, and dressing; civil justice; animal rights; neighborliness.

I focus here on Leviticus, because it takes us directly to the heart of the matter. Many or most Christian scholars have long accepted Julius Wellhausen's deeply negative view of the Priestly Code, that it tends toward "denaturalisation" and "abstracts from the natural conditions and motives of the actual life of the people in the land of Canaan. . . . "[18] I hope to show that the opposite is the case: Leviticus articulates, perhaps more fully than anywhere else in Scripture, a theologically profound vision of the complexity and interdependence of the created order. Further, it grapples with the difficult question of how humans may responsibly participate in that order.

We find the key in the divine declaration that is arguably the climax of the book: "I shall remember my covenant with Jacob, and yes, my covenant with Isaac, and yes, my covenant with Abraham I shall remember – and the land I shall remember" (26:42). It is within the context of *covenant relationship* that God considers and values – "remembers" – the land. That biblical understanding may be correlated with a notion frequently evoked by Wendell Berry and others, namely, of the "membership" of all creation, "a membership of parts inextricably joined to each other, . . . receiving significance and worth from each other and from the whole."[19]

The notion of membership implies the obligation also to *re*-member, to work at healing the wounds inflicted on the land by all its human inhabitants. Being at home on the land, then, means living with the reality and consequences of sin. Likewise, the Priestly tradition of Leviticus[20] reckons with sin from first to last. It assumes the existence of rupture within the harmony of creation, both the regular disruption of sin and the great disruption of exile, with which, according to the vision set forth in this book, Israel is threatened even before entering the land to possess it.

A PATTERN OF PATTERNS: LEVITICUS 19

The genuine problem that Leviticus presents is its difficult theological grammar; its language is remote from that of "ordinary" religious discourse, in our society and probably in ancient Israel as well. In this matter, readers of our generation might have a real advantage over our predecessors, because the studies of Jacob Milgrom and Mary Douglas (followed now by numerous others) have opened the way for an entirely fresh and appreciative reading of Leviticus. Their most important contribution is the recognition that the Priestly tradition speaks not the language of the discursive intellect, but rather that of the embodied imagination. Unlike the preachers of Deuteronomy, the authorial voice in Leviticus offers little of either explanation or motivation; "I am YHWH (your God)" is about the extent of it. The thought pattern is associative, correlative – in Mary Douglas's term, "mytho-poetic": "Instead of explaining why an instruction has been given, or even what it means, it adds another similar instruction, and another and another, thus producing its highly schematized effect. The series of analogies locate a particular instance in a context. They expand the meaning.... Instead of argument there is analogy."[21] Thus by means of "strings of concrete examples,"[22] the text delineates the right ordering of the world, or of the microcosm that is Israel, its people and land.

The notion of analogy is as central to the work of agrarian writer Wendell Berry as it is to Mary Douglas's reading of Leviticus. It is crucial for understanding why there is a vital connection between the health of soil and the health of human communities. Both "belong to a series of analogical integrities that begins with the organelle and ends with the biosphere."[23] A healthy farm is *like* an ecosystem and is nested *within* an ecosystem. Therefore, a concern for pattern necessarily complicates a proper concern for agricultural production. There is, as Berry notes,

> a reciprocating connection in the pattern of the farm that is biological, not industrial, and that involves solutions to problems of fertility, soil husbandry,

economics, sanitation – the whole complex of problems whose proper solutions add up to *health*: the health of the soil, of plants and animals, of farm and farmer, of farm family and farm community, all involved in the same internested, interlocking pattern – or pattern of patterns.[24]

In Leviticus, the most concise and rhetorically powerful evocation of the community living responsibly on its land is chapter 19.[25] It consists of a series of directives, addressed to the whole people Israel, all subsumed under the heading "You shall be holy, for I, YHWH your God, am holy" (19:2). Elsewhere in Leviticus, holiness is the special characteristic of the sanctuary and the priests who attend it, but here in the Holiness Code (chapters 17–26), that notion is democratized and vastly extended, so it looks something like Berry's notion of health: multiple interlocking patterns, or "integrities," of people and land. J. Joosten notes that the holiness of ordinary Israelites derives from the same source as does that of the sanctuary and the priests:

> [T]he Israelites are hallowed by the holy presence of YHWH among them and by observing the commandments. What is striking is that the commandments allowing the Israelites to attain holiness are not exclusively of a ritual nature, nor even limited to the religious domain. All the different areas of life, religion and ethics, but also economics, politics and social affairs are brought into subjection to the divine will.... [H]oliness is an ideal toward which the Israelites must strive and not an acquired quality.[26]

In Leviticus 19, the eighteen directives that follow the initial demand for holiness range from the acme of the ethical – "You shall act lovingly to your neighbor, as [to] yourself" (19:18) – to the agricultural: "You shall not mate your animals in two kinds nor seed your field in two kinds" (19:19); there is to be no mixing of species, plant or animal. While most of us would see all the difference in the world between those two prescriptions, the Priestly editor apparently does not; one immediately follows the other, without distinction. I suggest that the key to understanding the unity of these diverse prescriptions lies in the fact that the chapter as a whole is a highly condensed exemplar of analogical thinking. By means of a string of concrete examples, the writer is showing what holiness looks like on the ground. It is a matter of reckoning deeply, imaginatively, and creatively with the stuff of ordinary life. Contrast, then, the generalized exhortation to righteousness of the Deuteronomic "preacher" – "Righteousness, righteousness you shall pursue" (Deut. 16:20) – with this very specific charge of the Holiness Code: "Righteous scales, righteous weights, righteous *ephah*, and righteous *hin* will be yours; I am YHWH your God who brought you out of the land of Egypt" (Lev. 19:36). Israel's measuring practices are proof that it has left Egypt behind.

The charge to be holy needs to be nuanced and specified for all the various situations of daily life, because what enables Israel to live with God in its midst is precisely a refined ability to distinguish the holy from the "profane" (*profanus*, literally, that which remains "in front of the temple," outside the sacred precinct), and further, to distinguish between different levels of holiness, the most intense being that of the holy of holies, the innermost sanctum of the temple, accessible only to the high priest on one day each year (Leviticus 16). For the sake of its own well-being, and even survival, Israel and its priests must judge accurately who or what is fitting to come into close (or closest) proximity to God. According to the Priestly tradition, Israel is poised on the knife's edge between the two domains, a position as precarious as it is privileged. Leviticus has something like a doctrine of real (divine) presence, yet God's very immanence to Israel implies the need for constant vigilance: "My Sabbaths you shall keep and my holy place [*miqdāšî*] you shall revere; I am YHWH" (19:30). Here *miqdāš* refers to the sanctuary proper, but it may also allude indirectly to the land. For the Holiness writer, the whole land is the place of God's dwelling: "YHWH's holy presence radiates outward from the sanctuary throughout the entire land and imposes its demands on all the inhabitants."[27] Accordingly, there is no place in the land that ordinary Israelites are not obliged to revere. Only by constant mindfulness of the holy in its varying intensities can this people live fittingly on the land with which it is entrusted.

Each of the holiness instructions in Leviticus concerns matters of concrete practice. This is true even of the famous injunction to neighborly love, although that is not evident from the standard rendering, "You shall love your neighbor as yourself." The unusual Hebrew syntax – the verb '-*h-b* followed not by the definite (direct) object marker but rather by the preposition *l-* – suggests an active connotation: "You shall *act lovingly to* your neighbor, as [to] yourself. I am YHWH" (19:18).[28] Loving actions are what is required, not an undemonstrated attitude. So far so good, but then there follow the prohibitions on interplanting two kinds of seed, interbreeding animals, and wearing a mixture of two kinds of cloth. What possible bearing could those practices have on Israel's holiness?

Milgrom argues persuasively that such mixtures are viewed as trespassing on the high-voltage holiness of the priestly sphere.[29] In ancient Near Eastern mythology and iconography, mixtures characterize the sacred realm. In Israel's own sanctuary, the ark is flanked by cherubim, those supernatural hybrids; the curtains and priestly garments are woven of blended linen and wool.[30] But mixtures must have occurred also in the realm of the ordinary. Probably Israelites, like other traditional farmers, practiced polycropping in order to maximize the productivity of small plots of thin-soiled land. Indeed, the very existence of a prohibition on sowing in two kinds would seem to imply that this was established practice, at least in some quarters.[31] Certainly, horses and asses were routinely interbred to produce mules. It would seem, then, that the Holiness writer is consciously countering cultural norms so as to eliminate encroachment on the sphere of the holy.

The Holiness writer is concerned with *practices*, but anyone reading with an agrarian mind-set has to ask, could the prohibition of sowing in two kinds ever be *practical*, in view of the well-known advantages of polyculture? That question is especially apt if (as seems likely) the writer is at home in a rural environment and therefore writes with real farmers and fields in mind.[32] An Israelite farmer working in the Holiness tradition would have to employ other means of soil maintenance and regeneration; in light of that, the emphasis (a few chapters later) on the land keeping its Sabbath year (Lev. 25:2) gains added significance.[33] Other practices not mentioned here, such as field fragmentation, crop rotation, and raising animals alongside crops, could make up for any negative effects of sowing in one kind only.

EXTENDING THE ANALOGY: GENETIC TECHNOLOGY

The practical applicability of the biblical prohibition on seeding in two kinds is pressing also in our own culture. It would be crude and overly literal to argue that the prohibition has found its ideal expression in industrial-scale monoculture, a practice that eliminates both small farmers and local food systems even as it exhausts the land. A better application may be reached by following the analogical style of reasoning that Leviticus itself evidences. As the good interpreters of Leviticus, including Origen and the traditional rabbis, have always recognized, its symbolic language prompts the reader to consider the deep structures of the world and relationships among the creatures. If, in the mind of the biblical writer, sowing in two kinds is inadmissible because it trespasses in the realm of the holy, then what might be the analogous practice in our own culture? I suggest that it may be the widespread use of genetic modification within our food system – more specifically, of transgenic technology, the introduction of foreign DNA into the chromosomes of food crops, resulting in such "mixtures" as corn that generates a human contraceptive (a so-called "pharma crop") or an insect toxin, *Bacillus thuringiensis* (Bt). Although transgenic technology was developed only in the 1970s and began to be planted commercially only in the 1980s, by the end of the century more than half of soybean and cotton grown was genetically engineered, as was 28 percent of corn.[34] We are dropping into established ecosystems organisms whose like has never been known, that cannot be called "creatures" in any genuine sense. Lawyer and environmental journalist Claire Hope Cummings uses language that may complement the notion of trespassing in the realm of the holy when she observes that transgenic technology is a "trespass on the public commons."[35]

Whereas traditional hybridization mixes genes among varieties within a species or between closely related species, transgenic engineering devises crosses between kingdoms: plant, animal, bacterial, and viral. A gene gun, electric shock, or other mechanical means is used to penetrate the cell wall, breaching the boundary that exists "to protect and insure organismal genomic integrity and stability."[36] For that reason, many, scientists and consumers alike, are concerned about the ecological and human health risks that may attend the technology. Among these are allergic and immune-system reactions to new substances such as Bt, since the insecticidal protein is distributed throughout the plant, including its edible parts. The instability of transgenes is also a concern: They mutate rapidly and also cause mutations in the host organism, so that the unexpected and even unknown consequences of a transgenic event may greatly outnumber the one intended consequence that makes the "product" marketable. Further, transgenes travel easily, both in pollen and through incautious handling of seed, and they show up in places they are not expected and very much not wanted, for example, in the field of an organic farmer, ruining not just the value of a crop but a whole business. The mobility of transgenes may even be a threat to biodiversity and thus, to food security on national and international scales. In a landmark survey conducted in 2004, the Union of Concerned Scientists found that non-genetically modified seed stock of corn, soybeans, and canola were already "pervasively contaminated with low levels of DNA sequences originating in genetically engineered varieties of those crops."[37]

Another concern is social: Who controls the technologies, and who profits from them? Is it the poor (as the promoters of genetic engineering often assert), or the seed and chemical giants, Syngenta and Monsanto? Ecologist Jules Pretty observes that "first-generation" technologies, those that spread widely in the last decade of the twentieth century, "have tended to provide substantial private benefits for the companies producing them."[38] Since they are attended by substantial risks that are currently ill-defined, it is not surprising that some of the world's desperately hungry nations reject genetically engineered crops even in the form of food aid; in 2002, Mozambique, Zambia, and Zimbabwe refused U.S. shipments specifically for that reason.[39]

However, "the transgenie ... [is] out of the bottle,"[40] and there is little doubt that the technology will play some role in addressing the problem of feeding a population that is likely to grow by two or three billion in the coming decades, when there will no longer be the option of bringing under cultivation large new areas of rich, watered land. The dimensions of a full solution are not yet known, although one point around which considerable hope (and publicity) has constellated is the transgenic phenomenon of "golden rice." Bacterial and maize genes are injected into the rice cell to enable the production of beta-carotene, a precursor of vitamin A. Since rice is the primary food of nearly half the world's population, the potential benefits of such a nutritional boost must be taken seriously. In an important initiative designed to institute benefit sharing, the inventors of golden rice assigned the key technology rights to Syngenta, for large-scale seed production, on the condition that farmers in developing countries could plant the rice and earn up to U.S.$10,000 without paying royalties. Nonetheless, large questions remain: whether a cultural resistance to orange-colored rice can or should be overcome, whether its irrigation needs are sustainable, and whether promoting diverse, small-scale farming would not better alleviate poverty and provide a balanced diet.[41]

What have not received enough public attention or funding are other forms of genetic technology that can be used to speed and improve traditional breeding processes and increase genetic diversity for food crops. For example, "wide hybridization" is an induced mating of two different plant species, a domesticated annual and its wild perennial relative, which may bring out the best attributes of both: for instance, the high yield of a domestic grain and the perennialism of a related wild grass. Sophisticated techniques, such as backcrossing (mating a hybrid with one of its parents), are used to overcome the obstacle of sterility that often results from chromosome incompatibility. Molecular markers may also be exploited in order to select for desirable traits without waiting for plants to reach maturity. Such techniques are in fact the only means currently available for introducing complex attributes. Biologist Mary Eubanks, who breeds high-protein, drought-tolerant corn, comments:

> Transgenic technology is reasonably well developed for traits controlled by single, dominant genes; whereas recessive genes and quantitative traits are still largely the domain of conventional plant breeding. Therefore, important genes for most traits affecting a plant's ability to cope with environmental stress, such as those for drought tolerance, will be found among available genetic resources and crop wild relatives.[42]

Similarly, breeders at The Land Institute make use of wide hybridization in the development of perennial grain crops that are viable for broad commercial and domestic use. Because perennialism is "an intricate life path that goes well beyond a single trait, let alone a single gene," transgenic modification is

not useful in the early stages of this work. However, breeders do not exclude
the possibility that it might in the future have some limited utility in refining
simple inherited traits: "For example, if a domesticated perennial wheatgrass is
successfully developed but still lacks the right combination of gluten-protein
genes necessary for making good-quality bread, gluten genes from annual
wheat could be inserted into the perennial plant."[43]

Researchers who use these latter forms of technology do so mindful that the
organisms we eat have come into being through their own "life paths" that are
as intricate and beautiful as the one that lies behind *Homo sapiens*. Their aim
is not to overcome by brute force the essential protective barriers that guard
the biological integrity of different life forms, but rather to capitalize on the
phenomenon of natural hybridization, often going back into a crop's ancestral
history in order to create improved hybrids. These plant breeders may never
have read Leviticus, but those of us who have may observe in their work a
regard for the integrity of the created order that is fundamental to the Priestly
and Holiness traditions. Such a regard should guide us in determining what
might constitute holiness with respect to our culture's scientific, agricultural,
and eating practices.

FARMER, FAMILY, AND FIELD

The thinking of the Holiness Code is ecological in Aldo Leopold's sense; its
point of orientation is the web of relationships uniting the various members
of the land community: earth, animals, and humans.[44] The writer assumes
that their identities interpenetrate, and everyone knows it, so there is no
need to explain how or why the same rule with the same wording applies to
all. "You shall observe my statutes: your domestic beasts you shall not mate
in two kinds, your fields you shall not seed in two kinds, and cloth of two
kinds – a *sha'atnez* blend[45] – shall not show up [literally, rise up] on you"
(Lev. 19:19). The prohibition on mixtures draws the analogy among activities
variously in the field, in the breeding pen, and at the loom. Similarly, it is
forbidden to cut the *pē'â*, "the edge," of either field (19:9) or human head
and beard (19:27). We would reason that shaving clean (or not) is a matter
of personal or cultural style, at most a ritual observance, whereas harvesting
clean is an ethical matter: How will the landless have a share in the land's
bounty? But for this writer, both proscriptions have the same rationale (of
sorts): "I am YHWH." Because we put the two kinds of trimming in different
categories, we miss the force of the analogy, which could prompt reflection on
the likeness between the male Israelite and the field, both being possessed of
pē'ôt, "edges."

So how is the farmer like the farm? That question is not fanciful or archaic, but it is likely to occur only to the agrarian mind, such as that of Wendell Berry's "Mad Farmer," who articulates "a human intelligence of the earth that no amount of technology can satisfactorily replace":[46]

> Sowing the seed,
> my hand is one with the earth.
> . . . .
> Hungry and trusting,
> my mind is one with the earth.
> Eating the fruit,
> my body is one with the earth.[47]

The analogy between farmer and field is implied also in the Holiness Code's instruction that fruit trees must remain "uncircumcised" ('ărēlîm, Lev. 19:23) for three years after planting. Some standard translations simply remove the metaphor entirely and render the word as "forbidden" (NRSV, NJPS). But the word choice is neither arbitrary nor meaningless. Jacob Milgrom suggests, based on both close reading of the metaphor and actual horticultural practice, that it refers to removing fruit from the juvenile tree while it is still in the bud; for him the (un)circumcised fruit "provides another example of how religion penetrated into folk idiom."[48] Yet, if the principle of analogy is operative, then even more might be said. The writer is using the strong language of covenantal prohibition to draw a boundary around that which is not yet available for use; the young tree is set outside the covenant community for its own protection until it comes of age. As with the farmer and the field, hearers are invited to stretch their imaginations to perceive that humans and trees are distinct from one another but also related in their creaturehood and their vulnerability. Heeding the divine instruction entails accepting what Wendell Berry calls "the discipline of unity" among the creatures, ourselves included; the only alternative to that acceptance is "the hideousness and destructiveness of the fragmentary."[49]

These analogies forge a link between the Israelite male and the field. A complementary analogy, the most striking in all of Leviticus, has as its subject the person whose social position is diametrically opposed to that of the adult male landowner, namely, the unmarried female: "Do not defile your daughter by prostituting her, so the land may not commit prostitution and the land be full of depravity [zimmâ]" (19:29). As with the previous example, the lapidary style of the prohibition prompts us to wonder, how are this land and this daughter alike? How does abuse of the one resemble abuse of the other? The Holiness Code is addressed to the average Israelite, someone who would consider selling a daughter into prostitution only as a last, desperate measure, seeing no other way for any member of the family to survive. Not surprisingly, the social situation that must underlie the biblical prohibition has its industrial counterpart in our culture. In Thailand, Costa Rica, and other countries with high levels of rural poverty, "sex tourism" is a thriving industry. Customers fly in – mostly businessmen from North America and Western Europe – to enjoy services offered by teenage (or younger) girls, many of them the daughters of impoverished subsistence farmers, or farmers who have lost their land. Moreover, 800,000 to 900,000 people are trafficked across national borders each year (some 18,000 into the United States), of whom approximately 70 percent are forced into the commercial sex industry. Eighty percent of the victims are female; half of them are children.[50]

No parent makes a free decision to sell a child into prostitution, any more than a farmer makes a free decision to "prostitute" the land for small, short-term gain. In the deepest sense, those decisions are made by a culture that in its economic aspect is characterized by what the Holiness writer calls zimmâ, "depravity," which connotes both depraved acts and the sickness of mind and imagination that generates them. On the implication of the land as whoring, my student Scyller Borglum comments: "The land would have given up what was precious and valuable for a paltry sum and given it to whoever offered money. In fact chances are, that which was precious and treasured could be taken without any permission at all."[51] A depraved economy such as the one that now holds the whole globe in thrall is dangerous equally to land and to daughters, to farm families altogether, for all have become commodities, interchangeable goods, valued only for their fleeting contribution to the profits or pleasure of the relative few who have prospered.

Perhaps the most thoroughgoing application of the likeness between farmer and field is in the laws of redemption (Leviticus 25), which treat analogously the enslaved farmer and alienated land. Of all Israel's religious institutions, land redemption and (associated with it) the fiftieth-year Jubilee have the greatest potential for creating widespread social change in an agrarian society, for their purpose is to prevent the opening of a gulf between rich and poor with the establishment of a permanent, landless underclass. Leviticus 25 sets forth the practical consequences of the Holiness tradition's central theological tenet, that both the people and the land of Israel belong exclusively to God (vv. 23, 55). God has settled Israelites as resident aliens on familial "holdings"; the term 'ăhuzzâ is consistently used by the Holiness writer (including twelve times in this chapter: vv. 10, 13, etc.) to designate land held by a farm family on the condition of obedience.[52] God's "ownership" of Israel derives from Israel's deliverance from bondage in Egypt; henceforth, neither the people nor the land can be permanently alienated from YHWH.[53] While that deliverance was God's direct action, the operation of redemption as a socioeconomic institution in Israel requires human cooperation from within the kin group. That is, institutionalized redemption requires many small acts of *imitatio Dei*.[54]

Leviticus 25 reads almost like a narrative, tracing the several stages of economic loss (and accompanying personal disaster) that an Israelite farmer might experience; delineation of each of the several descending stages begins with the poignant phrase *kî-yāmûk 'āḥîkā*, "When your brother is low" (vv. 25, 35, 39, cf. 47). The existence of such a detailed legal code indicates that the social problem it treats was serious, found in many or most rural communities known to the Holiness writer. The first stage is redemption of the land (vv. 25–28), set in motion when an impoverished farmer puts up a portion of the ancestral holding as collateral for a loan (likely for the purchase of seed)[55] secured from a creditor outside the kin group, and then, because of a poor harvest, is unable to repay it. His closest "redeemer" (*gō'ēl*, v. 25), a relative with means, is expected to enact the option of purchasing the right of usufruct, of working the land and taking its yield until the Jubilee Year; at that time, it reverts to the original owner. If the Jubilee, which comes every fifty years, is yet a long time off, then probably it would be the indebted farmer's son who eventually "return[s] to his holding" (v. 28).

If the farmer's fortunes continue to decline, so that the whole property is lost, then this "brother" farmer must subsist with relatives as a "resident alien" (*gēr wĕtôšāb*, v. 35), a tenant farmer. Milgrom argues that the indigent farmer lives in his own home and works his own land, and the extended family offers subsistence in the form of exemption from interest on either monetary or food loans (vv. 36–37).[56] The status is clearly a vulnerable one, and so God's own authority as redeemer of the people Israel is adduced (v. 38); the status of resident alien is the same one that all of "you" occupy in the land that YHWH owns (v. 23).

The third and lowest stage is reached when the impoverished brother cannot maintain his family even on these conditions and therefore is sold, entering the household of either a fellow Israelite or an alien. If the purchaser is an Israelite, then the conditions are to be those of a hireling, not a slave (vv. 39–43), who may still have the chance of working off the debt.[57] Again, God's past action of redeeming Israel from Egypt is the basis on which intra-Israelite slavery is strictly forbidden. But if an Israelite is sold into the hands of a foreigner, then it is imperative that a family member – a brother or uncle or cousin – act as redeemer (vv. 47–49). Then the redeemed slave can work at paying off his debt to his relative, with the Jubilee Year serving as an absolute terminus.

The obligation for a human redeemer to take responsibility in the case of the *enslaved Israelite* echoes in even stronger terms the call for a relative to redeem the *land*. Multiple verbal echoes between the two passages (vv. 24–28, 48–54) are underscored by the fact that the whole section is framed on either side by YHWH's assertion of the theological rationale for redemption: "For the land is mine" (v. 23); "For the Israelites are slaves to me" (v. 55). Neither farmer nor field is finally eligible for sale. The analogy between them establishes the theological understanding that YHWH redeems Israel, at a national level and also at a familial and individual level, and further, redemption is accomplished directly by God (first in the exodus and then through the periodic Jubilee) and also through the agency of those Israelites who accept the divine charge to imitate God's own holiness (19:2). Like the prophets, the Holiness writer makes a theological assertion that is meant to exert weighty social and economic pressure in every community throughout the land.[58]

EATING TO BLESSING OR TO DAMNATION

The most obvious thing that commends Leviticus for an agrarian reading is its deep interest in how Israelites eat. Nowhere else in the Bible is it so clear that the writers, like the contemporary agrarians, recognize eating as *the* definitive cultural act.[59] It is at the same time a religious act, and all these writers treat thoughtless eating as sacrilege. Possibly the most important and dangerous thing about our own historical moment is that now for the first time a great social swath across the globe – the society created and sustained by the industrial economy – is eating sacrilegiously in that sense; we are "drawing our lives out of our land" without thought of return.[60] If we continue to do so, we will perish from our heedlessness, a possibility that the Leviticus tradition faces squarely.

As Mary Douglas saw long ago, the dietary regulations of Leviticus are not primarily instrumental (i.e., their aim is not hygienic), nor are they an arbitrary amalgam of items, each to be explained independently (as, for instance, in the allegorical approach[61]). Rather, taken as a whole, they constitute a *system of communication*, a symbol system that says something about holiness, and at the same time, about the nature of creation. Holiness entails observing the order that is inherent in creation, and keeping its categories distinct. In the famous third chapter of *Purity and Danger*, Douglas proposed that the key to the distinction between clean and unclean animals is full conformity (clean) or only partial conformity (unclean) to class; the dietary laws are signs pointing to "the oneness, purity and completeness of God."[62]

One of the several ways that Douglas's reading of Leviticus has changed through the years is that her anthropological approach to the dietary regulations has been informed by Jacob Milgrom's ethical view of them. According to Milgrom, the regulations implicitly maintain that "animal life is inviolable except for a few edible animals, provided they are slaughtered properly (i.e., painlessly, Lev. 11) and their blood (i.e., their life) is drained and thereby returned to God."[63] In sum, the dietary laws are "the Bible's method of taming the killer instinct in humans."[64] In *Purity and Danger* (1966), Douglas rejected an ethical interpretation in favor of a symbolic ("anthropological") one.[65] In her book-length study of Leviticus written nearly forty years later, the dichotomy between those approaches has disappeared completely. Now she too attaches great importance to the restrictions on animal bloodshed; they stem from God's own compassion for all creatures, human and nonhuman. Although the analogical style does not favor direct moral exhortation, there is a kind of moral vision inscribed in its symbol system: "The idea of goodness in Leviticus is encompassed in the idea of right ordering. Being moral would mean being in alignment with the universe, working with the laws of creation, which manifest the mind of God."[66]

Our need to eat presents us with our primary opportunity to work with the laws of creation. Season by season, we have no obligation more immediate than producing and consuming food in wise and respectful ways. Chapter 11 of Leviticus sets our obligation to creation in plain view, and even the placement of the chapter contributes to its effect. This, the fullest statement of the dietary regulations, appears precisely at the center of Torah: the middle letter of the Five Books is found in Leviticus 11:42. That might be something more than sheer coincidence, since the final editing of Torah seems to have been done by Priestly/Holiness writers, with their delight in literary craftsmanship and design.[67]

A more certain indication of authorial intention is the careful phrasing in Leviticus 11, which establishes the fact that we eat only in the context of creation. Its subtext is unmistakably Genesis 1, as multiple verbal echoes indicate: "And YHWH spoke to Moses and to Aaron, saying to them: 'Speak to the Israelites, saying: This is the animal you may eat out of all the domestic beasts that are on the earth . . .'" (Lev. 11:1–2). "On the earth" – that phrase, absent from Deuteronomy's less fully crafted version of the dietary regulations, appears tellingly seven times in this chapter (11:2, 21, 29, 41, 42, 44, 46).[68] It is a reminder, taking us back to the sixth day of creation, when the earth was first covered with plants and mobile ("creeping") creatures, and humans were blessed and charged to "exercise mastery" with respect to fish, fowl, and "every animal that creeps on the earth" (Gen. 1:28, cf. 1:26). The climactic repetition of the phrase "on the earth" in Leviticus 11 occurs in a statement that draws most of its distinctive wording from Genesis 1: "This is the instruction for *quadruped* [*běhēmâ*] and *fowl* ['*ôp*] and every *animal being* [*nepeš haḥayyâ*] that *creeps* [*rōmeśet*] in the waters, and for every being that *swarms* [*šōreṣet*] *on the earth* ['*al-hā'āreṣ*], in order to *make a distinction* [*lěhabdîl*] between the unclean and the clean, and between the edible animal and the animal that is not to be eaten" (Lev. 11:46–47). Most of these allusive words are repeated multiple times in Leviticus 11, to the point of awkwardness. A further connection with Genesis 1 is the tag phrase *lěmînô*, "according to its kind" (11:14, 22, et passim), which occurs (with variations) a total of nine times – only one less than in the creation story itself. Moreover, the ungainly phrase "seed-for-seed that will be seeded" (11:37)[69] recalls in its very excessiveness the Priestly writer's insistence on the self-seeding system set up in the beginning.

The pronounced pattern of allusion makes it clear that Leviticus 11 is picking up where Genesis 1 (as modified by Genesis 9) left off.[70] In Chapter 3 of this book, I proposed that in the context of Genesis 1, human mastery denotes sharing responsibility for the integrity of the food chain ordained on the sixth day of creation. If that responsibility is to be maintained, then it is necessary to update Genesis 1 to take account of the postdiluvial addition to the human food chain. The first covenant with Noah makes the animals available for consumption: "Every creeper [*remeś*] that is alive may be yours for food" (Gen. 9:3). So, the dietary regulations as formulated here make it the special obligation of Israelites, specifically as flesh eaters, to observe and protect the fruitfulness of creation. The work of the Priestly legists reflects careful study of the created order and, in turn, makes further study requisite, even to this day. Jacob Milgrom boldly asserts: "[T]he real contribution of this Priestly theology is that it manifests the beginnings of an ecological doctrine,"[71] the teaching that God's will may (and must) be discerned in creation as well as in the revealed word.

For humans, as Mary Douglas has long insisted, eating is a powerful and complex mode of communication, a fact to which our own culture is strangely blind: "We simply do not know the uses of food, and our ignorance is explosively dangerous. It is more convenient for us to take a veterinary surgeon's view of food as animal feed, to think of it as mere bodily input, than to recognize its great symbolic force."[72] In Israel, by contrast, food is a primary communicator of the covenant. The dietary regulations as formulated in Leviticus 11 cover the great sweep of covenant history from Noah to exodus, as is evidenced by an outrageous pun that appears in the verses immediately framing the stipulations. At the outset, the criteria for edible animals are given thus: "Every one that has a hoof and a split of hooves and brings up cud [*ma'ălat gērâ*] ... " (11:3). The phrase sinks in; it is repeated five additional times in the descriptions of the animals (11:4 [2x], 5, 6, 26). Then, at the very end of the stipulations, comes the seventh, climactic appearance of the participle, but this time its subject is God, and its object Israel: "I am YHWH, who brings you up [*hamma'āleh 'etĕkem*] from the land of Egypt to be God to you, and you shall be holy, for I am holy" (11:45). The length of that divine self-identification is unique in Leviticus; "I am YHWH (your God)" elsewhere suffices.[73]

More remarkable is the choice of the verb: *hip'il* of the root '-*l*-*h*. To denote God's role in the exodus, Torah normally uses *hôṣē'tî* – *hip'il* of the root *y*-ṣ-' – and always thus when God speaks in the first person (cf. Lev. 26:13, 45). The sole exception is here, and the apparent reason, as Gary Rendsburg has seen, is to create an inclusio around the dietary laws.[74] But to what effect?

Mary Douglas gives the important clue: an analogy is operative here. Douglas draws it thus: "[O]nly the clean animals and only the people of Israel are to be consecrated."[75] However, Leviticus does not attribute holiness to animals, even if they must be ritually slaughtered — only to God and (in the Holiness Code) to the people.[76] Maybe it is better to see the correspondence between two acts of divine creation: of the quadruped who brings up cud, and of the people Israel, whom God brings up from Egypt. Unlikely as it seems, the distinctive anatomy of the edible animal is held up as a reminder of God's greatest action on behalf of Israel. The inclusio is witty yet not frivolous; it "digests" the essential message of Leviticus 11: eating meat – a rare enough event for most Israelites – is an occasion for Israel to practice covenantal faithfulness. God's own covenant loyalty, *hesed*, of which the exodus is the outstanding example, is discernible also in the availability of meat.

If that is the message here, then we may well find it indigestible. Our own culture, especially in North America, certainly operates the most death-dealing meat market the world has ever known. Considered within the context of creation, it epitomizes our ingratitude for what God has done. Every member of the land community suffers within a system in which fish, poultry, and quadrupeds are born and fed, fattened, killed, and packaged in factories,or a series of factories, in a process completely abstracted from their natural habitats and life cycles. The single aim of the system is to slash to the sparest minimum the costs to the producer, while the real costs are literally exorbitant, far beyond what the world can afford. The immediate human cost is paid by the mostly nonunionized workers who struggle to handle 7,100 pigs or 144,000 chickens in a single eight-hour shift, with no toilet breaks and no health insurance. Tens of thousands (at least) of injuries are sustained each year on the killing, "carcass disassembly," and packing lines. Eighteen migrant workers are found living in an unfurnished one-bedroom apartment; rent and supplies for the processing line (everything from knife sharpener to hairnet to rubber boots) are deducted from the paycheck.[77] Ronald W. Cotterill, director of the Food Marketing Policy Center (University of Connecticut), has described working conditions as "now clearly more dangerous and debilitating than at any time since Upton Sinclair wrote *The Jungle*" in 1906.[78]

Suffering, disease, and wasteful death for so-called domesticated animals is also a large part of the cost of our eating habits and food production system. The abandonment of long-standard practices of animal husbandry in favor of "concentrated animal feeding operations" (CAFOs) has led to the emergence of new epidemics, such as BSE ("mad cow disease"), which is communicable to humans; moreover, old diseases have spread to an unprecedented extent. "Plague" was the description applied to Europe's 2001 outbreak of foot-and-mouth disease, a form of nonlethal animal flu that is preventable by vaccine and treatable by ordinary veterinary care. In this case, however, ten million animals were destroyed, millions of them not infected, because their market value had plummeted and trade policies demanded it.[79] Colin Tudge observes the irony that hygiene laws designed to maintain food in a state of asepsis "are superimposed on a system of food production and distribution that seems specifically intended to generate and spread infection, or at least could hardly do the job better if it had been."[80]

But infectious disease is only the tip of the iceberg of suffering that is built into industrial systems of animal confinement and slaughter. Eighty million of the 95 million hogs slaughtered each year in the United States are the product of CAFOs. The scale is gigantic: 60 percent of the hogs are processed "from birth to bacon" by just four companies. They never feel soil or sunshine, and rarely the touch of a human hand.[81] A 500-pound sow spends an adult lifetime – measured in terms of litters and terminated after the eighth, if she survives that long – in a metal crate seven feet long and twenty-two inches wide, covered with sores, her swollen legs planted in urine and excrement.[82] On the kill-floor at Smithfield's Tar Heel plant, hogs are stunned, slashed, hoisted, and scalded at the rate of 2,000 per hour. When the four-pronged stunner misses its mark, then the flailing animal may be dropped alive into the scalding tank. "The electrocutors, stabbers, and carvers who work on the floor wear earplugs to muffle the screaming."[83] Indeed, animal suffering and human suffering is intertwined; the Tar Heel plant has a 100 percent annual turnover among its five thousand employees, most of them immigrants. The uncompromising stricture found in Leviticus on the slaughter of animals might serve as a commentary on our current practices: "If anyone from the house of Israel who slaughters an ox or a sheep or a goat in the camp or who slaughters it outside the camp does not bring it to the entrance of the Tent of Meeting, to offer it, an offering to YHWH before the Tabernacle of YHWH, *as blood* it shall be accounted to that man; he has shed blood. And that man shall be cut off from the midst of his people" (Lev. 17:3–4).

The cost of our eating is paid even in the distortion of agriculture itself, to service the meat and dairy industries. Beef cattle now consume half the world's wheat, most of its corn (a grain they do not naturally eat), and almost all of its soybeans. In turn, the agricultural industry is the largest consumer of water in North America. In addition to these extractions from the earth, the meat industry is responsible for dangerous inputs, including massive direct pollution of soil, water, and air from intensive "livestock units." In California's Central Valley, 1,600 dairies produce more effluents than a city of 21 million people. In 1997, the Senate Agriculture Committee reported that the total manure waste produced by U.S. animal industries was 1.3 billion tons: 130 times the amount of human waste processed in the nation.[84] Workers inside the factories and also nearby residents suffer high rates of respiratory and sinus problems, as well as nausea and diarrhea.[85]

How Israel eats is a covenantal concern. From the perspective of Leviticus, whether Israel eats at all is in the long term a function of covenant faithfulness practiced among three parties: God, land, and people. The book concludes with a series of blessings and curses that set forth two possible futures for Israel, and eating is central to both. If Israel chooses obedience, then this is God's promise:

> you will eat your bread to surfeit
> and dwell securely in your land . . . .
> You shall eat old [grain] long stored. . . . (Lev. 26:5, 10)

The verb *'-k-l,* "eat," occurs seven times in this chapter (vv. 5, 10, 16, 26, 29 [2×], 38). Notably, even God's satisfaction with the people is expressed in a striking image of divine ingestion:

> I will make my dwelling in your midst,
> and my throat will not expel you [*wĕlō'-tigʿal napšî 'etĕkem*]. (v. 11)[86]

The alternative is portrayed in a series of images that express the diametric opposite of consumption yielding satisfaction. Further, they depict a dramatic reversal of the actions that God has earlier taken for Israel. God who once *broke* the yoke of Egypt (v. 13) now *breaks* Israel's "pride" (*gĕʾôn,* v. 19), a term that here as elsewhere (Isa. 4:2) denotes the fruitfulness of her land. Lest that not be clear, God translates the metaphor of breakage:

> When I *break* for you the staff of bread,
> ten women will bake your bread in a single oven.
> And they will dole out your bread by weight,
> and you will *eat* but not be satisfied. (Lev. 26:26)

Finally, the language of consumption plunges to its nadir:

> You will *eat* the flesh of your sons
> and the flesh of your daughters you will *eat*. (v. 29)

When that happens, God will find it impossible to stomach Israel: "My throat will expel you" (v. 30). Expulsion is, of course, no empty metaphor; it is reified when Israel is scattered among the nations (v. 33), *eaten* by an enemy land (v. 38), even as enemies *eat* the seed that Israel sowed in her own land (v. 16). Moreover, this metaphor recalls another unforgettable image of bodily expulsion that appears in the instruction about sexual violations: "And the land became defiled, and I held it accountable for its iniquity, and the land vomited out its inhabitants" (18:25; cf. 18:28; 20:22). The land is a semi-autonomous moral agent. Though it can be victimized by its inhabitants, it remains accountable to God even for the defilement it suffers at human hands. Ultimately for the land, divine presence trumps human presence. The land, which retains its healthful instinct for God, must finally expel the unhealthful presence and make up the Sabbath years that Israel failed to observe.

So the land retains a capacity to act for God, even when humans have forfeited their high yet humble calling to work with God. As with other odd notions we have encountered in Leviticus, this one is not antiquated, even if it is very much the minority view in our culture. It is well expressed in a poem-prayer by Wendell Berry:

> Those who will not learn
> in plenty to keep their place
> must learn it by their need
> when they have had their way
> and the fields spurn their seed.
> We have failed Thy grace.
> Lord, I flinch and pray,
> send Thy necessity.[87]

❧

Covenantal Economics: The Biblical Case
for a Local Economy

Piety is deepest practicality, for it properly relates use and enjoyment. And a world sacramentally received in joy is a world sanely used. There is an economics of use only; it moves toward the destruction of both use and joy. And there is an economics of joy; it moves toward the intelligence of use and the enhancement of joy.

(Joseph Sittler)[1]

The stability, coherence, and longevity of human occupation require that the land should be divided among many owners and users. The central figure of agrarian thought has invariably been the small owner or small holder who maintains a significant measure of economic self-determination on a small acreage. The scale and independence of such holdings imply two things that agrarians see as desirable: intimate care in the use of the land, and political democracy resting upon the indispensable foundation of economic democracy.

(Wendell Berry)[2]

THE VALUE OF A LOCAL ECONOMY

Agrarians in every culture must reckon with the issue of land possession, usually as a vexed issue. The fact that land possession is a central (arguably *the* central) issue of the Hebrew Scriptures thus confirms their fundamentally agrarian character. And of course the issue remains vexed; the intensity of the conflict over possession of the land once called Canaan is probably greater today than it was in the Iron Age, and certainly more people and religious perspectives are involved. When I wrote this, armies of Israel and the Islamic movement Hezbollah were battling in Lebanon, while a Christian preacher from Texas promoted the Israeli cause among North American evangelicals: "Do not give the land away. It belongs to you. It is God's heritage to you."[3] An agrarian reading of the Bible also yields an understanding of land as a heritage that comes ultimately from God, and the consequences of such a reading have inescapable political and economic as well as religious dimensions. However, the presuppositions of the agrarian writers, ancient and modern, pose a basic challenge to the kinds of thinking that prevail in almost all modern cultures and therefore figure, even to this day, in struggles over the "Holy Land." Their thinking is challenging because agrarians do not assume, as states and other militarized entities (including at times the militarized church) almost invariably do, that the only important political or moral question regarding land possession concerns political *sovereignty over land.* Rather, they place priority on the *care of land,* asking whether or not practices of land tenure and use serve that end.

Here we shall explore the theological premises and economic intentions of the system of tenure of arable land endorsed by the Bible, which differs radically from the one that now prevails in the European Union, Canada, the United States, and Brazil,[4] and whose effects ramify throughout the globe. It is the contrast between, on the one hand, a system whose chief aim is the subsistence of local farming communities and, on the other hand, a corporate system of land management and food production that has resulted in the steady and now far-advanced impoverishment and dissolution of rural communities. The ideal shared by most biblical writers, in Torah, the historical books, and the Prophets, is that arable land is covenanted by God to the people Israel; the central feature of the "internal economic system" pertaining to the covenant is "the preservation of multiple family holdings in relative equality and freedom."[5] Extended families and kinship groups were settled on modest hereditary (patrimonial) plots of land, engaging in subsistence agriculture and supported by networks of mutual assistance and trade. The land was the tangible evidence of the covenant, and therefore the ideal of God's covenant with every Israelite meant that land possession and management should be radically decentralized. As Christopher Wright observes in his classic study: "The relationship between Israel and [YHWH] was vested, initially at any rate, in the socio-economic fabric of household-plus-land units. . . . It was by belonging within a household, with its portion of land as the proof of its share in the people of [YHWH], that the individual Israelite shared in the privileges and protection of this relationship."[6] In early Israel, most people seem to have known the social coherence of that kind of local and regional economy.[7] Thus the Shunammite woman replies when Elisha offers to secure her a favor from the king or the commander of the army: "In the midst of my people I am dwelling" (2 Kgs. 4:13). Her kinfolk provide all the protection and support she requires; to her, the political and military organization of the state is "irrelevant," or perhaps something to be resisted.[8]

The most obvious difference between the kind of land tenure system advocated by the biblical writers and the one that dominates our culture is an immense discrepancy of scale. In contrast to a network of small freeholdings held in perpetuity, the watchword for industrial-scale agriculture (as expressed by a former U.S. secretary of agriculture) is "Get big or get out."[9] The vast majority of small farmers in the United States have gotten out, mostly involuntarily. After World War II, there were 6 million farms. The numbers change so fast that it is hard to keep track of the rate of demise, but over 4 million of those are no longer family farms.[10] Thirty years ago, when Wendell Berry wrote *The Unsettling of America*, he lamented the fact that only 4 percent of the population was making a living from farming (in 1920, the figure stood at 50 percent).[11] Now it is less than 1 percent; but even that statistic is misleading with respect to the extent of consolidation. In 2002, 1.6 million farmers grew 6 percent of the food in the United States; 94 percent came from farms owned by a mere 400,000 farmers.[12]

A second (and related) difference between these two systems of land tenure and management is the discrepancy between the intimate care of land that is characteristic of small-scale farming and what Wendell Berry has described as the disastrous "generalization of the relationship between people and land" that is an inevitable consequence of industrial agriculture. That system of land tenure

> has divided all land into two kinds – that which permits the use of large equipment and that which does not.... Those lands that are too steep or stony or small-featured to be farmed with big equipment are increasingly not farmed at all.... That these lands can often be made highly productive with kindly use is simply of no interest; we now have neither the small technology nor the small economics nor the available work force necessary to make use of them.[13]

The standard rationale for industrial agriculture, energetically promoted by the multinationals that profit from it, is that it is more efficient; it can feed the world and do so cheaply. Yet, in fact, small farms everywhere, in North America and also in the Third World, are more productive than large ones, for multiple reasons. An industrial soybean farm may produce more beans per acre, but the small farm, planted with six to twelve different crops, has a much higher total yield, both in food quantity and in market value. Plants do favors for each other. In agrarian cultures in Mexico and northern Central America, farmers have traditionally interplanted "the three sisters": corn, beans, and squash. The corn provides trellises for the beans, the squash leaves discourage weeds and retard evaporation, and the beans fix nitrogen that enhances soil fertility for all three crops. Polycropping and even the planting of diverse varieties within a species also help with pest control; the different crops create more habitational niches for beneficial organisms, and harmful organisms are unlikely to have an equally devastating effect on every crop.[14] Small farmers often integrate crops and livestock, rotating pasture and planted fields in a single system of recycled biomass and nutrients.

The difference in productivity between small farms and industrial farms is not slight. In every country for which data is available, smaller farms are shown to be 200 to 1,000 percent more productive per unit area.[15] Moreover, small farming is more productive because the quality and even the quantity of labor and land care is higher when workers invest themselves in their own farm and community. Farmers who expect their families to have a future on the land do not willingly mortgage that future by robbing soil and water of their long-term health. Productivity and cost-effectiveness are durative qualities, although the short-term "success" of agribusiness depends upon ignoring that truth.

Smaller farms also generate more prosperity for nearby rural towns, where farmers buy supplies and in turn find markets for their produce. In Brazil, towns that once turned away members of the grassroots Landless Workers Movement (MST) have welcomed them because of their history of building schools, clinics, and houses, which has boosted the economies of depressed regions. As a result of this wide acceptance, members have won land titles for some 350,000 farms in 2,000 settlements.[16]

A third contrast between the kind of land tenure envisioned by the Bible and the system we currently practice has to do with the loss of vocation, or more properly, the *destruction* of vocation within rural communities. Now, after some sixty years of industrial agriculture in North America,[17] we have largely lost the practice of farming as craft, since most of the people who possess(ed) the skills of the craft can no longer afford to farm. From a biblical perspective, farming is the primary human vocation, "serving and preserving" the fertile earth (Gen. 2:15), and that labor is not merely altruistic. As many passages attest, the land itself is the medium or even the agent through which we may experience life as divinely blessed, or conversely, accursed (Gen. 3:17; 4:11; Leviticus 26; Psalms 72; 37). Any economy that negates this essential vocation is necessarily unjust, for "justice and vocation are inseparable," as Berry perceptively notes. "It is by way of the principle and practice of vocation that sanctity and reverence enter into the human economy. It was thus possible for traditional cultures to conceive that 'to work is to pray.'"[18]

The injustice of our system is evident to anyone who has visited rural America, where 25 percent of Americans still live in what many of them now describe as a "colony."[19] Colonial economies are notoriously extractive, and North American farmland functions in most places almost exclusively as a source of wealth flowing *out* of local communities, in direct contrast to the biblical model of communities first maintaining themselves and then engaging in a mutually advantageous exchange with urban populations. The contemporary dynamic is one of comprehensive local impoverishment; not just food but also opportunities for income and thus, inevitably, people move steadily from rural areas to the city. Today most small towns in America's grain belt are severely underpopulated. Many are virtually ghost towns, with no school, post office, or grocery store. Most farmers who have managed to stay on the land do so as renters or low-paid employees of the multinational corporations; the term "bioserf" has been coined to describe their situation.[20] In both the United States and Britain, the suicide rate among farmers is twice that of the general population; in other parts of the world it may be even higher.[21] Rural residents experience significantly higher rates of depression and mental disorder, and studies have shown "exceptionally large increases" in the incidence of substance abuse and domestic violence.[22] More organized and ambitious forms of violence are also coming out of the American heartland, as reported by Joel Dyer in his sobering journalistic investigation of the antigovernment movement, undertaken in the wake of the Oklahoma City bombing. He argues that the multifaceted movement, some elements of it driven by religious ideologies, offers to the victims of the "economic genocide" a twisted message of hope: "It's possible to fight back."[23]

Moreover, the injustice of current food policies in the industrial nations is felt widely in the Third World. Despite the food industry's claim to be feeding the world, chronic extreme hunger has increased since the mid-1990s, with 842 million people severely undernourished – even though there is, in absolute terms, enough food in the world for the current population. The situation is aptly termed "the paradox of plenty";[24] even though production is high, the profits remain in the hands of large farmers and corporations. The United States and Europe dump agricultural surpluses on poor countries, where local farmers cannot compete. The tragic irony is that such "food aid" increases both poverty and hunger. Internationally recognized economists such as Stephen C. Smith, Amartya Sen, and Jeffrey Sachs assert boldly that the elimination of hunger worldwide is still a realistic goal, but only if local and regional economies are strengthened.[25]

THE ECONOMICS OF PERMANENCE

My premise is that we are in grave danger from our mainstream culture's total divergence from the biblical ideal of healthy local communities with local food economies; the rest of this chapter shows how "the idea of a local economy"[26] functions within biblical thought about land possession. The key idea – really a complex of ideas – is most often summed up with the Hebrew word *naḥălâ*. Throughout the Bible, this is the word that most often characterizes divine or human title to the land of Canaan, an entitlement "that has continuity with the past and ties with a sacred heritage."[27] Originally, Canaan is designated as YHWH's *naḥălâ*, a claim that probably dates back to the beginning of Israel. It appears in Moses's Song at the Sea, possibly the oldest poem in the Bible:

> You will bring them in and plant them on your mount of possession [*har naḥălātĕkā*],
> . . . the sanctuary, O Lord, that your hands have established. (Exod. 15:17)

Here, Canaan as a whole is conceived as a holy mountain and a sanctuary for Israel's God, long before the temple has been built. From this perspective, the land itself is the primary sanctuary, with the temple standing as a symbol or replica of it.[28] In the ancient religious context, the claim that Canaan is YHWH's *naḥălâ* was polemical; in the epic poetry of ancient Canaan, the high god Baal uses the cognate word (*nḥlty*, "my entitlement") to claim the same territory.[29]

In turn, Canaan becomes Israel's covenantal allotment, held on the condition of obedience from generation to generation. Conceived as *naḥălâ*, the land of Canaan and any part of it is the possession of all Israel (Deut. 4:21; 15:4, etc.), of a tribe (Josh. 11:23; 17:6, etc.), or of an ancestral house within Israel (Josh. 24:28; Judg. 2:6; 1 Kgs. 21:3, etc.). It is in this last sense, as the property of a family through the generations, that *naḥălâ* is a genuinely agrarian concept. Such an understanding of land ownership is among the fundaments of an "agrarian worldview," defined by Eric Freyfogle, an expert in property law, as "one that respects the land and its mysteries, that honors healthy, enduring bonds between people and place, and that situates land users within a social order that links past to future."[30] Because the complex of ideas represented by the single term *naḥălâ* focuses on land possession, elements of that complex enter into discussions about political sovereignty in a national sense. However, I am highlighting its neglected aspect, for the biblical development of the concept points not only, and maybe not primarily, to possession "from above," based on conquest, but also to possession "from below," based on care.

Indeed, the notion that land possession is conditional upon care is itself profoundly challenging to all modern states, just as the biblical writers intended it to challenge the states they knew, including their own. If land care were really a priority for states and other militarized bodies, then other aspects of the nationalistic agenda would have to be excluded or drastically modified, including the practices of war. Long-term or permanent devastation of land is one of the tragic *effects* of the Middle Eastern wars of this generation. At the same time, if Jews, Christians, and Muslims in each of our communities were to place priority on land care and nurturance of the local economy, then there would be much less *cause* for war in every part of the globe. Economist Herman Daly (formerly of the World Bank) offers this prescription for our healing: "To avoid war, nations must both consume less and become more self-sufficient. But free traders say that we should become less self-sufficient and more globally integrated as part of the overriding quest to consume ever more. That is the worst advice I can think of."[31]

The future of humanity may now depend upon our grasping this neglected notion of land possession based on care and applying it to every part of the globe, and we may begin that work by seeing how the biblical idea functioned in historical context. The word *naḥălâ* expresses the "spirituality" of the Israelite village, in the sense that Tim Gorringe uses that term. Places have an "inner spirituality, which marks them off from every other place, and puts its impress on its citizens." Spirituality in this deepest sense shapes "the whole of everyday life" in a given culture "for good or ill, writ[ing] itself into the land":

> There are spiritualities which give rise to Cotswold villages, Italian hill towns, compact Indian cities, to the Parthenon, the Dome of the Rock, to Chartres, and the Meenakshi temple, and there are spiritualities which give rise to the unsustainable cities of Assyria and Babylon, to slums, the enclosing of rivers, Disneyworld, and the carving up of cities by grotesquely misnamed "freeways."[32]

The spirituality that wrote itself into the highlands of Canaan in the Iron Age was genuinely agrarian because it reflected the characteristics and the exigencies of the place from which it emerged. Archaeologist Carol Meyers observes: "In an environment with limited water and usable land, the establishment of fixed and theologically sanctioned patterns for family land tenure was an essential component of societal stability."[33] This steep, thin-soiled, highly variable country is hard to farm well and easy to ruin – quite like the Appalachians, whose tragic ruin has given rise to some of the best agrarian thinking in North America.[34] In addition to the more or less routine difficulties of all Middle Eastern agriculture – seasonal aridity and frequent drought – the corduroy pattern of slopes and small plains and valleys where the Israelites settled means extreme variation in rainfall, wind patterns, and solar radiation even within small areas, and as a result wide differences in the density and composition of vegetation. (A case in point is the contrast between the two slopes rising on either side of Shechem/Nablus: the verdant north-facing slope of Mount Gerizim and the bare south-facing slope of Ebal, traditionally places of blessing and curse respectively.)[35] In ancient times, only farmers with intimate knowledge of their particular plot of land – the kind of local knowledge that should pass from generation to generation with the land itself – would have been likely to prosper and to prosper their land over the long term.

Local knowledge comes into action through kindly use. "Kindly use" is Wendell Berry's term for the discipline of caring for land in its particularity. Berry himself farms land that is sloping and therefore fragile; being partly wooded, it must be worked in patches and plots, not the vast, supposedly uniform tracts that industrial agriculture requires in order to be "economical." If Berry's experience of land resembles that of ancient Israelite farmers, it is not wholly surprising that his description of kindly use suits not only Kentucky but also the topography of Canaan and the mind-set disclosed by the Bible:

> [K]indly use is a concept that of necessity broadens, becoming more com-plex and diverse, as it approaches action. The land is too various in its kinds, climates, conditions, declivities, aspects, and histories to conform to any generalized understanding or to prosper under generalized treat-ment. . . . Kindly use depends upon intimate knowledge, the most sensitive responsiveness and responsibility.[36]

Kindly use of land is the economic discipline observed by people who expect their "seed" to be thriving on the same small farm for generations to come. That dream can be fulfilled only through an economics of permanence (to use Schumacher's felicitous phrase),[37] in contrast to industrial agriculture's economics of extraction and total consumption.

Because the land itself is various in its character and needs, "kindly use . . . becom[es] more complex and diverse . . . as it approaches action." Within the Bible, the best place to glimpse something of the breadth of the concept, as it was conceived and may have functioned within Israelite villages, is through the several law codes found in Torah, all of which show a keen awareness that land care is part of the covenanted life. The first and earliest of them, the Covenant Code in Exodus (Exodus 21–23), may reflect a period a century or so after the founding of the monarchy, when pressures generated by the state were beginning to be felt. Legal codes often emerge in times of transition, when basic cultural understandings are threatened from within or without. The social environment represented here is the village engaged in mixed farming, with grain fields, vineyards, and animals on smallholdings, small enough that relations with neighbors – and their goring, wandering, or overburdened animals (Exod. 21:28–32; 23:4–5) – require regular community oversight. The fragility of the smallholder economy at the time of codification is indicated by the fact that the very first issue taken up here is slavery: "When you buy a Hebrew slave, for six years he shall be in servitude; and in the seventh year he shall go free, at no cost" (21:2). Israelites might be sold into slavery by financially desperate parents (21:7), for their own debts (Lev. 25:39), or for acts of theft (Exod. 21:37–22:3 [22:1–4 Eng.]). The six-year limit on working the slave is matched by the limit on working the land: "Six years you shall seed your land and gather its yield; but the seventh year you shall fallow it and leave it alone – and the vulnerable of your people will eat, and what they leave the animal of the field will eat; thus you shall do for your vineyard and for your olives" (Exod. 23:10–11). Kindly use binds together and benefits every member of the land community.

The Holiness Code of Leviticus[38] highlights the benefit of the land itself, even in the potential absence of humans. The seventh-year "Sabbath-ceasing" (*šabbat šabbâtôn*) is emphatically "for the land" (Lev. 25:4, 5); at the same time, it is "a Sabbath for YHWH" (v. 4). William P. Brown has argued that the Sabbath "transforms private land into an eminently public domain."[39] However, in the conception of Leviticus, arable land is not for a moment private. It could more accurately be said that the seventh year simply clarifies what the land always is: God's domain. This passage includes the most strident assertion in the whole Bible that the fertile land of Canaan belongs to God: "The land shall not be sold in perpetuity, for the land is mine," God declares to Israel; "You are resident aliens with me!" (25:23). The whole land is imbued with the holiness that derives from God's sanctuary. As J. Joosten observes, the people Israel "are represented in the image of asylants granted the right to settle on temple lands. . . . Anyone established in the land . . . must, therefore, adapt his actions, his words and his thoughts to the holy presence of the God of Israel."[40]

Even though the people Israel may fail to participate in the rest and renewal of Sabbath and consequently be scattered among the nations, the land will do so nonetheless. It will "accept [or: enjoy, *tirṣeh*] its Sabbaths all the time it is desolate" (Lev. 26:34). The Holiness writer perceives that the land cares how it is used or misused. It demonstrates a kind of moral sensitivity – even agency – "vomiting out" those who defile it, be they Canaanite or Israelite (18:25–28). The sensibility that perceives land as a living being in the full sense is distinctly agrarian. Norman Habel identifies the social model implied in the Holiness Code as "an agrarian theocracy" and comments: "As a jealous landowner, YHWH desires responsible tenants who will maintain an attitude of reverence and concern for the very soil and soul of the land."[41]

Though rarely, if ever, found in the mainstream, that sensitivity to land as a moral agent has even now not entirely died out. Recently I visited a former cotton plantation in Eastern North Carolina, where Simon Rich now practices a form of "holistic management" based on principles developed by African farmer and biologist Allan Savory.[42] He explained what motivates him: "I want to help the land do what *it* wants to do and has not been free to do for at least 150 years." Like the Holiness writer, Cy Rich has the imagination to see that the land has a capacity to enjoy itself, and the practical intelligence to figure out the necessary economic conditions for it to have joy. For lack of a culture that nurtures it, that kind of agrarian imagination may go to ground and become inactive for a time, only to crop up once again – often, under the threat of devastation.

One could multiply examples of commandments that bespeak keen sensitivity to the needs of the nonhuman members of the land community. The last several chapters of the Deuteronomic law code are full of them: for instance, the prohibition on cutting down fruit trees when laying siege to a city: "Now is the tree of the field human, that it can get away from you in the siege?" (Deut. 20:19). Both the commandment and the question reflect the agrarian imagination of those by and for whom the codes were formulated. Even after Israel began to be urbanized, most people (perhaps 85 percent of the population) were still village farmers.[43] But that does not mean that the ancient states of Israel and Judah were ideal (or even healthy) agrarian societies. On the contrary, there is good literary evidence that a community of small freeholdings was an endangered economic species through most of the biblical period: most obviously, all three legal codes in Torah include provision for the liberation of debt slaves or the redemption of slaves and/or family land. Outside the legal codes, at least two texts (1 Kings 21 and Psalm 37) articulate the "spirituality" of Israel's *naḥălâ* culture, and both show a traditional economy struggling and, for the present, failing to survive within an exploitative national economy.

ECONOMIES IN CONFLICT

The story of Naboth's vineyard is the most famous account of confrontation over the land rights of an Israelite farmer. Although the narrative is unique in the Bible, it is a mistake to view this as an isolated incident: one greedy king (Ahab) taking advantage of a noble but regrettably naïve hayseed. Rather, this is an emblematic tale of two economic systems or cultures in conflict, each with a different principle of land tenure. The ancestral household ideology has run up against a royal ideology – formerly of Canaan, subsequently adopted by Israelite monarchs, beginning with David – that asserts the king's right to lay claim to land or distribute it at will.[44] "Now *you*," says Ahab's wife Jezebel, "will enact sovereignty [*ta'áśeh mĕlûkâ*] over Israel" (1 Kgs. 21:7). Every word in this narrative is chosen for maximum impact; that care suggests that its subject is of the utmost importance both to the writer and to the intended audience.

Ahab is "king of Samaria" (1 Kgs. 21:1), the elegant capital city built by his father, Omri. However, the vineyard he is after lies in Jezreel, the richest agricultural region of the country, close to the major trade route running through Megiddo. "And Ahab said to Naboth, 'Give me your vineyard so I can have it for a vegetable garden, for it is close to my house. And let me give you in its stead a better vineyard – or if it is good in your eyes, let me pay you its price in silver'" (21:2). Ahab approaches this as a simple real estate deal: The vineyard is an exchangeable and interchangeable commodity. That is antithetical to Naboth's understanding, and he refuses categorically. The relevant category is religion: "It would be defilement/pollution [*hǎlîlâ*] for me from YHWH if I were to give my ancestors' *nahǎlâ* to you!" (21:3). This is the only sentence Naboth ever speaks, and it sums up forcefully the theology of covenantal economics. While he uses the first person singular, Naboth is speaking for the whole community-through-time of those who experience God's blessing as they live on and work this one small piece of land, "my ancestral entitlement." In complete contrast to Ahab, Naboth has a complex notion of property ownership, one that is well expressed in David Klemm's description of "property as material grace":

> Property as material grace both is and is not one's property; it is a possession that is not one's possession. Moreover, I want to argue that the paradoxical experience of both owning and not owning one's own property precisely signifies the moment at which the divine depth of meaning and power breaks into the structure of acquiring, using, and exchanging property. Property as material grace is given and received as a living symbol of divinity.[45]

Ahab appears in this exchange as a mild-mannered weakling, who goes off pouting, "sullen and resentful" (*sar wĕzā'ēp*, 21:4), and lets Jezebel do the dirty work of getting rid of the recalcitrant Naboth. Yet, there are reasons to suspect that Ahab does not say everything he thinks; maybe Jezebel is the designated executioner in a plan he intended from the outset. First, if the king were sincere in wanting to rip up a vineyard to plant vegetables, then he would be self-indulgent, and furthermore, stupid. Raisin cakes, grape honey, and wine were staples of the Israelite diet; vegetables were not. Indeed, there may be a negative judgment implied with respect to Ahab's very mention of a "vegetable garden" (1 Kgs. 21:2). The only other biblical occurrence of the phrase appears in Deuteronomy's statement that the promised land of Israel "is not like the land of Egypt, . . . where you would sow your seed and water it with your foot, like the vegetable garden" (Deut. 11:10). That explicit statement of contrast was likely known to the writer of the Naboth story, who shared the same "Deuteronomistic" literary and theological traditions. The inference to be drawn is that Ahab would make Israel too much like the land of Egypt.[46]

More importantly, a good vineyard is far more valuable than a garden. The work of decades, not a summer, it is a sign of permanence, an investment in the future of a place and a people.[47] However, the historical record makes it clear that Ahab was neither stupid nor a weakling; rather, he was one of Israel's most important military figures. He mounted successful campaigns against the powerful kingdom of Damascus and was the first Israelite king to engage Assyrian forces, apparently with success. In 853 b.c.e., Ahab brought an army of 10,000 infantry and 2,000 chariots – huge for its time – against Shalmaneser III at Qarqar on the Orontes; he is the only Israelite king who merits mention on an Assyrian monument. As a warrior, Ahab bought his nation a long period of freedom: Samaria did not fall to Assyria for another 130 years.

Ahab's wars were fought over the comparatively scarce arable land, the tradable goods it could produce, and control of the trade routes. With that in mind, one might suspect that the proposed royal vegetable garden is a scam. The king has a large professional army to support, as well as an expensive "lifestyle." While Ahab speaks of his "house," the narrator tells us that it is *hêkal* (21:1), "a palace," an unparalleled designation for the home of an Israelite king – and a second home at that. Likely, Ahab intends not to tear out the vines but rather to appropriate their yield and produce wine, first for his own table and then for the export economy. The prophet Amos, prophesying against the elite of Israel about a century after Ahab, decries those who lie on ivory banqueting couches on "Mount Samaria," the royal acropolis, and drink wine straight from the kraters (Amos 6:4–7). Nathan MacDonald has focused attention on the phenomenon of royal feasting in Israel as a significant factor in consolidating and maintaining power: "The king's table was very important for creating and maintaining political support amongst the ... elite."[48] Lavish spreads of food and wine were thus not just a form of indulgence: They were also an investment intended to yield social capital in both the domestic and the international spheres. The queen of Sheba had her breath taken away, not only by Solomon's ability to tell her anything she wanted to know, but also by "the food of his table, and the seating of his servants, and the standing of his servants and their attire, and his cupbearers ... " (1 Kgs. 10:5), and the happy result of her breathlessness was a trade agreement. As MacDonald observes, those who can commandeer the food and wine for such feasts are the same ones "who will be able to participate in and profit from international trade, further boosting their power and prestige."[49] It is no coincidence that when Ahab defeated the king of Aram, in the story immediately preceding ours, the terms of the treaty included Ahab's right to set up markets in Damascus (1 Kgs. 20:34). The treaty itself was a mistake for Ahab; an anonymous prophet condemned him for making an ally of a king whom God had proscribed, and "the king of Israel went to his house sullen and resentful" (20:43) – exactly as he would do after his encounter with Naboth, the second and final instance in which Ahab's behavior elicits a direct prophetic condemnation.

Both feasting and trade required the appropriation and redistribution of food commodities on a large scale, and thus the conversion of Israel's economy from one focused on local subsistence to a state-controlled economy designed to generate surpluses of the key crops. Regarding the intensification of the economic conversion during Ahab's reign, Tamis Rentería observes:

> Pressures on Israelite peasants increased throughout Ahab's 20 year reign and into the reigns of Ahaziah and Jehoram. Israel was on the downward swing of ... the "adaptational cycle," moving from expansion of production to depletion of resources with no sign that elites intended to heed negative feedback processes by changing their productive strategies.... Even when a severe drought hit Palestine during Ahab's reign, the king, according to 1 Kings 18, worried about food for his horses, oblivious that the peasant masses were starving.[50]

The very fact that the "king of Samaria" has a palace *in Jezreel* may be a further reason to suspect that Ahab aspires to more than vegetables when he accosts Naboth: He means to break the traditional land tenure system at its power base. The new-style kingdom founded by Omri required that the old centers of power be won over, neutralized, or eliminated. Moving the capital away from the ancient hill-country cities of Shechem and Tirzah was a strategic way of bypassing the old urban elite. And Ahab may well have decided that moving into the midst of the country's richest patrimonial lands was the way to undermine the rural elite and secure new crown lands.[51] Looking at the story from that perspective, it becomes evident that Naboth is a person of influence; that is why Ahab targets him, and why Naboth finds the courage to refuse the king. The "elders and nobles" whom Jezebel enlists in the plot against him are men who once "sat" with him (*hayyōšěbîm*, 21:8), exercising political and judicial authority at the city gate.[52] Evidently, the royal house has created a rift within the old power structure, doubtless by granting favors or lands to those who cooperate with them. In the end, they garner enough support to sentence Naboth to death "before the people" and have him publicly stoned (21:13).

When a king who is politically and militarily successful is portrayed as a fool and a weakling – a vegetable-eating king who goes off "sullen and resentful" – this is political satire. Satire is characteristically used to point out a weakness in a system that is still apparently strong, a weakness that, the satirist wagers, will eventually prove fatal. What this narrative reveals, then, is that when Ahab "enacts sovereignty" in a way that defeats the local economy, he sets in motion a destructive mechanism that he himself is unable to arrest; eventually it will bring down his own royal house. But the first step in the wider collapse is when, as the narrative shows, the community of the non-elite becomes divided against itself. It is not possible to subtract the essential economic functions from a community and expect mutual trust, goodwill, and aid among neighbors to remain. A healthy economy is part of an authentic local culture, and lacking that, as Wendell Berry observes, "a place is open to exploitation, and ultimately destruction, from the center."[53]

There is a sharp irony in the way the Deuteronomistic historian sums up this royal career: "There was no one like Ahab, who *sold himself* to do evil in the eyes of YHWH" (1 Kgs. 21:25; cf. v. 20). Like a debt slave who loses successively his patrimony and the freedom of his person, Ahab forfeits his own proper entitlement, a kingship that is meant to maintain his people in freedom.[54] But whereas the hapless debt slave "is sold" (*yimmākēr* [*nipʿal*], Deut. 15:12; cf. Lev. 25:39), Ahab voluntarily "sells himself" (*hitmakkēr* [*hitpaʿel*]).[55] With that, he seals his own doom and that of the royal household (1 Kgs. 21:21–24).

POSSESSING LAND

If the story of Naboth's vineyard is the Bible's paradigmatic *narrative* account of the undermining of the subsistence economy, then Psalm 37 is the primary *poetic* response to that sabotage. The psalmist speaks to and for the "vulnerable" (*'ănāwîm*), who, it seems, are currently landless. Therefore, this agrarian poem looks toward change in matters of land tenure:

> For evildoers will be cut off,
> but those who hope in YHWH, *they* will possess land [*yîršû-'āreṣ*]. . . .
> The vulnerable will possess land,
> and they will take delight in an abundance of *šālôm*. (Ps. 37:9, 11)

Land possession is the poem's recurrent theme; the phrase *yîršû-'āreṣ* (with variations) occurs five times (vv. 9, 11, 22, 29, 34). Psalm 37 is generally undervalued by theological interpreters, because it is taken to be the worst kind of "wisdom literature": a somewhat random collection of truisms[56] that may not be so true after all:

> I have been young and now I am old,
> but I have not seen the righteous one forsaken
> nor his seed begging bread. (v. 25)

Walter Brueggemann considers this a "psalm of orientation"; "it reflects a community for whom most things work."[57] However, that reading fails to take account of the note of keen expectation that runs throughout; the tone of the psalm is encouragement for the dispirited, not contentment with the *status quo*. Far from being sanguine, the poem acknowledges that there is reason for apprehension and even mourning. Lines such as these show its kinship with the psalms of lament, prayers uttered under intense pressure from enemies:

> Let anger go and abandon rage;
> do not become heated; it only does harm.
> . . . Just a little longer, and there will be no wicked one;
> you shall examine his place – and he is gone. (vv. 8, 10)

The psalm seeks to nurture hope in God while calling vividly to mind the elements of a traditional world that is threatened or eclipsed, namely, the world of the Israelite village. "One of the functions of the music or formality of poetry is to make memorable," Wendell Berry observes;[58] perhaps it is no coincidence that the form used here is the strictest available within Israelite poetry: an alphabetic acrostic, which lends itself to recitation and retention. Memory, imagination, faith – these are the common stock that remains to the endangered community. So, this poet uses images designed to evoke a farmer's experience in order to create a solid foundation for hope:

For like grass [the evildoers] will quickly dry up,
and like green herbage they will wither.
Trust in YHWH and do good;
settle the land and graze on faith [*ûrĕ'ēh 'ĕmûnâ*]. (vv. 2–3)

"Graze on faith" is surely one of the most arresting metaphors in the Bible, when it is correctly translated; "enjoy security" (NRSV) and "remain loyal" (NJPS) are not compelling alternatives. But the effect of the metaphor is not to spiritualize the divine promise that unfolds from here (although that is how "inheriting the earth" is most often understood, at least by Christians). To the contrary, the appearance of the grazing metaphor near the beginning of this liturgical poem underscores the concreteness of the psalmist's vision, offered to people whose food supply is in jeopardy. "Unless you hear the mouth eating, you cannot hear the mouth crying," according to a Ugandan proverb,[59] another form of traditional literature that deals with the most basic elements of existence.

The psalm speaks to those who look to God for legal justice that will secure their claim to land:

Rely on him and he will act,
and bring forth like light your vindication
and your judgments like noonday. . . .
Do not become heated over the one who advances himself,
the man who executes illegal schemes.
. . . [Those who hope in YHWH] will not be disappointed in an evil time,
and in days of famine they will be satisfied.
. . . The wicked borrows and does not pay back,
but the righteous is gracious and giving.
For the blessed will possess land,
but the accursed will be cut off.
A landowner's steps [*miṣ'ădê-gĕbĕr*][60] are established by YHWH,
and he wills his way. (vv. 5b, 6, 7b, 19, 21–23)

The poet is clear eyed about the economic situation. "The wicked borrows and does not pay back" – that is the regular practice not just of irresponsible individuals but also of extractive economies. Yet communities that endure are "gracious and giving"; they cultivate modest habits of use and accumulation, and with those, the generosity that is often the remarkable grace of the poor:

Better the little the righteous [*ṣaddîq*] has
than the glut of many wicked folk. (v. 16)

"Righteous" here is likely a technical term, denoting those who have legal rights, even if they are currently being violated. So these are hopeful words for the *'ănāwîm*, the "vulnerable," trapped in a killing system that still appears to be strong, though it has already far outreached itself. (In this reading of the psalm I follow Jacqueline Osherow, in her stunning poetic monologue "Psalm 37 at Auschwitz.")[61] In such a situation, hope cannot mean naïve expectation of personal prosperity, nor even perhaps one's own survival. Rather, it means looking to the inevitable collapse of the system, with the visionary realism that often emerges among the oppressed, knowing that on the other side of that destruction there may be life within a radically different kind of social and economic system, one that might truly be called "community":

> For the arms of the wicked will be broken,
> but YHWH upholds the righteous.
> YHWH knows the days of the honest,
> and their entitlement [*naḥălâ*] will be enduring. . . .
> Hold to integrity and regard the honest,
> for there is a future [*'aḥărît*] for the peaceful citizen [*'îš*].[62]
> But transgressors will be annihilated altogether;
> the future of the wicked is cut off. (vv. 17–18, 37–38)

"A future," as this agrarian psalmist conceives it, denotes something concrete, whose dimensions are theological, legal, social, physical. The Israelite poet would likely concur with Eric Freyfogle's judgment that "[f]ew tasks offer more promise than the crafting of a new understanding of what it means to own land."[63] Freyfogle shows that the sharp distinction between public and private property that dominates Western legal thought and practice is false. For in virtually every instance of land use, "public and private influences intermingle. So varied is this intermingling that we do not really have two categories of lands. We have a continuum."[64] Although he maintains that "the public has a legitimate interest in how all lands are used," Freyfogle does not argue for more public land as such. Rather, he foresees and advocates a "marked reduction" of both public land and private land "as we now know them. . . . We do not need a shift of land from one type of ownership to the other. We need instead an end to the categories themselves. We need to craft new, intermediate forms of land management, and then shift lands from both sides into the center."[65]

Some of the most creative agrarian work now being done is the protection of farmlands, and especially smaller farms, so that they do not become housing developments or second homes for urbanites with ready cash. At the same time, those who live in cities and suburbs must have a stake in the countryside that is both emotional and economic. The common biblical metaphor for the relationship between a city and its surrounding villages is that of a mother and her daughters (Num. 21:25; Josh. 15:45, 47, etc.); it connotes mutual belonging, affection, benefit, and need.[66] That image should be embraced and promoted by those of us who, farmers or not, sense the "deadly impermanence"[67] of the global economy and seek sustenance outside it, for ourselves, and even more, for our children.

Transformed models of land ownership are being developed and implemented, including regulations and easements on private property that restrict some forms of alteration and protect wetlands, forests, and arable land. Some family farms are being purchased by public and nonprofit conservation trusts operating at various levels: national (the American Farmland Trust), state and provincial (e.g., Maine Farmland Trust, Ontario Farmland Trust), county and regional. The suburban town of Weston, Massachusetts, ten miles from Boston, has developed an educational farm on town-owned conservation land. The town contracts with a nonprofit community farming organization to run the farm, and local youth work in its various commercial enterprises (firewood and timber, maple syrup, organic flowers, fruits and vegetables), gaining both employment and skills training.[68]

Moreover, farmers' markets and membership farms (Community Supported Agriculture, "CSAs") are now enabling small farmers in exurban areas to stay on the land, while urbanites and suburbanites have the pleasure and tangible benefits of investing in their "breadbasket" communities. In dramatic contrast to the general statistics for family farm collapse in the United States, the number of small farms that sell directly to their neighbors increased by 20 percent between 2001 and 2007.[69] The number of farmers' markets increased from 340 in 1970 to 3,700 in 2004.[70] Anathoth Community Garden in Cedar Grove, North Carolina, is a CSA that demonstrates another potential benefit of community farming, namely, the healing of rifts along economic, ethnic, and racial lines. In this small rural community, such rifts had led to a murder, apparently provoked by racism. Out of the community's agitation and grief came a vision: A lifelong member of the community, a woman whose grandfather had been born into slavery, offered five acres of land to Cedar Grove United Methodist – once known as "the rich white church" – for the purpose of planting a community vegetable garden. Now Asians, Mexicans, Hondurans, African and European Americans, Christians and non-Christians, poor and relatively rich, work that land together, and have weekly dinners on the ground. The older farmers contribute their local knowledge and their manure – things that no one had seemed to value before. The food goes to those who need it most; some need it very badly. A community that a few years ago was riven by fear is now growing in trust and joy. In biblical terms, the people of Cedar Grove are reclaiming their *naḥălâ*, which is, in its widest sense, the means of livelihood and blessing in community bestowed and received as the gift of God.[71]

7

&

Running on Poetry: The Agrarian Prophets

CROWN AGRICULTURE IN EIGHTH-CENTURY ISRAEL

To those who speak to the many deaf ears attend.
To those who speak to one,
In poet's song and voice of bird,
Many listen; but the voice that speaks to none
By all is heard:
Sound of the wind, music of the stars, prophetic word.

(Kathleen Raine)[1]

In the widening circle of those who attend to the message of the new agrarians, it is common, almost instinctual, to characterize their message as "prophetic" witness the first chapter in this volume).[2] Like the biblical prophets, the contemporary agrarian writers expose folly and idolatry, various forms of bad faith that are endemic to their (and our) society. Like the prophets, they express their grievances and hopes in terms that are inseparably economic, political, and religious. And further, they, like the prophets, alert those who can hear to the close or immediate threat of social collapse; they see and say that we are at a tipping point, either toward life on drastically different terms or toward death on a massive scale. Yet, if the message of the new agrarian writers may rightly be called "prophetic," the more important fact is less widely recognized: The message of the earliest prophetic writers of the Bible was distinctly "agrarian." The eighth-century prophets Amos and Hosea were probably the world's first agrarian writers, followed within a few decades by the Greek farmer-poet Hesiod, who resembles the biblical prophets in his complaints about corrupt judges and princes (*Works and Days*, lines 250–65), and also about the loss of ancestral inheritance (namely his own).

Victor Davis Hanson's illuminating study of eighth-century B.C.E. Greece suggests both similarity and difference between the socioeconomic conditions there and in Israelite society of the same period. In Greece, as in the Canaanite city-states, the Late Bronze Age had been characterized by a system of palace-controlled agriculture, which demanded cash crops and appropriated the surplus; in both cases, this system began to totter about 1200 B.C.E. It took nearly four centuries for a significant number of independent Greek farmers to establish themselves on their own land – as in Israel, on small plots of marginal land that had not been previously farmed. The emergent agrarian culture, though not free of pressure from the old landed aristocracy, proved to be a powerful force in the wider culture; Hanson argues that it "created the surplus, capital, and leisure that lay behind the entire Greek cultural renaissance."[3]

It seems likely that the Israelites developed a viable small-farming net-work several centuries *earlier* than the Greeks – probably in the twelfth and eleventh centuries, when Israelites settled in upland villages independent of the Canaanite city-states. However, by the eighth century the culture of Israelite small farmers was beginning to crack under pressure from their own monarchs, who had created new systems of centralized agriculture. Despite the outcry of the prophets – first Amos and Hosea, and then, in the next generation, Micah and Isaiah of Jerusalem (the latter being perhaps the first urban agrarian)[4] – that pressure would not be relieved short of the destruction of Israel and Judah.

For Jews and Christians seeking to situate themselves theologically and ethically in the current social milieu, it is of the greatest significance that these earliest prophetic writings express a certain understanding of land and its proper use, whose basic elements are these:

- Fertile soil is a gift and trust from God.
- Our relationship to the soil, demonstrated primarily in our practices of food production and consumption, is fundamental to every other aspect of human life.
- Misuse of the gift of land, including maltreatment of those who work the soil, will ultimately undo every political structure, no matter how sophisticated, stable, and powerful it appears to be. In the subversive dictum of Qoheleth (Ecclesiastes), who lived in Jerusalem half a millennium after the agrarian prophets: "The advantage of a land in everything is this: [even] a king is in service to a field [*melek lĕśādeh ne'ĕbād*]" (Eccl. 5:8 [9 Eng.]).[5]

Amos and Hosea spoke out in response to a growing threat to that still-common cultural understanding. Their message may be instructive for us, because their social situation bears some resemblance to our own. Like us, they lived in a vigorous society that for some decades enjoyed considerable success in pursuing domestic and foreign policies that were enriching for the elite but difficult or disastrous for small farmers. It was a time of economic and territorial expansion, with the great powers, Aram (Syria) and Assyria, at least temporarily in eclipse. During the eighth century, the minor states of Judah and Israel reached their greatest geographic extent since Solomon's reign. The national economy was active, with international trade drawing heavily upon the agricultural products of the region. From the perspective of those at the top of the power structure, it was an encouraging time, with the religious establishment endorsing the policies of state.

So Amos and Hosea stood under a clear political sky and forecast the approach of a devastating storm:

> Look, the eyes of the Lord YHWH are on the sinful kingdom,
> and I will annihilate it from off the face of the fertile soil [*'ădāmâ*].
>
> (Amos 9:8)

> There comes an east wind,
> the wind of YHWH blowing up out of the wilderness,
> and its fountain will dry up and its spring be desiccated. (Hos. 13:15)

These threats the prophets spoke, in Kathleen Raines's words, "to none." At the time, there was no reason for anyone in power to listen; and for decades following, no evidence seemed to support the prophets' reading of the historical moment. It is therefore remarkable that some gave them credence. Doubtless it was among the small farmers (who constituted the overwhelming majority of the Israelite population)[6] that their sayings, speeches, and stories were collected and passed on until at length the storm hit.

This sudden outburst of rural prophecy, apparently unprecedented in the depth and range of its vision and replete with language and images that evoke the experience of farmers, seems to have been prompted by a large-scale transformation of both the land and the rural economy. Archaeological evidence and also multiple strands of the biblical text attest to the development of a centralized system of commodity agriculture controlled by the crown. The old subsistence economy, as it had been practiced in semiautonomous villages cooperating within regional networks, was supplanted by intensified and specialized agriculture. The new system was designed to maximize production of the three most important commodities: grain to feed the cities (the state's administrative and trade centers), and wine and olive oil, the more expensive products, to provide export revenue and to satisfy (directly and indirectly) the taste for luxury now cultivated among the few who were rich.[7]

Farmers felt the burden and constraints imposed by the government in several ways. Taxation-in-kind of agricultural products (e.g., "exactions of wheat," Amos 5:11; "the king's mowings," Amos 7:1) was compounded by conscription for labor gangs and military service, and also by appropriation of valuable metals for military purposes; iron that might have been used for plowshares was turned into swords (see Isa. 2:4; Mic. 4:3; Joel 4:10 [3:10 Eng.]).[8] Altogether, the demands of the centralized government may well have consumed half or more of a family's labor and production capacity.[9] In a bad agricultural year (about three years out of ten in that semiarid land),[10] many families would have been unable to feed themselves and also meet the demands of the state. So the crown literally gained ground for centralized agriculture through acquisition of the ancestral lands of small farmers who went into debt and put up their land as collateral. Land thus extracted from freeholders was reassigned to the new aristocracy in the process known as latifundialization ("the making of wide estates").

In the old rural economy, those who were relatively well-off would have resided in the villages. As members of the same community with the indigent, they would have been immediately confronted with the claim of the needy, who were probably their kin. In biblical tradition, Boaz exemplifies the prosperous landowner who responds to such a claim from his kinswoman (by marriage) Naomi. Amos himself may be another example; he is described as being "among the *nōqĕdîm* from Tekoa" (Amos 1:1), a term that probably designates those who bred sheep on a large scale.[11] By contrast, the new estates often belonged to absentee landowners, living in the royal cities of Jerusalem and Samaria. The Samaria "ostraca" (pottery sherds bearing written notations) attest to the practices of the new regime. Evidently used to record incoming shipments from the estates of one or another royal functionary, the ostraca sketch "a picture of a capital peopled by the king's retinue and mulcting the neighboring countryside."[12]

Correspondingly, the archaeological evidence from rural sites points to the spread of specialized agriculture in the eighth century. In the hill country of Judah and Israel, many wine and oil manufacturing installations from this period have been identified; in some cases, storage towers and large houses with multiple grain pits are found nearby.[13] Surveys of the slopes around Jerusalem show that at this time the natural limestone terracing was built up into structures designed to conserve and direct water, control erosion, and thus enable intensive planting of orchards and vineyards.[14] Throughout

Judean territory, archaeologists have unearthed over one thousand jar handles from the eighth and seventh centuries, each inscribed *lmlk*, "belonging to the king," and bearing the name of one of four cities. These cities must have held regional storehouses for wine and oil; the handles attest to royal oversight of the commodities that were the produce of royal estates or else were extracted from the peasants as taxes and tariffs.[15]

It was during the lengthy expansionist reigns of Jeroboam II of Israel (ca. 786–746 B.C.E.) and Uzziah of Judah (ca. 785–733 B.C.E.) that both Amos and Hosea began their public work. The Chronicler, writing of the latter monarch, casts a positive light on the practice of regionally specialized agriculture under royal control: "And Uzziah built towers in Jerusalem . . . and he built towers in the wilderness and hewed out many cisterns, for he had many cattle. And in the piedmont and on the plain he had plowmen, and vinedressers in the hills and in the Carmel – for he was a lover of arable land [*'ōhēb 'ădāmâ*]!" (2 Chron. 26:9–10).[16] Amos and Hosea viewed the royal love of land more critically than did that royalist historian of a later period. As residents of rural districts,[17] they would have witnessed the appropriation of the land and those who worked it; many formerly free peasants became serfs, doubtless on land their own families had long held. Speaking from firsthand knowledge, they show what state-run agriculture meant to the small farmer. In the diversified farming characteristic of the village-based economy, families had grown nearly all their own food and obtained the rest through cooperative trade networks. In the more "efficient" system of commodity-driven agriculture, families were forced to purchase their most important dietary staple in the grain market, without benefit of the ethical constraints that perforce inform business among neighbors and kin. Amos graphically evokes the new situation:

> Hear this, you who devour the needy,
> in order to finish off the vulnerable of the land,
> saying, "When will the New Moon [festival] be over, so we can market
>   grain,
> and the Sabbath, so we can open sale on wheat?" –
> making the *ephah* too small and the *shekel* too big,[18]
> cheating with trick scales,
> buying the destitute with silver
> and the needy for a pair of sandals –
> "and we will market the refuse of the wheat!" (Amos 8:4–6; cf. Mic.:10–11)

For all but the wealthy, wheat and barley were the chief sources of protein and of nutrition altogether; what happened in the grain market was for them literally a matter of life and death. Therefore, Hosea proclaims that blood crimes are rife in the land:

> There is no truth and no covenant loyalty
> and no knowledge of God in the land.
> Cursing and deception and murder
> and stealing and adultery are rampant;
> bloodshed follows upon bloodshed. (Hos. 4:1b–2)

Likely for Hosea all these accusations point to crimes with an economic base; as we shall see, adultery is for him a favorite metaphor for economic irresponsibility. When the covenant community is thus undone, the whole "land community"[19] of Israel suffers from its destruction:

> Therefore the land mourns [or: withers]
> and all who inhabit it languish –
> among the wild beasts of the field and among the birds of the sky,
> and even the fish of the sea are gathered in.[20] (Hos. 4:3)

A new way of thinking gradually established itself in Israel and Judah, on the margins, often outside the cities: a prophetic challenge to royal authority so far-reaching that it could envision the end of kingship and even of Israel's tenure in the land. The books of the eighth-century agrarian prophets are a benchmark in that process; although prophets had been abroad in the countryside at least since the days of Saul (e.g., 1 Sam. 10:5, 11–12), theirs were evidently the first prophetic messages to be preserved verbatim. Their words were poetic – evocative, memorable – and unavoidable; they reached the royal sanctuary (Amos) and even the king's court (Micah and Isaiah). The questions to be explored here are how agrarian poetry served as the primary vehicle for inscribing a new social vision in the eighth century, and further, how the poetic traditions generated by Amos and Hosea might yet retain power to prompt reflection and action in response to our present agricultural crisis.

POETRY AND SOCIAL CHANGE: THE BOOK OF AMOS

> The herdsman sings ancestral memories
> And the song makes the singer wise,
> But only while he sings
> Songs that were old when the old themselves were young,
> Songs of these hills only, and of no isles but these.
> . . . .
> Our words keep no faith with the soul of the world. (Kathleen Raine)[21]

The earliest prophet-poets spoke in terms analogous to what the Scots-English poet Kathleen Raine calls "the ancient speech" of the isles and highlands of Scotland – that is, a language deeply connected to a culture and a place – in their case, the village culture of rural Israel and Judah. Stephen Cook has argued persuasively that the eighth-century prophets were not "revolutionaries," envisioning an entirely new form of social organization. Rather, they were "activist-traditionalists . . . , defending old ideas with new vigor and imagination."[22] The analogy of Scotland is apt; in its contemporary campaigns for land reform, that country demonstrates with unique clarity how agrarian poetry may be instrumental in social change.

At the end of the twentieth century, about six hundred families owned half of Scotland's 19 million acres; eighteen families owned 10 percent of the land.[23] In several instances, indigenous communities of crofters (tenant farmers), assisted by public sentiment and later by a government-established land fund, have succeeded in purchasing the land that they work from absentee lairds (rural landlords).[24] An early success was the purchase of the Hebridean Isle of Eigg in 1997. Theologian-activist Alastair McIntosh, a founding trustee and now chronicler of the buyout, says that in its early years, the campaign ran on "a trickle of widows' mites," and then he adds: "But there was that other factor: we also ran on poetry."[25] The Celtic tradition of poetry and song played a role in raising public consciousness; modern bards articulated the ancient and enduring link between people and land, a link with religious as well as political and economic dimensions. The local bardic tradition "wound itself up to full declamatory volume" in the seven-year struggle over Eigg, and likewise, in a thirteen-year battle against a "superquarry" project on the Isle of Harris that would have reduced the National Scenic Area of Mt. Roineabhal to gravel. McIntosh recounts: "The *Stornaway Gazette* published Gaelic poems about the beauty of Roineabhal and letters from islanders as well as visitors lamenting the proposed desecration. . . . Ian Stephen, the Benside poet, wrote of how Roineabhal had long been used as a line of sight when fishing far out to sea. He concluded laconically, 'Maybe we'll lose / only our bearings.'"[26]

The Scottish campaigns regenerated a tradition of artful and reverent speech about the land as God's creation, a possession common to the whole people, not "owned" so much as held in trust by one generation for those to come after – an idea that is paralleled by the biblical concept of *naḥălâ*, "ancestral inheritance."[27] In time, this way of speaking proved empowering to a degree that members of a deracinated urban culture can hardly credit, accustomed as we are to words that "keep no faith with the soul of the world." It is precisely for that reason that the Scottish campaigns may suggest to biblical readers something of how the Israelite prophets came to exercise public influence in their own culture. Amos and Hosea, Isaiah and Micah evoked religious and literary traditions already ancient in the eighth century, and maybe that is why their disparate efforts did not dwindle away but instead coalesced into a social movement and a body of prophetic literature whose impact continues to be felt more than two and a half millennia later.

Much has been written about Amos as the champion of the poor, but from an agrarian perspective, what may be most important is the little-noted point that Amos's prophecy is to a remarkable degree oriented to the fertile soil.[28] The most striking linguistic marker of this orientation are the ten occurrences of the word *'ădāmâ*, "arable land" (Amos 3:2, 5; 5:2; 7:11, 17 [3×]; 9:8, 15 [2×]).[29] That word marks both the starting point and the end point for Amos's vision for the people Israel on their own land. In its very first occurrence, it recalls God's promise to Abraham:

> Only you have I known from all the families of the *'ădāmâ*;
> therefore I shall visit upon you all your iniquities. (Amos 3:2)

"All the families of the *'ădāmâ*" – the phrase has only two other occurrences in the Bible, in God's promise of blessing through Abraham and his descendants (Gen. 12:3, 28:14). Amos's signature rhetorical strategy is the dramatic reversal of traditional symbols, images, and stories that the political and religious establishment adduced to support their interpretation of the national interest. At Bethel – literally, "the house of God" – the prophet confronts the priest Amaziah, whose description of that ancient shrine shows where his own first loyalties lie: "It is a king's sanctuary, and it is a house of [the] kingdom" (Amos 7:13). With hammering repetition, Amos demolishes that false understanding of both land and religion, shared by priest and king, and announces its inevitable consequence:

> Jeroboam will die by the sword,
> and Israel will surely go into exile from off its *soil* [*'ădāmâ*].
> ... Your wife will be a whore in the city,
> and your sons and daughters will fall by the sword,
> and your *soil* will be portioned out by lot,
> and as for you – on ritually unclean *soil* you will die,
> and Israel will surely go into exile from off its *soil*. (7:11, 17)

Amos's persistent references to the soil give precision to his condemnation of Israel's political and religious system. It is not "the rich," categorically conceived, whom he damns, nor is it established religion *per se*. Rather, his words expose the ideology and inner workings of a complex social system that alienated ordinary Israelites from their inherited land. It took out of their hands, if not always the land itself (although that happened frequently enough[30]), then at least crucial decisions about its cultivation, and also much or most of its marketable produce. Klaus Koch (following Albrecht Alt) suggests that "Amos had in mind a particular *constitutional ideal*," a view already old in his time, "that equal rights of participation in the actual soil of the promised land belonged to Israel, with all its members, as the people of [YHWH]."[31] For the state to dispossess the small farmers "means rising against the Almighty and the order he has created through salvation history."[32] That disturbance is so fundamental that the land itself will react against it:

> Over this shall not the land shake,
> and everyone who dwells in it mourn;
> and all of it rise up like the Nile,
> then fall back and sink like the Nile of Egypt? (Amos 8:8)

As we have seen with the Priestly writers,[33] Amos does not conceive of the world as having components that are neatly separable into discrete categories: moral, physical, social, religious. Israel's political disorder is a disturbance of creation itself – an understanding reflected likewise in the scattering of creation hymnody through the book (4:13; 5:8–9; 9:5–6).

To epitomize the pernicious workings of the crown's redistribution system,[34] the prophet-poet employs another favorite catchword: *'arměnôt*, "strongholds" (1:4, 7, 10, 12, 14; 2:2, 5; 3:9 [2×], 10, 11; 6:8). Using the word multiple times in his oracle against the royal citadel of Samaria, Amos quickly sketches the dimensions of the system and declares its fate:

> Proclaim upon the *strongholds* in Ashdod,
> and upon the *strongholds* in the land of Egypt,
> and say, Gather together upon the mountains of Samaria
> and see the great upheavals within her,[35]
> and those who have been oppressed in her midst.
> They do not know how to deal honestly – an utterance of YHWH –
> those who store up violence and plunder in their *strongholds*.
> Therefore, thus says the Lord YHWH:
> A foe – and all around the land!
> And it will deprive you of your strength
> and plunder your *strongholds*. (3:9–11)

J. A. Dearman argues that here the term *'arměnôt* designates public buildings that served as storehouses for goods appropriated for crown use and distribution. It was in a room of such a "stronghold" on the royal citadel of Samaria that excavators found the ostraca used to record wine and oil supplies.[36] Amos calls upon Israel's historical oppressors, Egypt and the Philistine city-state of Ashdod, to witness the abuses perpetrated by their emulators, the king and governmental leaders of Israel: centralizing power and extracting wealth from people who are treated as subjects, not citizens.

The soil-centered character of Amos's prophecy is finally underscored in the vision of restoration that concludes the book:

> And I shall restore the fortunes of my people Israel,
> and they will rebuild devastated cities and settle down.
> And they will plant vineyards and drink their wine,
> and make gardens and eat their own fruit.
> And I shall plant them on their *soil*,
> and they will not again be pulled up out of their *soil* –
> that which I gave to them, says YHWH your God. (9:14–15)

Those who consider Amos to have been exclusively a prophet of doom assign these verses to a later hand; Julius Wellhausen scornfully dismissed them as "roses and lavender in place of blood and iron."[37] It is probably impossible to determine who wrote such passages, but the more important question is whether the turn toward hope that appears in Amos and the other prophetic books represents anything more than a failure of nerve. Robert Coote, in a frequently cited study, offers a detailed reconstruction of three supposed stages of composition within the book of Amos, yet he takes no position on the authorship of these final verses. Instead, he comments on the intention that apparently underlies them: "In place of the society that is destroyed another society must be built, and the earlier prophets were concerned with the new society as well as the old."[38] Imagination and faith combine to give poetic expression to the conviction that the God who formed Israel will somehow find a way for its life to continue.

Alastair McIntosh speaks directly to why those who seek to create the conditions for fundamental social change require a wide scope for the religious imagination. Among several "rules of strategy" for community work, he recommends:

> Look at the stars. . . . Let the small picture blur, reorganise and re-emerge in relation to the big picture. Let yourself hear the old myths and also the new ones coming forward. Discern, then navigate. Never be so vain as to expect to reach the stars, but do set your course by them. That way, even when on a small scale things seem to be going wrong, when you're losing the battles, life and what is life-giving will be on your side because you're onside with it, and you'll invariably end up winning the war.[39]

The soil-centered tradition of prophecy that begins with Amos is in fact oriented to the stars. Through the strategy of reversal that characterizes the whole book, those who "convert [*h-p-k*] justice into wormwood" (5:7)[40] are confronted with

> the God who makes the Pleiades and Orion
> and turns [*h-p-k*] utter darkness into the morning
> and darkens day to night,
> who calls for the waters of the sea
> and pours them out on the face of the earth –
> YHWH is his name,
> the One who causes ruin to burst upon the strong,
> so ruin comes upon the fortress! (5:8–9)

Buried in the threat of destruction is a call to align with the power that undergirds both political history and creation itself.

"from me is your fruit": the book of hosea

The book of Hosea is not an obvious candidate for an agrarian reading, since it offers nothing comparable to Amos's vivid descriptions of peasants ground under the heels of landowners (Amos 8:4–6). The targets for Hosea's virulent attacks are kings, royal officials, and, above all, religious leaders:

> Your people has a case against the priests;[41]
> you shall stumble by day,
> and the prophet shall stumble along with you, by night.
> ... Because *you* have rejected knowledge,
> I reject you as my priest.
> because you have forgotten the teaching of your God,
> I – yes, I – forget your children. (Hos. 4:4–6)

While Amos is widely acknowledged as the social justice prophet *par excellence*, Hosea is treated as a religious reformer in a narrower sense. Virtually every study cites Canaanite " fertility religion" as the focus of his outrage; Hosea is a rigorous opponent of Baal worship and proponent of the strain of thought and practice ("Yahwism") that becomes biblical orthodoxy. Stephen Cook observes: "Forced to choose his battles, Hosea must have trained his prophetic focus on pronouncing [YHWH's] ownership of a land that many others claimed for the Canaanite god, Baal. In doing so, he subordinated his concerns about Israelite farmers' rights to their allotted portions of this land."[42]

The notion that Hosea chooses between the *theological* issue of divine land ownership and the *social justice* issue of farmers' rights may say less about the prophet than about Western religious practice and biblical scholarship. In our context, it is relatively rare to see a concern with religious orthodoxy converge with zeal for social justice – within the work of a single individual, a congregation, even within one denomination. But the present fact of divergence attests not to their incompatibility but rather to the fragmentation and overspecialization that characterizes every aspect of industrialized culture, including its faith communities. Hosea is as much a prophet of social justice as is Amos,[43] and he is equally concerned with the separation of farm families from their land. However, while Amos speaks directly and unmistakably about extortion in the marketplace, Hosea focuses more on the way in which the religious establishment lends respectability to the market economy, which sets the state's interests over those of the people. He develops an elaborate metaphorical complex to evoke the multiple ways in which Israelite identity is fundamentally bound up with YHWH and at the same time with the arable land and its produce. Using the raw language of abusive sexuality and illegitimate offspring, he depicts the loss of social and religious integrity when the intergenerational connection between the Israelite family and its land is severed.

Poetry, as George Steiner says, is "maximal speech";[44] potentially every word is loaded with connotations to be exploited by the poet and the interpreter. From an agrarian perspective, it is noteworthy that the land figures in this prophetic poetry from the very "beginning of the word of YHWH through Hosea":[45]

> Go, take for yourself a woman of fornications, and children of
> fornications,
> for the *land* ['*ereṣ*] has in fact fornicated away from YHWH. (1:2)

Scholars have long agreed that Hosea's marriage represents Canaanite fertility religion, which was supposedly characterized by sacred prostitution or other forms of imitation of the *hieros gamos*, the sacred marriage between the god Baal and his "earth goddess" consort.[46] The problem with this suggestion, however, is the lack of solid literary or archaeological evidence, either that the land was thus construed or that a highly sexed Canaanite cult existed. Alice Keefe (following Jo Ann Hackett) has argued persuasively that tendencies toward both gender polarization and theological polarization have generated the scholarly construct of "Canaanite fertility religion" as "the inferior yet 'seductive' other which must be resisted and excluded."[47]

So if it is not safe to assume the widespread existence of cultic sex in Israel of the biblical period, then what kind of fornication is it that enrages Hosea's God, and why should the *land* be thus accused? Alice Keefe reads Hosea's poetry in its full cultural context, recognizing that his language has socioeconomic dimensions that cannot be divorced from its religious import. "When Hosea proclaims that Israel has become an *'ēšet zᵉnûnîm* – a woman/wife of fornications – ... he is speaking of a class of powerful men aligned with the interests of the monarchical state, whose mercantile dealings threatened to precipitate the dissolution of a traditional way of life in Israel."[48] The image of Israel as woman is a "symbolic alibi"[49] that draws upon "the homology between woman and land [that] is a well-known feature of the religious imagination of agrarian peoples."[50] The crucial point is that Hosea's trope of fornication refers not simply to apostasy but to the whole religio-political system of state-controlled agriculture and international trade, run by an urban-based elite and endorsed by priests and prophets at the central shrines. Venality and greed are reconfigured as rampant sexual impropriety. Of priests and people alike (4:9), Hosea, in typically graphic style, proclaims:

> A spirit of fornication has led them astray,
> and they fornicate out from under their God.
> On the mountaintops they sacrifice.... (4:12–13)

Hosea may be innovative in how far he stretches the metaphor of disordered sexuality, female and also male (4:15; 5:3, 7; 7:4), to characterize (or caricature) participation in an exploitative religious, political, and economic system. Yet he draws on literary precedents, specifically the story of Baal Peor (9:10, cf. Num. 25:1–18), which is itself an extended allegorical representation of illicit worship as an act of fornication: "... and the people began to 'whore' [*liznôt*] toward [or: with] the daughters of Moab" (Num. 25:1). Again, stories that tell of the matriarchs placed in sexual danger (Genesis 12, 20, 26), the rapes of Dinah (Genesis 34) and the princess Tamar (2 Samuel 13), and the rape and dismemberment of the Levite's concubine (Judges 19) all attest to the existence and legibility of "a literary convention in which the female body figures the social body," especially for the articulation of vulnerability, violation, dissolution.[51] Beginning with the parable of his own shattered family and "children of fornication," Hosea augments the literary convention with the new elements of disinheritance (with a son named "Not-My-People," 1:8) and profiteering ("You have loved a harlot's fee on all the threshing floors of new grain," 9:1). Thus he alludes to the collapse of the traditional Israelite household ("father's house"), a unit of people and land bound together in perpetuity, under the pressure of the new market and export economy, which enriched the few at the expense of the many.

Hosea's sexual imagery is what commands the attention of contemporary readers, although alongside it and sometimes conjoined with it are direct references, equally vivid and frequent, to farming, food production, and consumption of the primary trade commodities, "grain and wine and oil" (e.g., Hos. 2:10, 24 [8, 22 Eng.]; 3:1–2; cf. 2:7, 11 [5, 9 Eng.]):

> Fornication and wine and new wine steal the heart.[52] (4:11)
> They do not cry out to me with their heart;
> rather, they wail on their couches,
> adulterous[53] over grain and new wine. (7:14)

Although Wolff sees here a reference to sexual laxity ("their adulterous beds"),[54] the context suggests that these couches are for reclining at table, where the appropriated goods are consumed. The (previously cited) oracle against the priests and people gives a similar picture:

> They eat and are not sated;
> they swill yet do not burst.[55] (4:10)

Hosea depicts what is happening at the sanctuaries, likely behind closed doors, but the profusion of references to eating and drinking suggests that he is as concerned with disordered consumption as with orgiastic sex (if, in fact, any of those references are literal). An advantage of Keefe's interpretation is that it does not depend upon positing cultic practice ("fertility religion") for which there is no clear evidence. However, it develops the implications of what we do know, namely, that there was a clear connection between Israel's food economy and the priesthood. As in Egypt and Babylon, priests were state officials who played an important role in the national economy, especially with regard to the harvest. They issued loans to farmers to pay for animals and seed. They calculated and collected taxes in the form of agricultural products; these might be stored, redistributed to forced labor gangs and soldiers, or exported.[56] Since few sacrifices involved total destruction of goods, it is more accurate to see the sanctuaries as places for *food processing*, along with storage and redistribution: "At sanctuaries throughout Israel, priests slaughtered and butchered livestock, decanted wine and olive oil, and parched grain."[57]

Against that background, it is evident that a number of Hosea's images express God's antipathy for the involvement of the sanctuaries in commodity agriculture. The transport of goods from farm to sanctuary will cease:

> Therefore I am about to block up your way with thorns
> and I shall erect a fence about her, and she will not find her paths.
> She will pursue her lovers but not overtake them. . . .
> And I will cause all her celebration to cease:
> her pilgrimages and her New Moons and her Sabbaths and all her
> festivals. (2:8–9a, 13 [6–8a, 11 Eng.]; cf. Amos 2:13)

Israel's new agricultural practice marks the end of its cultural distinctiveness and thus portends the end of its national life:

> They sow wind and harvest whirlwind,
> standing stalk – it has no ears; it yields no flour.
> Perhaps it yields; strangers swallow it.
> Israel is swallowed up.
> Now they are among the nations, like a vessel no one wants,
> for they themselves have gone up to Assyria;
> a wild ass off by himself, Ephraim hires lovers. (Hos. 8:7–9)

Hosea's agrarian sensibility is apparent even in his preference for the designation "Ephraim" for the northern kingdom of Israel (e.g., 7:1, 8, 11; 8:9, 11; 9:3, 11, 13 [2×], 16). The prophet-poet plays with the possibilities the name evokes; in the passage just cited, it is the wild ass (*pere'*) of Jacob's deathbed blessing.[58] But Hosea dwells especially on the resonance between *'eprayim* and *pĕrî*, "fruit," and in the following chapter that resonance is developed into an extended meditation on Ephraim's abuse and loss of the blessing of fruitfulness:[59]

> Yes, you have fornicated away from your God;
> you have loved a harlot's fee on all the threshing floors of new grain.
> Threshing floor and wine vat will not feed them,
> and new wine will fail them [Heb.: her].
> ... But Ephraim will return to Egypt,
> and in Assyria eat what is unclean.
> ... They will not pour out wine to YHWH...
> Like grapes in the wilderness, I found Israel.
> Like the fruit that first ripens on the fig, I saw their ancestors....
> Ephraim – like a bird, their glory flies away
> from birth and womb and conception.
> And if they should bring up their children, then I shall bereave them of
> 　　every one....
> Yes, Ephraim, [obliged] to bring out his children to the slayer.
> Give them, YHWH – what will you give?
> Give them a bereaving womb and shriveled breasts!
>
> 　　　　　　　　　　　　　　　(9:1–4a, 10–12a, 13b–14)

"Wordplay is in this case a matter of life and death,"[60] and the poem offers a radical vision of the death of the nation. Having thus cancelled Jacob's ancient pronouncement of "blessings of breasts and womb" (Gen. 49:25) on Joseph, the father of Ephraim, it concludes:

Ephraim is stricken,
their root is dried up; fruit [*pĕrî*] they cannot produce.
Even if they give birth,
I shall kill the treasures of their womb.

My God rejects them, for they did not listen to him –
and they will go wandering among the nations. (Hos. 9:16–17)

SEXUALITY AND AGRICULTURE

Hosea 9 shows a seamless blending of the themes of sexuality and eating, of offspring and harvest, of love and worship and economics and international politics. His impassioned treatment of these inseparable aspects of Israel's life marks Hosea as the prophet whose vision coincides most closely with that of contemporary agrarian writers and others concerned with the depredations wrought on both the earth and community life. The similarity is particularly evident in the work of Wendell Berry, although as far as I know he never cites the biblical prophet. Repeatedly Berry brings together the same two themes or images that occupy Hosea: on the one hand, marriage, family, sex; on the other, agriculture and the fecundity of the land. Thus in discussing the "rule of industrialism," and the concomitant collapse of community, he observes:

> [O]f all the damaged things probably the most precious and the most dam-aged is sexual love. For sexual love is the heart of community life. Sexual love is the force that in our bodily life connects us most intimately to the Creation, to the fertility of the world, to farming and the care of animals. It brings us into the dance that holds the community together and joins it to its place.[61]

Sexuality is damaged by its isolation from other responsibilities and plea-sures of the common life, as a result of the "dismemberment of the house-hold" that is characteristic of industrial society. If the shattering of a sta-ble household-based economy is the social reality that lies behind Hosea's prophecy, then it is especially apt to reflect on Berry's notion that the house-hold has traditionally been "the formal bond between marriage and the earth"[62] – a practical, extensive bond that unites not just one couple but also children and other household members, more distant descendants and forebears, and the larger contemporary community, as well as "the sources of all these lives in memory and tradition, in the countryside, and in the earth."[63] Because all of these are bound together in the household, "there is an uncanny *resemblance* between our behavior toward each other and our behavior toward the earth."[64] The willingness, conditions, and means that enable exploitation of the one are like those that enable exploitation of the other.

Perhaps it is the homology of sexual love and farming that leads Hosea to use the metaphor of prostitution. To his agrarian mind, sexual activity outside the ties and responsibilities of community life is a figure for appropriation of the earth's bounty by the elite, to the impoverishment of the countryside: "Strangers swallow it" (8:7). After the extended parable of the promiscuous woman (Hosea 1–3), Israel is described as a "[male] fornicator" (*zōneh*, 4:15), Ephraim as a cheating "trader" (*kěna'an*, 12:8 [7 Eng.])[65] who brags about his exploits – in the latter case, not in bed but in the commodities market:

> Ah, I have grown rich; I have got me wealth.
> All my profiteering won't get me! (12:9 [8 Eng.])

Similarly, Berry describes the proponents of modern agribusiness as "the pornographers of agriculture"; like sexual pornographers, they thrive on mining cultural rifts.[66]

As frankly as they depict the sick imagination of the despoilers, both Hosea and the new agrarians offer also glimpses of a radically different vision of a renewed world. Hosea begins a tradition in which other prophets will follow, notably Jeremiah (Jer. 31:31) and Jesus (Mark 14:24); he envisions renewal in the form of a divinely initiated covenant, a bond of affection and responsibility, which here explicitly links Israel with every living creature:

> And I will make for them a covenant on that day,
> with the animals of the field and with the birds of the heavens and the
>   creeping things of the fertile soil,
> and bow and sword and war I will abolish from the land ['*ereṣ*],
> and I will let them lie down in safety.
> And I will marry you to me forever. . . .
> And it shall happen on that day that I will answer – an utterance of
>   YHWH –
> I will answer the heavens, and *they* will answer the earth ['*ereṣ*].
> And the earth will answer the grain and the new wine and the oil,
> and they will answer Jezreel. (Hos. 2:20–21a, 23–24 [18–19a, 21–22 Eng.])

Commentators are at some loss with this passage, which has no close parallel in the Bible. Wolff notes that the series beginning with God and ending with Jezreel "follows the route of human nutrition," and he suggests that "the background of these verses indicates a genuine scientific representation of relationships within nature."[67] Hosea is indeed tracing the chain of Israel's rain-fed agriculture, but his intent is polemical and theological: to show that it is YHWH and not the Canaanite storm god Baal (2:18 [16 Eng.]) whose responsiveness makes Jezreel (literally, "El/God sows") the richest agricultural district in the land. It is doubtful that Hosea's interest is scientific, at least in the narrow sense that modern society construes scientific inquiry, as distinct from the arts. Hosea, a poet and likely a priest, works here within a tradition of sacred poetry already long established in the land of Canaan, whose theme is the "converse of heaven with earth," an image for the blessing of fertility. He must have known, at least in fragmentary form, the *mythos* of cosmic communication that found exquisite expression in the epic cycle of Baal, which was composed in Northwest Canaan in the second millennium.

The importance of the theme is indicated by the fact that it occurs three times in the Baal epic cycle, in the speech of either the storm god Baal or the high god El:

> For I have a word I will tell you,
> A message I will recount to you,
> A word of tree and whisper of stone,
> Converse of Heaven with Earth,
> Of Deeps to the Stars.
> I understand the lightning Heaven does not know,
> The word humans do not know,
> And Earth's masses do not understand.
> Come and I will reveal it.... [68]

As a poet, Hosea inherited or acquired from this ancient literary tradition[69] a concept of divine knowledge that is worked into the cosmos yet remains hidden from humans. That concept adds depth to Hosea's seminal complaint: "There is no truth and no covenant loyalty and *no knowledge of God in the land*" (Hos. 4:1).

Notably, a form of the millennia-old tradition of the converse of heaven with earth reasserts itself in Wendell Berry's novel *Remembering*,[70] in a mystical vision experienced by farmer and writer Andy Catlett. Having lost his right hand in a farming accident, Andy alienates himself from family and neighbors. Eventually he comes home, physically and emotionally, seeking forgiveness. Walking out onto his land at daybreak, he experiences the place as both familiar and changed:

And now above and beyond the birds' song, Andy hears a more distant singing, whether of voices or instruments, sounds or words, he cannot tell.... He understands presently that he is hearing the light.... The light's music resounds and shines in the air and over the countryside, drawing everything into the infinite, sensed but mysterious pattern of its harmony.

From every tree and leaf, grass blade, stone, bird, and beast, it is answered and again answers. . . . The world sings. The sky sings back. It is one song, the song of the many members of one love.[71]

Hosea, speaking against the background of a poetic and religious tradition already ancient in the eighth century, and Berry, mindful of our current state of agricultural disruption, enable us to overhear a conversation ongoing in the cosmos, to witness a chain of mutual responsiveness that culminates in the blessed event of healthy land producing a sufficiency of food. Hosea instructs us that it is God who initiates and directs that conversation. Although, for the present, industrial farming may have all but ended meaningful conversation between human communities and the earth, destruction does not have the final word in Hosea's prophecy. The book concludes with a call to repentance and discernment about our relationship to the Source of life:

> Turn back, O Israel, to YHWH your God, for you have stumbled in your
> guilt.
> Take with you words and return to YHWH. . . .
> . . . From me is your fruit gotten.
> Whoever is wise should understand these things; the discerning should
> know them. (14:2–3a, 9b–10a [1–2a, 8b–9a Eng.])

Both Hosea and the contemporary agrarians call for repentance, a change of thought and action rooted in love, which includes, but extends far beyond, the personal sphere. The highest agrarian priority, then, is the cultivation of affectionate minds, "committed to the preservation and nurturing of the good (no matter how small)."[72] Hosea already expresses the agrarian insight that when affection is fully developed, it becomes an *economic* disposition, orienting our desires to the Source of life. Thus we may accept the healthful and ultimately joyous discipline of participating in an economy whose goal is not self-aggrandizement but praise for all that is given us in trust.

8

❧

Wisdom or Sloth? The Character of Work

There is the bad work of pride. There is also the bad work of despair –
done poorly out of the failure of hope or vision.... Good work finds the
way between pride and despair.

(Wendell Berry)[1]

A WASTING DISEASE

There is no serious question that the chief effective causes of land degradation
worldwide, and of the ecological crisis in general, are human work and population growth. Those two are directly connected, and the connection lies in
the area of agriculture. Population growth as we have experienced it since the
mid-twentieth century is largely a result of the vast increases in crop yields
made possible by the invention of the process for fixing nitrogen in ammonia
fertilizer compounds.[2] In turn, a population of six and a half billion (and
growing) has led to the large-scale conversion of previously untilled land to
agricultural use; that conversion currently constitutes the greatest threat (even
above global warming) to healthy ecosystems worldwide.[3] It is apt, therefore,
that contemporary agrarian writers give considerable attention to the character and quality of work and to the attitudes, healthy and unhealthy, that
underlie it.

U.S. Poet Laureate Donald Hall writes of his grandparents and their farming
community in New Hampshire:

> The farm produced little money, and my grandfather wore my father's old
> hand-me-downs; everywhere rags of poverty flourished like skunkweed.
> Still, my grandparents appeared to enjoy their work, which did not extend
> human consciousness but occupied or absorbed it. Elsewhere there were
> miserable farmers who should not have been farmers, who lacked the voca-
> tion for it and never got their work done, or did it so late that it failed: Green

139

wood burns badly; hay without nutriment makes poor milk. The old people spoke of feckless farmers not with contempt for laziness but in hushed and nervous tones as if they spoke of an illness. If work was life, working badly was a wasting disease.[4]

The notion that bad work is a wasting disease is revealing. In an earlier age, "consumption" denoted a disease that wasted the body; the same term now names the sickness that lays waste the earth. The current rampancy of our society's consumption is obvious; less so is the fact that it is conjoined with a certain quality of work. The character of work in industrial society may be illumined by the concept of *sloth* and its converse – which is not *work* merely, but *good work*.

Sloth is the most distinctly biblical and theological of the traditional "seven deadly sins," the only one without a counterpart in Greco-Roman philosophy. The concept of sloth as sin is now unfashionable or incoherent. As suggested by New York playwright Wendy Wasserstein's wry book-length apologia for sloth, complete with a plan for "getting started,"[5] sloth might be viewed as an amiable and even healthful alternative to the norm of frenetic activity in our culture. But the biblical sages take a different view. They recognize that work inadequately done is destructive of both the individual and the community:

> Even one who is slack in his work–
> he is kin to a vandal [literally, a master-destroyer]. (Prov. 18:9)

> The fool folds his hands
> and eats his own flesh. (Eccl. 4:5)

Medieval theologians were long interested in sloth (or *acedia*, as they called it),[6] but it has received little fresh attention in subsequent centuries. An important exception is Karl Barth's extensive reexamination of the nature of sloth, which begins with the surprising claim that sloth plays "the leading role ... in world history, in every sphere of human life."[7] Contrary to the normal identification of laziness with inactivity, Barth views sloth chiefly as a sin of commission, not omission; it evidences itself in foolishly assertive action. According to Barth's analysis, the basic dimension of sloth is *stupidity*, specifically the stupidity of believing that "we can authoritatively tell ourselves what is true and good." For religious people, that means thinking that we have already been so enlightened by the Word of God that we have no need "to hear or practise it afresh" (413). The stupidity of sloth masquerades as "the 'wisdom of the world'" (1 Cor. 1:20); it has a strange ability "to attract, to magnetise and thus to increase" (417, 414). That is why it operates as a powerful force in history, "wast[ing] and destroy[ing] all the goodness that is really given"

(413). Sloth, in Barth's analysis, is the undoing of God's good work of creation and preservation of the world.

In addition to stupidity, Barth outlines several other dimensions of sloth: *inhumanity*, the refusal to act as neighbor and kin to others, including the failure to be responsible toward those who precede and follow us in this world (444); *dissipation*, remaining inactive when action is necessary (452); and anxious *care*, ultimately in the face of death (468). In the Western world, such anxiety often conceals itself in the drive for success and "the high concept of conscientious work" (473). Ironically, a care-ful life is at once fundamentally threatened and fundamentally shaped by death; it is "a wasting and perishing existence" (471).

Barth's analysis is specifically christological: He interprets each of these dimensions as a refusal to embody a truly human life as it is seen in Jesus Christ. Yet, his conception of sloth is congruent with readings of contemporary culture that are not exclusively Christian, nor even theological. Writing about global warming, James Gustave Speth observes that our society's absorption in the present – what Barth would call our "inhumanity" – is "at war with one of the two central principles of environmental ethics – the proposition that we have duties to future generations." (The second principle is "Aldo Leopold's proposition that we have duties to other species.")[8] Similarly, the "stupidity" and even the "dissipation" of sloth are manifest in the bravado that purports to offer simple solutions to our most basic and persistent physical challenge, that of eating adequately and responsibly from generation to generation. We are warned already in the third chapter of the Bible (Gen. 3:17–19) that this challenge is unremittingly difficult. Eating with difficulty is a condition of life outside Eden; presumably, it will be with us as long as we endure as a species. Yet, the agricultural industry has convinced most people in our society (many of whom would regard the Bible as authoritative in other areas) that food production is a simple matter: The problem of feeding seven or eight billion in a world that is warming will be resolved by more applications of nitrogen fertilizer and herbicides, by genetic modification of life forms. This is still industrial orthodoxy, despite multiple indicators that these current "solutions" entail even bigger problems, such as the fifty or more dead zones in the oceans tied to the resulting surplus of biologically active nitrogen,[9] the dangers to human health and the environment emerging from the vast *terra incognita* of GMO (genetically modified organism)-based agriculture,[10] and the newly named phenomenon of Colony Collapse Disorder – the sudden massive die-offs in North America and Europe of commercial honeybees, the indispensable pollinators for apples, pears, soybeans, and many other crops.[11] The one thing that can be said with assurance is that the practices currently dominant in agriculture have not made our food supply secure for the long-term future.

The concept of sloth is useful for thinking, in terms both agrarian and theological, about a style of life and work that is pursued without regard for the enduring health of community and place. Sloth is a deadly sin, because it is opposed to love. (Significantly, in Aquinas's theological vocabulary, the antonyms for *acedia* are *caritas*, "love," and *gaudium*, "joy.")[12] Sloth may disguise itself as "conscientious work" and meet with various forms of public approval or success. But work that is not motivated by love for the life of the community, beyond the temporal and spatial confines of one's own small life, cannot free either worker or community from profound anxiety ("care").

It takes some imagination to confess poor work as sin, because "claiming the truth that reveals this sin requires a wholly revised view of the world."[13] I shall try to show that the two extended biblical depictions of good work aim at such a revised view of the world. Those are the description in Exodus of the design and construction of the tabernacle, the portable sanctuary for the wilderness, and also the portrait of the "valorous woman" that concludes the book of Proverbs. As we shall see, those lengthy accounts offer yet another way of naming the disposition directly contrary to slothfulness: That way is *wisdom*, which inspires and directs work that honors God, confers dignity on humans, and shows knowledge and respect for the material world as God's own well-crafted work.

BEGINNING WITH WISDOM

"The built environment is a product of vision," says Timothy Gorringe, in his theological study of architecture and community design.[14] Nowhere is this better evidenced than in the Priestly tradition in Exodus. In seven highly detailed chapters (25–31), the design for the tabernacle is laid out, communicated directly by YHWH to Moses, "when Moses was on the mountain for forty days and forty nights" (24:18). Then some time later, Moses assembles "all the congregation of the Israelites" and the divine intention is realized. At the end of six more detailed chapters (35–40), the tabernacle is standing, fit to host God's luminous Presence; "and the Glory of YHWH filled the tabernacle" (40:35).

The exhaustive detail makes these chapters less a description than a verbal blueprint. The only close parallel in the Bible is Ezekiel's vision for another sanctuary, the Jerusalem temple (Ezekiel 40–48), to be rebuilt after its destruction by Nebuchadnezzar's army – an architectural vision that likely owes a debt to these chapters in Exodus. Biblical narrative on the whole makes scant appeal to the visual imagination; that rule only underscores the importance of this first and paradigmatic exception, even if its detail seems boring to most modern readers. The fact that multiple echoes of the Priestly creation story (Gen. 1:1–2:4a) appear in this account of the tabernacle's design and construction[15] offers the best clue to its purpose. The wilderness sanctuary is a microcosm, an image of the world as viewed from Sinai. It seems that the Priestly writers are seeking to build in our minds a fresh vision of the world as God's creation.

The tabernacle is meant to be the first thing that Israel makes in freedom, a project designed to counter the demeaning work of Egypt, where Israel did "hard labor" – always a negative term in the Bible[16] – "in mortar and in brick and in every kind of field labor" (Exod. 1:14). As it turns out, however, the first thing Israel makes in the wilderness is the golden calf. The story of that costly reversion to demeaning work (Exod. 32:1–35) is sandwiched between the two halves of the tabernacle account, separating the divine *instructions* for the sanctuary and its priestly service from their *execution*. It provides the drama that gives vividness to the whole; the story of Israel's delusional work throws into high relief the details of the demanding but (literally) edifying work of envisioning the world anew.

Perhaps the single most important requirement set down for the work of construction – and, for contemporary readers, perhaps the most opaque – is periodic *rest*. The instructional section concludes with the fullest iteration of the Sabbath commandment in the Bible (Exod. 31:12–17), and likewise, the actual construction begins with the solemn injunction that all Israel observe "total Sabbath," *šabbat šabbātôn*, on penalty of death (35:2). Sabbath marks the definitive separation between slavery in Egypt and the epoch that is formally inaugurated at Sinai. Israel is not to be a total-work culture, regardless of whether the compulsion is external or internal. Moreover, the Sabbath imperative suggests that the basis on which work may be judged "good" goes beyond its direct products – in this case, a portable sanctuary and a mode of worship acceptable to God – to include also the effect on human character that is an inevitable by-product of labor. Throughout Exodus, Sabbath serves as a reminder of creation: "Between me and the children of Israel it is a sign for all time, that for six days God made the heaven and the earth, and on the seventh day he stopped and was refreshed" (31:17). Sabbath is a sign posted at crucial intervals in the tabernacle account, marking Israel's domestic economy as a renewing economy that memorializes God's work in creation, in contrast to an industrial economy that exhausts workers and material goods, both of which it tellingly calls "resources."[17]

Because the character of the worker affects the quality of the work, Moses' instructions emphasize the personal disposition of those who offer their contributions: "Take up from among yourselves a contribution for YHWH, *everyone whose heart is willing,* and let them bring it, . . . gold and silver and copper, and blue and purple and crimson [yarns]. . . . And *every person wise of heart among you,* let them come and make all that YHWH has commanded: the tabernacle, both its tent and its covering, its clasps and its planks . . . " (35:5–6, 10–11). Like Sabbath observance, generosity and wisdom mark this work as absolutely unlike slave labor in Egypt, and equally unlike the thoughtless abandon that produced the golden calf. Bezalel, the chief designer of the tabernacle, is the exemplar of wise work: "[God] has filled him with a divine spirit [evidenced] in wisdom and insight and knowledge, and in every craft: to conceive designs for working in gold and silver and copper and in stonecutting for setting and in woodcarving, to work in every kind of designer's craft, and to instruct . . . " (35:31–34). The ascription of wisdom is more pervasive in this account than in any other place in biblical narrative, including the story of Solomon: "And every woman wise of heart spun with her hands, and they brought their spinning, the blue and the purple and the scarlet, and the fine linen. . . . And Moses called Bezalel and Oholiab and everyone wise of heart, in whose heart God had put wisdom, all whose heart elevated them, to enter into the craftwork, to do it" (35:25; 36:2; cf. 36:1, 4).

It is appropriate to speak of the artisans as possessed of wisdom (and not just "skill"),[18] because the biblical writers share the understanding common to most traditional societies that the active form of wisdom is good work. Wisdom does not consist only in sound intellectual work; any activity that stands in a consistently productive relationship to the material world and nurtures the creative imagination qualifies as wise. The modern failure to honor physical work that is skilled but nonetheless "ordinary" has resulted in the devaluation and humiliation of countless workers. Moreover, probably everyone on the planet is now affected, directly or indirectly, by industrial society's widespread disconnection from the physical world as a source of meaning and therefore a focus of love. In her classic study of the imagination, twentieth-century philosopher Susanne Langer observes that a great threat to mental security is "the new mode of [industrial] working," which is "too poor, too empty, for even the most ingenious mind to invest it with symbolic content. Work is no longer a sphere of ritual; and so the nearest and surest source of mental satisfaction has dried up. . . . Technical progress is putting Man's freedom of mind in jeopardy."[19] By contrast, the biblical writers recognize that careful practical work is the best expression of our freedom and safeguard of our sanity. In a healthy society, such work is the means most consistently available for people to practice holiness of life, to imitate God's enabling and sustaining care for the world: "YHWH *by wisdom* founded the earth" (Prov. 3:19).

Wise work has its limits, material as well as temporal. "Morning by morning" in the Exodus tabernacle narrative, the "wise" among the people "multiply" their contributions, bringing them before Moses until there is more than enough to complete the work of construction. Then Moses calls a halt: "Let neither man nor woman do any more craftwork for the contribution to the sanctuary!" (Exod. 36:3–6). The detail is curious. Our logic might lead us to question the narrative's realism, considered from a certain perspective: Where did the Israelites in the wilderness get all those raw materials? It is likely, however, that the Priestly writer is following a different kind of logic, to insight of a wholly different order. Underlying the whole story is the logic of sufficiency, a way of thinking and living first set forth in the manna story. That story establishes the economy for the wilderness, and this one gives further definition to the economic understanding of the Priestly tradition. Two points are relevant. First, in an economy where everyone has enough, everyone can afford to be generous, and more than that, there is an impulse to be generous ("all whose heart elevated them," 36:2). Second, the influx of materials for the construction of the tabernacle reflects the essential character of God's sanctuary as a place of abundance. A poet whose imagination is riveted on the temple in Jerusalem celebrates the experience of pilgrims thus:

> How precious is your active love [ḥasdĕkā], O God,
> and human beings – in the shelter of your wings they take refuge!
> They are sated with the richness of your house,
> and you give them drink from the torrent of your delights.
> For with you is the fountain of life;
> in your light we see light. (Ps. 36:8–10 [7–9 Eng.])

At the sanctuary every human need is met and more. By giving without stint for construction of the holy place, the people are already entering into the flow that pours from the "fountain of life." Yet in the divine economy, and therefore in the world in all its parts, abundance is not incompatible with thrift. Indeed, over the long term, the experience of abundance *coincides* with thrift and is utterly incompatible with waste; that is why Moses declines to accrue a gross excess of materials. Material restraint is another step in establishing Israel's economy of sufficiency on a permanent basis.

The place of practical wisdom in economics is central to the writings of the prescient and unconventional economist E. F. Schumacher. The following observation could almost serve as a commentary on the present passage from

Exodus, as its representation of wisdom evidenced in good work challenges our own cultural habits:

> The exclusion of wisdom from economics, science, and technology was something which we could perhaps get away with for a little while, as long as we were relatively unsuccessful; but now that we have become very successful, the problem of spiritual and moral truth moves into the central position.
>
> From an economic point of view, the central concept of wisdom is permanence.... Nothing makes economic sense unless its continuance for a long time can be projected without running into absurdities.... Permanence is incompatible with a predatory attitude which rejoices in the fact that "what were luxuries for our fathers have become necessities for us."[20]

The incorporation of wisdom into economic thinking would exclude such absurdities as "scientific or technological 'solutions' which poison the environment or degrade the social structure and [humanity]" and "ever-bigger machines, entailing ever-bigger concentrations of economic power"[21] – that is, all the products of sloth, no matter how well disguised by energetic effort.

The interplay of generosity and thrift within the tabernacle account is further illumined by Schumacher's positive understanding of what he calls "the culture of poverty." He contrasts that cultural model with the modern conceit of a culture of affluence, which is attractive but delusory; it cannot serve as a model for the world as a whole. "All real cultures" – those that incorporate traditional wisdom and a lived experience of nature into their practical economic systems – have observed a distinction between "ephemeral goods" and "eternal goods." People have lived frugally with respect to the former, directing whatever excess there was, and at the same time enriching their lives, through the common project of celebrating the eternal – for instance, by building a cathedral or a great mosque.[22] It is tempting to view the extravagance of such structures purely as a reflex of the power of established religion, and doubtless that has played a significant role in their construction or operation at various points in history. But what Schumacher sees, along with Susanne Langer and the Priestly writers, is that communities may be nourished and instructed by the buildings they construct and with which they subsequently live.[23]

For good and for ill, buildings are a major part of human culture and productive activity. (Notably, they are the only artifacts that the biblical writers ever describe in detail.) It is estimated that in the United States, almost 40 percent of all raw materials and energy are directed to the construction and operation of buildings; they account for one-third of our CO_2 emissions and one-sixth of our water usage. Their impact altogether is so significant that, as David Orr says, the fundamental issue underlying building design is "the kind of people we intend to become." In the coming decades and centuries, the challenge and the imperative is for "a remaking of the human presence on earth,"[24] so that our built environment exists in harmony with our natural environment. Meeting that challenge will require (doubtless) the development of new technologies and, at the same time, the recovery of a traditional sensibility and sense of value. In other words, it will require the engagement of wise and willing hearts – in the metaphorical physiology of the Bible, the organ from which all good work proceeds.

A VALOROUS WOMAN

The biblical picture of good work would not be complete without the climactic poem of Proverbs (31:10–31), which celebrates 'ēšet-ḥayil, "a valorous woman" – not "a capable wife" (NRSV, NJPS). That translation, now standard, is not only colorless but also misleading to contemporary English speakers, for whom the word "wife" no longer has an inherent connotation of economically and socially productive work. But as terms such as "midwife," "fishwife," and even "housewife" reveal, the word once could denote a woman, married or not, viewed in relationship to her work and to her community through her work. The Hebrew word 'iššâ is the general term for "woman," though it may also identify her in relation to a husband (e.g., Gen. 2:24). In the present instance, the 'iššâ is married, yet the poem only touches on that fact, focusing instead on her effectiveness in running a prosperous agrarian household. Further, the word ḥayil denotes power, most often military power, as in the stock phrase gibbôr ḥayil, "a mighty man of valor" (Judg. 6:12; 1 Sam. 9:1, etc.). On one occasion, it describes the social and economic standing of a man, Boaz of Bethlehem (Ruth 2:1); he in turn gives the honorific 'ēšet-ḥayil (3:11) to the gutsy young widow Ruth when she comes to him on the threshing floor – certainly not at that point "a capable wife"!

The poem is an alphabetic acrostic, an 'aleph-to-tav ("A-to-Z") statement of her work and character:

> A valorous woman – who can find?
> Her price is higher than corals.
> Her husband's heart is secure with her,
> and he does not lack booty.
> She renders him good and not evil
> all the days of her life.
> She searches out wool and flax
> and works with eager hands.
> She is like a trader's fleet;

from afar she brings her food.
She rises while it is still night
and provides "prey" for her household and "statutes" for her
      young women.
She plans a field and takes it;
by the fruit of her palms she plants a vineyard.
She girds her loins with strength
and makes firm her arms.
She judges that her trading is good,
and [so] her lamp is not extinguished at night.
Her hands she reaches out with the spindle,
and her palms hold the spinning whorl.
Her palm she spreads out to the poor,
and her hands she reaches out to the needy.
She does not fear snow for her household,
for all her house is clothed in crimson [wool].
Coverlets she makes for herself;
of fine linen and purple is her clothing.
Her husband is known at the gates,
when he sits with the elders of the land.
Linen garments she makes and sells;
sashes she gives to the merchant.
Strength and splendor, her garment;
she smiles at the day to come.
She opens her mouth in wisdom
and faithful teaching is on her tongue.
She is watching over the activities of her household;
she does not eat the bread of sloth.
Her children arise and pronounce her blessed;
her husband praises her:
"Many daughters have done valiantly,
but you have surpassed them all.
Charm is a lie, and beauty a vapor.
The God-fearing woman is the one who should be praised.
Celebrate her for the fruit of her hands;
and let her works praise her in the gates." (Prov. 31:10–31)

This is the Bible's most extended description of the regular activity of an ordinary person. It is significant that a book that purports to be "the proverbs of Solomon" (Prov. 1:1) concludes by celebrating a nonroyal figure. The book might fittingly have ended with the passage that immediately precedes the poem, "the words of Lemuel king of Massa, which his mother taught him" (31:1–9).[25] Yet by virtue of its length, climactic position, and poetic craft, this poem honoring the industry and accomplishments of a plain Israelite citizen trumps that instruction from a foreign queen. Lemuel's mother cautions, "Do not give your power [ḥēlekā] to women" (v. 3), but that admonition is immediately cast in an ironic light by the celebration of the Israelite "woman of power" (ḥayil). The twenty-two verses of the poem are a kaleidoscope of shifting images, all of them suggesting social value and a power that is not domesticated in any narrow sense. The woman who is more valuable than corals (v. 10) is, moreover, like a merchant fleet (v. 14), a wild animal hunting prey at night (v. 15), a warrior arming for battle or bringing home booty (vv. 17, 11). She is lawgiver and teacher to her household (vv. 15, 26). The images evoke roles belonging typically to males, sometimes to kings, and even to God![26]

Yet despite its consistent emphasis on (benevolent) power, some readers find this representation of the woman demeaning. Joseph Blenkinsopp describes it as "the petit bourgeois portrait of the ideal wife ..., or perhaps ... an unattainable, male fantasy of the perfect spouse, who does her husband proud and brings up a clutch of perfectly adorable children while engaged in a daunting range of managerial tasks." He considers it to be "the product of a particular social class with a very limited and sclerotic view of human relations."[27]

The children's appeal, whatever it may have been, is never mentioned in the poem. But a more serious problem with Blenkinsopp's characterization is anachronism. Read in its own social context, the poet's representation is far from sclerotic. Rather, it is actively subversive of the claims of the imperial economy that had come to dominate Israel in the postexilic period. Assigning a certain date for the poem's composition is impossible; both the linguistic style and the agrarian work described would fit what we know of almost any time in the Iron Age, or later. However, most scholars would date the final editing of Proverbs to approximately the fifth century B.C.E.; by that time what was left of Israel, following the Babylonian destruction of Jerusalem, had become the Persian province of Yehud. It does not matter whether the sages who gave the book its final form composed a new poem for its conclusion or adopted a piece that had long been in circulation.[28] By promulgating it anew, and giving prominence to this depiction of a woman successfully running the family farm, they made a statement that was likely intended to challenge the economic status quo.

What was the economic situation of the typical farm family in Yehud under its Persian overlords? The most direct attestation comes from the memoir of Nehemiah, the Jewish governor in Jerusalem, beginning in the twentieth regnal year of "the Great King" Artaxerxes I (444 B.C.E.). He recalls a food crisis, or a series of crises, that prompted an outcry among the common people, women and men both: "Our fields and our vineyards and our houses we are pledging to get grain. . . . We have borrowed money to pay the king's tax – against our fields and our vineyards! . . . We are subjecting our sons and our daughters to slavery . . . and there is no power in our hands" (Neh. 5:3–5). A few, including some Jews, prospered, but the majority of residents of Yehud lived at the level of subsistence and easily fell below it. In "good" times, their small surplus went into the provincial and imperial coffers;[29] those who could no longer carry the tax burden hocked their land and their children in order to survive.

According to Persian imperial ideology, conquered lands came wholly under royal authority; wine, oil, grain, and woolen cloth were paid as taxes-in-kind. The goods were appropriated for the export trade or used by government and military personnel, both soldiers garrisoned in Yehud and those in transit to the field (most likely, in Artaxerxes I's campaign against Egypt). Archaeological surveys indicate that the number of small farms and villages in the Shephelah (the western foothills) and the upper hill country increased in the fifth century, and this may reflect an imperial initiative to increase the agricultural productivity of the province and integrate it more fully into existing military, economic, and communications systems. Land was deeded to the farmers of Yehud, but the burden of that status weighed heavily against the privilege: Landowners could be drafted for military service and corvée (gang labor). It is likely that many or most men spent months at a time away from the farm, working on such imperial projects as road and fortress construction, and even the rebuilding of Jerusalem, once Artaxerxes I established it as the provincial seat.[30]

Read against that social background, the poem about the valorous woman asserts, in the face of imperial power, the continued relevance and viability of the traditional family-based economy of Judah and Israel. A woman providing amply for her own household and even operating a small cottage textile industry is a sort of fantasy, if the reality for most people was commodity production for the empire.[31] But it is not (*pace* Blenkinsopp) a petit bourgeois male fantasy. Rather, this poem sets an ideal before a whole people living on the edge of subsistence: women householders deprived of the benefit of adult male labor, perhaps for months at a time; men conscripted for service away from home. Both women and men might well have been encouraged by this beautiful depiction of a farmer directing "*her* house[hold]" (vv. 15, 21, 27) – a telling departure from "father's house" (*bēt 'āb*), the normal term for the Israelite family unit – and making it thrive through the work of her hands. Those energetic and expert hands are this woman's outstanding physical feature. They are mentioned seven times – the number denoting completeness – as the poet highlights their activity and productivity: diligently sorting wool and flax (v. 13), planting a vineyard – an excellent investment (v. 16), taking up spindle and whorl (v. 19, twice), reaching out to the poor and vulnerable (v. 20, twice), yielding "fruit" (v. 31).[32]

As many have noted, the woman is the real-life counterpart to the figure of personified Wisdom (*ḥokmôt*), who "builds her house" and invites the "naïve" (*petî*) to come and feast (Prov. 9:1–6). Similarly, the valorous woman puts flesh and a face on sayings that were likely common among Israelites:

> Woman's wisdom [*ḥokmôt*] builds her house,
> but folly destroys it with its own hands. (14:1)

> By wisdom [*ḥokmâ*] a house is built,
> and by understanding it is made firm,
> and by knowledge rooms are filled
> with every kind of goods, precious and lovely. (24:3–4)

The kind of practical wisdom evoked here is less an individual quality than a cultural disposition, the common possession of a people. Because, as the proverbs suggest, "understanding, knowledge" is fully integrated into the economy of the household, that social capital is itself endangered whenever the community's economic health and independence is threatened.

Fresh insight into the interplay between knowledge and economics in cultures both local and imperial comes from anthropologist and agrarian James C. Scott, in his exploration of the concept he names *mētis*, or "practical knowledge." He takes the word from Homer (himself a bard with agrarian sensibilities[33]); *mētis* denotes the special kind of intelligence displayed by Odysseus, typically (but inadequately) rendered in English as "cunning" or "wily." Scott comments:

> Broadly understood, mētis represents a wide array of practical skills and acquired intelligence in responding to a constantly changing natural and human environment.... The emphasis is both on Odysseus's ability to adapt successfully to a constantly shifting situation *and* on his capacity to understand, and hence outwit, his human and divine adversaries.[34]

The semantic range of *mētis* corresponds closely to that of the Hebrew word *ḥokmâ*; both denote practical wisdom, skill, craftsmanship – a kind of intelligence bred through generations of work done in particular places, with particular materials, in response to concrete and immediate problems. It is the practice of "the art of the locality":[35] "To speak of the art of one loom, the art of one river, the art of one tractor, or the art of one automobile is not preposterous; it is to point to the size and importance of the gap between general knowledge and situated knowledge."[36] The context for Scott's treatment of *mētis* is instructive; he is making the case against "imperial knowledge," the kind of general, "scientific," oversimplifying claim to knowledge about agriculture that has underwritten modern state-run agricultural projects such as Stalin's forced collectivization, Nyerere's "villagization" in Tanzania, or China's Great Leap Forward. Scott argues that both human societies and the natural world are endangered by "the *combination* of the universalist pretensions of epistemic knowledge and authoritarian social engineering," which is "implicit in the logic of scientific agriculture and explicit in its colonial practice. When schemes like these come close to achieving their impossible dreams of ignoring or suppressing mētis and local variation, they all but guarantee their own practical failure."[37]

The valorous woman of Proverbs represents situated knowledge, and the contrast Scott draws between that and imperial knowledge may suggest why this poem secured a permanent place in Israel's tradition precisely during the rule of the Great Kings of Persia, whose Achaemenid Empire brought political unification for the first time to the vast stretch of diverse lands and cultures stretching from the Indus to the Aegean, from the Black Sea to the Red Sea. The logic of empire is centralization of information and social control; its essential processes are acculturation of local populations and appropriation of goods. Local knowledge, however, is difficult to control, since it is by definition dispersed and relatively autonomous. Nor can it be appropriated from without;[38] mētis or ḥokmâ can be learned only from inside the community. The skill that enables the woman to "plan a field" well and plant it productively is indigenous knowledge; it comes from participation in a community that belongs on and to the land through generations.

It is noteworthy that this representation of a wise woman comes in the form of a poem. As several contemporary agrarian writers point out, people who are scrupulous in the care of land are frequently exacting and imaginative in their use of words. There is reason for the coincidence: Good farming and good speech are both forms of local knowledge, skills held in community and "developed from the cradle by imitation, use, trial and error."[39] Both involve a sense of propriety, of fitness, that does not derive from abstract rules or purely scientific reasoning. J. D. van der Ploeg comments on "the importance of metaphor" to Andean potato farmers. A cluster of bipolar concepts are used to describe the state of the soil; for example, *alta/baja* (high/low) implies not just the altitude of a field but also how it lies with respect to the wind, and even the degree of its fertility. The pair *dura/suavecita* (hard/soft) conveys both relatively objective information – the extent to which a plot has been tilled – and a more subjective judgment about how well the land has been cared for, with the result that "she" may be "grateful for the respect paid earlier to her." These concepts are accurate and informative only for people who know how to weigh one against the other in relation to a particular field. Their fluidity is the very quality that allows for active interchange and interpretation as part of the communal work of farming, and for flexibility in responding to the different needs of different plots of land.[40]

Wendell Berry likewise points to the relevance of crafted speech to farming. In this case, the context is more obviously "poetic"; asked about his own beginnings as a writer, he comments:

> I listened to the old people. I always loved to listen to the old people, and I heard a lot of talk. At least until the 1980s, I was working in the fields a lot with people whose language had not been the least bit touched by the media. They spoke a beautiful language, direct and strongly referential, as far as possible from "pure poetry." I grew up around people who would entertain themselves by talking. There'd be a crew at work and something remarkable would happen, and they would start telling about it as soon as it was over. Three or four would each tell a different version of it, and they'd be trying to get the language right.[41]

Careful speaking is an important part of the valorous woman's community-building activity:

> She provides . . . statutes [$ḥōq$][42] for her young women.
> . . . She opens her mouth in wisdom;
> and faithful teaching [the teaching ($tôrâ$) of covenant devotion ($ḥesed$)]
>   is on her tongue. (Prov. 31:15, 26)

These several words belong to the vocabulary of covenant; her speech carries a communal memory that extends back to Sinai. The echoes of covenant language are a reminder of how serious is the business of running an Israelite household. As Christopher Wright has shown, in addition to being central to social and economic life, "the household was an integral part of Israel's 'land theology.'"[43] People and land together were bound to God in covenantal relation, and the landed household was at the center of that system. Moreover, it was the only part of that system that perdured from the settlement through the fall of Jerusalem and beyond – a fact that is crucial for consideration of the poem's import. In the absence of nation-state and king, with the roles of prophets and priests greatly diminished, the postexilic household assumed (or resumed) larger significance as "the locus of manifestation of God's blessings."[44] The household was the place where religious identity was defined and nurtured through instruction and other forms of religious observance. The opening[45] and closing poems of Proverbs both represent the mother of the family as a teacher, sharing fully with her husband in the work of maintaining both the household and the covenantal identity of its members.[46]

If children rise up with public accolades for their mother (31:28), it is because she protects their life in community, preserving their identity in both religious and material terms. If her works merit recitation "at the gates" (v. 31), it is because of their public and enduring significance. This woman, who "does not eat the bread of sloth" (v. 27), is a consummate practitioner of the economics of permanence as Israel understood it, maintaining the integrity of her household, keeping her family on the land. Barth perceives correctly that sloth is a powerful destructive force in world history, but the biblical poet asserts that good work is even more powerful. In the words of a contemporary agrarian poet,

> ... the world survives
> By the survival of
> This kindly working love.[47]

9

The Faithful City

Seek the *shalom* of the city to which I have exiled you, and pray on its behalf to YHWH, for in its *shalom* is *shalom* for you.

(Jer. 29:7)

The Holy One, blessed be He, said, "I will not enter the heavenly Jerusalem until I can enter the earthly Jerusalem."

(Babylonian Talmud, Ta'anith 5a)

When hope sets out in its desperate search for reasons, it can find them now.

(Wendell Berry)[1]

CITIES OF FARMERS

Modern agrarians seek to "re-member" the land, but they cannot afford to forget the city, with half the world's population now living in cities. Certainly North Americans cannot do so, since four out of five of us (including myself) reside in metropolitan areas.[2] Even within the confines of the much less deeply urbanized world of the biblical writers, the city is never long out of sight. For Israelites, as for virtually all other residents of the ancient Near East (except perhaps the most remote desert dwellers), the existence of cities was a fact already established for millennia. Scholars often cite the biblical suspicion of cities, and there is some truth to that. No city has an entirely positive reputation among the biblical writers; no capital city, including Jerusalem, escapes prophetic denunciation and predictions of doom. It is telling that according to the account of the Israelites' entry into Canaan, they were content to burn Jericho, the world's oldest continually inhabited city, rather than take it over for themselves.[3] Yet, the inference to be drawn is not that urban life altogether is unviable and should be discontinued. To the contrary, the combined biblical witness suggests that no great city is past praying for – certainly not Jerusalem (Ps. 122:6). Further, even Nineveh and Babylon, each in its own day identified as the axis of imperial evil, are held up in some part of the prophetic tradition (Jonah and Jeremiah respectively) as objects of divine mercy and therefore fitting subjects of compassion and intercessory prayer.

Prophetic judgment on any given city is rendered on the basis of how it treats those under its domination. Righteousness and justice are fulfilled when those who have some choice about how power is exercised remember those who have little or no choice. What is often overlooked is the extent to which the prophetic judgment of the city's righteousness (or unrighteousness) reflects a central agrarian concern. Righteousness is a question of who controls the land that feeds the city and fuels the royal trade economy, and who works that land; a question of who has plenty to eat and drink, and who does not; a question of who reaps the profits from the land's fruitfulness. To pose that question in terms of Israel's urban geography, one might ask about the relationship between the royal acropolis and its hinterland.[4] Does the city, the most widely visible symbol of royal sovereignty, provide for the needs of all those within its walls and its sphere of influence, or does it function as a colonial power, a parasite on the villages, near and far?

Nowhere is the distinctly agrarian concern for the city's righteousness more clearly expressed than in the oracles of the eighth-century prophet Micah of Moreshet, an agricultural village in the Shephelah region, thirty or forty kilometers southwest of Jerusalem. Micah was a younger contemporary of Amos and Hosea, and like them, he seems to have held a position of authority within the traditional village-based social structure.[5] Like them also, he dared to issue a direct challenge to the centralized power structures that constellated around the king, speaking for God on behalf of the rural population. Micah traveled to the capital during the reign of Hezekiah with this message for the Jerusalem elite:

> The voice of YHWH! To the city he calls out:
> ... Should I overlook in the house of the wicked storehouses of wickedness
> and the skimpy *ephah*,[6] deserving of a curse?
> Would [even] I be clear [of guilt] for wicked scales
> and a bag of deceptive weights?
> [The city,] whose rich are full of lawlessness,
> and whose inhabitants speak lies,
> and their tongue is treachery in their mouths –
> and so for my part I shall make you grievously ill,
> devastate you on account of your sins.

You yourself shall eat and not be satisfied,
and dysentery will strike you in your vitals.
You will come to the point of birth but not deliver,
and what you deliver I shall give to the sword.
As for you, you will sow but not harvest.
Yes, you will press olives but not rub on oil,
and grape drippings, but not drink wine.
They have adhered to the policies of Omri
and every practice of the house of Ahab,
and you followed in their counsels. (Mic. 6:9–16)[7]

No prophet offers a more vivid and thorough evocation and critique of the
state-controlled food economy. Micah shows how the royal storehouses get
filled with agricultural commodities, and how the farmers get swindled – or
worse. The allusion to "every practice of the house of Ahab" recalls the rigged
trial and death penalty that Jezebel arranged for Naboth, another rural leader
who dared to stand up against the king (1 Kings 21).[8] The oracle ends with
five "futility curses," which closely parallel those with which Deuteronomy
threatens Israel, should they break covenant with God (Deut. 28:38–41). The
Jerusalem elite are striking at the root of the covenant relationship, and the
prophet foresees that the punishment will fit the crime: In return for impov-
erishing their own people through the extortion of agricultural produce, the
city's leaders will go hungry, losing everything to the (Assyrian) enemy. In
fact, however, it seems that those in power heard and heeded Micah's message,
and so the final outcome was not what he anticipates here. According to the
Jeremiah tradition, composed a century or so later, Hezekiah changed his
policies and the city was saved (Jer. 26:18–19).

Alongside the litany of curses for disobedience, Deuteronomy sets forth
the fullest statement in Torah of the blessings that will "catch up with" Israel
(Deut. 28:2) when they keep covenant with YHWH. Blessing seems to come
unbidden, as the inevitable consequence of covenant obedience. Like the
futility curses, the blessings are counted in agrarian terms; blessing is evident
when food is available in abundance:

Blessed are you in the city,
and blessed are you in the field.
Blessed is the fruit of your womb, and the fruit of your soil, and the fruit
of your animals –
the young of your cattle and the offspring of your flock.
Blessed is your basket and your bowl.
Blessed are you at your coming in,
and blessed are you at your going out.

> YHWH will cause your enemies who rise against you to be stricken
> before you; by one road they will go out toward you, and by seven
> roads they will flee before you. (Deut. 28:3–7)

What is most notable with respect to a biblical understanding of the city is
that this proclamation of blessing envisions the full integration of the city with
its hinterland. The terms "city" and "field" would not have denoted for the
Deuteronomist two entirely separate settings and lifestyles, as they do for most
contemporary readers. Rather, as the passage suggests, the Israelite city and its
immediately surrounding fields formed a tight economic and defensive unit.
Many farmers lived within the city's protective wall and "commuted" with
their draft animals to work in fields within walking distance. Thus the picture
of people coming in and out of the city gate, their baskets full of produce
and grain for the grinding and kneading bowl, evokes the daily movements of
the vast majority of adult males resident in Israel's cities; and at harvest time,
as many women as could be spared from food preparation and child care
would have joined them. Although royal cities would have had a small elite
class of administrators, perhaps courtiers, priests and sanctuary attendants,
and also some artisans, in other cities, nearly everyone would have worked at
farming. The small cities that were not founded or built up by the monarchy –
for example, Bethlehem, literally the "house of bread" for nearby Jerusalem –
had a fairly uniform subsistence-level agrarian economy. As in the villages,
most of their inhabitants would have raised just enough food (in good times)
to eat and pay their taxes.[9]

Doubtless some urban farmers were working their own nearby land; within
the biblical story, Boaz of Bethlehem represents these moderately prosperous
landowners. It is likely, however, that others resided in the city precisely
because they were landless. Perhaps they had forfeited their ancestral lands
because of their inability to pay the exorbitant tax levies, or maybe they had
been driven out of their home territory into exile. (The book of Deuteronomy
itself may be largely the work of northern Israelites who fled to Jerusalem
around 722 B.C.E., when the Assyrian army destroyed their capital city of
Samaria.) Some of these city dwellers were not from "blue-blooded" Israelite
families and, therefore, had never held title to farmland. Probably this was the
situation of Uriah "the Hittite," King David's longtime companion in arms,
who was given a housing site just down the slope from the palace on the royal
acropolis. Others may have been second, third, or fourth sons in families
whose landholdings were too small or too poor to be divided.

Still others of those landless are represented by Ruth, the Moabite migrant
who found work in Boaz's fields during the barley and wheat harvests. Frank

Frick proposes that the "sojourners" or "resident aliens" for whom Deuteronomy repeatedly enjoins economic protection (10:18–19; 14:29; 24:19–21; 26:12) were just such landless peasants living in the city and working as sharecroppers for local landowners. "While they had originally been of different ethnic backgrounds, including autochthonous Canaanites along with immigrants from various countries, they became known collectively as *gērîm.*"[10]

Psalm 107 speaks of urban residents, giving powerful liturgical expression to the memory of landlessness and redemption (v. 2); they wander "hungry and thirsty, too" (v. 5), until at last they are gathered by YHWH (v. 3):

> He turned the wilderness into watered land . . . ,
> and settled the hungry there,
> and they established a habitable city.
> And they sowed fields and planted vineyards,
> and they made a fruitful yield.
> And he blessed them, and they multiplied greatly,
> and he did not let their cattle be few –
> though they had been few, and bowed down
> from oppression, misery, and grief. (vv. 35–39)

This poem or song, which would have been used for worship at the Jerusalem temple and perhaps elsewhere, offers another picture of the "habitable city" fully integrated with its hinterland. The health of crops, people, and animals is an indivisible wholeness, the urban *shalom* for which Jeremiah tells the Judeans exiled in Babylon to pray (Jer. 29:7).

It is evident from texts such as these that ancient Israel knew no deep rural-urban cleavage of the sort that industrialization has established so firmly that it now has the semblance of inevitability. Instead there was direct overlap and interdependence between both the populations and the economies of the city and its hinterland of villages. The latter supplied food and tradable agricultural commodities, while the former provided things only slightly less essential to an advancing agrarian society: a market where farmers could exchange any small surplus for tools and pottery from urban artisans, physical protection in times of crisis, access to work, and a social location for the landless. The rift that would have been widely and keenly felt was not between village and city as such but rather between the general populace and the very small ruling stratum that controlled the royal and administrative cities. That cleavage is reflected in such antiurban traditions as are found in the Bible. Yet even the harshest of them underscore the inherent interconnectedness of city and country. So, for instance, the caustic prediction that Micah addresses to those who "build Zion with bloodshed/and Jerusalem with iniquity":

... on account of you
Zion will be plowed [as] a field,
and Jerusalem will be ruins,
and the temple mount will become a hilltop shrine in the woods.

(Mic. 3:12)

The agricultural image clarifies the fact that despite the malicious extortion of rural wealth practiced by her civic leaders, Jerusalem is not superior to, or finally separate from, the villages and fields that feed her. They share a single destiny or, it may be, a common doom.

OUR URBAN AGRICULTURE

The health and viability of cities is no less an agrarian concern for us than it was for the biblical writers. At first thought, it seems impossible to draw any meaningful connection between our own urban scene and Iron Age Israel's cities of farmers. Probably none of those had a population larger than perhaps fifteen thousand (and most would have been much smaller),[11] whereas we see millions living in megacities across the globe. Moreover, it is our cities that will experience nearly all anticipated population growth, through both migration and natural increase.[12] Yet paradoxically, the very intensity of our urbanization may itself be a "doorway of hope" (Hos. 2:17 [15 Eng.]). Kai Lee observes that the dominance of the city and the evident threat it represents "is leading us to rediscover nature and the ecosystem services on which all humans rely."[13] A key element of this rediscovery is a heightened awareness that the city's health depends directly on the health of its hinterland. In some areas, urban planners and developers now work together with ecologists, recognizing that it is foolish, for example, to lay down water lines for housing developments without regard for water sources that may be many miles away.[14] Respect for the larger bioregion is the nonnegotiable condition for the city's continued existence. Wendell Berry summarizes well what such respect must entail: "The only sustainable city ... would live off the *net* ecological income of its supporting region, paying as it goes all its ecological and human debts. ... The balance between city and countryside is destroyed by industrial machinery, 'cheap' productivity in field and forest, and 'cheap' transportation."[15]

One of the most important and promising aspects of contemporary urban development is the recent rise of urban and peri-urban agriculture in Africa and Asia, and even in Europe and North America. Alongside organic agriculture, urban-area farming is the one aspect of the fragile agricultural economy that is consistently both productive for small farmers and beneficial for ecological systems. The existence of urban farming comes as a surprise to most Westerners, because the phenomenon has until recently been underreported, even in the substantial body of agrarian literature.[16] Yet urban agriculture and animal husbandry are, historically speaking, the norm; they probably began with the very first cities. As Halweil and Nierenberg point out, this is partly because cities are normally founded on the same wide, well-watered sites that are good for agriculture, and also because a large, settled population provides a perfect market for farm goods.[17] Excavation at Çatalhöyük in Central Anatolia, the most populous Neolithic settlement known, yields evidence of concentrated grain and pulse (legume) cultivation and domestication of animals. In the seventh millennium B.C.E. the site may have been inhabited by as many as eight thousand people.[18]

The historical peculiarity to be explained, then, is not the recent rise of urban agriculture but rather the *absence* of farming from industrialized cities throughout the twentieth century. As Berry's comment implies, the ready availability of "cheap" long-distance transportation had an impact, as did refrigeration and new legislation against urban livestock production. But the most decisive factor was the combination (in the nineteenth century, in Europe and the United States) of industrial and organic wastes into a single sewage stream, thus rendering wastewater too toxic for irrigation purposes.[19]

While that toxic effluent put an end to urban farming in the industrialized world a century ago, some cities are now discovering that extensive food production can make a positive contribution to waste management and can even heal toxic soils and water. Water spinach, a dietary staple, is grown by thousands of families living around sewage-contaminated Beung Cheung Ek Lake in Cambodia. Following ancient Asian practices of aquaculture, they are allowing the plants to recycle human waste into human nutrition, while at the same time providing fish habitat, controlling floods, and removing pollutants. Similarly, wastewater-fed aquaculture has provided fish for Calcutta's residents for some fifty years. Ten percent or more of the fish consumed comes from a 12,000-hectare pond cluster created out of a natural wetland at the edge of the city. Algae feeds on the sewage flow into the pond, fish feed on the algae, and the whole process dilutes the concentration of fecal bacteria found in raw sewage. In addition to generating saleable products, such an approach to organic wastewater treatment involves just a quarter of the cost of building and maintaining mechanical sewage plants. Aquaculture is practiced also in Eastern Europe; a duckweed pond in Kochcice, Poland, economically treats wastewater from 3,000 residents while producing a crop that is fed to livestock.

Such practices draw upon the ages-old recognition that sewage, treated intelligently, is an agricultural asset rather than a municipal problem.

However, some of the toxic waste challenges we face are unprecedented. When Hurricanes Katrina and Rita released into the soil high levels of toxins such as DDT, arsenic, and lead, urban farming was an innovative element of the response. In many parts of New Orleans, plantings of sunflowers, wild mustard, and oyster mushrooms, along with applications of compost, are now helping to sequester and break down these toxins.[20]

Disposal, which is now the fate of most material in North American urban waste streams, is literally a terrible waste, damaging to both the cities that export it and the rural regions, such as Appalachia, that receive it. New York City has taken the lead in creating a large-scale program in urban composting that could, by some estimates, produce enough compost to grow most of the vegetables the city's residents consume. A 2001 study by the NYC Department of Sanitation's Bureau of Waste Prevention, Reuse, and Recycling reported that an astonishing 55 percent of the waste stream that remains after curbside recycling is biodegradable.[21]

Urban crops are growing everywhere, under our noses. A United Nations–sponsored survey, published in 1996, found that cities worldwide were then producing about one-third of the food consumed by their residents;[22] since then, that figure may well have increased. Some of this food appears in local markets, but most is eaten by the families who raise it. In Havana, 90 percent of the produce consumed is grown in and around the city. The U.S. trade embargo and the consequent dearth of petroleum forced Cuba to feed itself, locality by locality. Yet even in Vancouver, a city with abundant external resources, a recent survey revealed that 44 percent of the residents grow food – ranging from herbs to nuts – in their own gardens, on their apartment balconies, or in one of the city's seventeen community gardens. When teamed with proper sanitation controls, intensive vegetable cultivation in urban settings maximizes scarce resources, using one-fifth as much irrigation water and one-sixth as much land as mechanized rural farming.[23]

Probably few U.S. citizens realize how much food has long come from metropolitan areas that are now experiencing rapid growth: According to a 1997 report of the American Farmland Trust, 79 percent of fruit, 69 percent of vegetables, and 52 percent of dairy products were grown in metropolitan counties or their immediate neighbors.[24] A substantial portion of our food resources thus lies directly in the path of suburban and exurban sprawl or has recently been swallowed by it, yet our current "construction habit" proceeds unabated by awareness of this potentially volatile conflict. If the recent trend continues (as is expected), then in the coming decades, much if not most U.S. population growth and construction – of highways, new residences, shopping areas and corporate centers – will occur in areas that Tom Daniels describes as "*the rural-urban fringe*, a hybrid region no longer remote and yet with a lower density of population and development than a city or suburb."[25] Already the extent of land conversion is vastly disproportionate to actual population increases: From 1982 to 1997, urbanized land in the United States grew by 47 percent, while the population grew by only 17 percent.[26]

For two centuries our nation has cultivated a romance with wide-open spaces; in recent years, that allure has taken the form of one- and two-acre lots for exurban homes, with their patios, pools, and lawns. We have reached the point in our history, however, when we must recognize that this romance, like every other, will issue in genuine love only through the practice of restraint. Those of us who live in metropolitan areas now face the challenge of learning to accept gladly the kind of compact dwelling spaces, centered growth, and mixed usage – combining homes, commerce, offices, and gardening in the same neighborhood – that will enable us to preserve open lands.[27] As Randall Arendt of the Congress for the New Urbanism urges, "we must broadcast the facts concerning the huge costs of financing low-density sprawl, as well as the benefits of attractive, livable, and accessible urban centers."[28]

But hearts are not won over by bare facts. We need to be able to imagine anew our cities and our own metropolitan lives. If we are to resist the attraction of sprawling residential acreage, then we need fresh counterimages on which to dwell: What might be "true, just and lovely, virtuous and praiseworthy" (Phil. 4:8) about our cities and our urban selves? The biblical writers offer us such images from their own reflection on the city that occupied the central place in Israel's religious imagination.

ICONS OF THE CITY

The Bible offers no "doctrine of Jerusalem," no general authoritative statement of that city's (or any city's) theological significance. Instead there are many vivid poetic images of Jerusalem – "Zion," as it is called from the perspective of the divine – especially from prophets and psalmists. The Zion images show the city as they conceived it: "a faithful city, filled with justice; righteousness would lodge in her" (Isa. 1:21). That is not a historical memory of Jerusalem as it ever was. Rather, it is an icon: a holy, healing image whose function is to invite worshipers into a different experience of the world and their own humanity. Icons are "grace-bearing matter," in Aidan Hart's words; they "affirm the role of the material world as a bearer of grace."[29] Zion is a city uniquely graced, "perfect in beauty, the joy of the whole earth" (Ps. 48:3 [2 Eng.]). And because of its iconic significance, Zion's beneficial influence can be felt in every place: "From Zion goes forth *tôrâ* [divine instruction]" (Isa. 2:3).

Two themes recurrent in the poetic icons of Jerusalem stand out as helpful for the project of imagining a city in its wholeness, in respectful relationship with its hinterland. First, as the locus of both the temple and the Davidic monarchy, Zion is the place where God's blessing reaches, one might say, its maximum concentration, and whence it flows outward in every direction. Second, Zion is the mother-city *par excellence*, whose relations of filiation, responsibility, and affection extend potentially throughout the world.

Blessing, as the biblical writers conceive it, is a kind of ecological phenomenon; it connects God and the creatures in a complex of interlocking relationships. Daniel Hardy and David Ford perceptively identify blessing as "a form of causality"; it is "the powerful yet respectful interaction" that sustains the world both physically and spiritually (a distinction no Israelite would have made).[30] God's faithfulness to the world, which the biblical writers call *ḥesed*, flows steadily: *kî lĕ'ôlām ḥasdô*, "his active love is forever" (Psalm 136). All creatures exist solely by virtue of that flow, and the psalms suggest that the nonhuman creatures respond to God with spontaneous praise:

> The heavens rejoice and the earth is glad;
> the sea roars, and its fullness.
> The fields exult and all that is in them;
> then all the trees of the forest ring out
> before YHWH when he comes. (Ps. 96:11–13)

For humans, and Israel in particular, blessing God is a moral act. It is something we learn to do, and by doing it we are formed or reformed according to our true nature. Blessing is essentially the transformative experience of knowing and honoring God as the Giver; it means valuing the steady flow that sustains the world even above the gift of life that each of us receives and is in time constrained to relinquish:

> For your faithfulness is *better* than life. . . .
> Indeed, I shall bless you with my life. (Ps. 63:4–5 [3–4 Eng.])

Taking a stand in the reciprocal flow of blessing moving between humans and God is the essential act of Israelite worship, as one short psalm suggests:

> Now bless YHWH,
> all [you] servants of YHWH,
> who stand in the house of YHWH by night.
> Lift your hands toward the holy place
> and *bless YHWH.*
> *May YHWH bless you from Zion,*
> Maker [*'ōśēh*] of heaven and earth. (Psalm 134)

The essential action is reciprocal: Israel blesses YHWH, the fitting response to God's incomparable gift of a world, and at the same time YHWH blesses Israel and the world from Zion. The final bicolon – including a Hebrew participle, the grammatical indicator of continuing action – suggests that blessing is God's current activity of sustaining the world; we might conceive it as metaphysical energy, fueling the process that later theologians would call *creatio continua*. Zion with its sanctuary is "the conduit through which the plenitude of divine blessings surges into the world."[31] Blessing travels out, with palpable effect, from the temple and the city to the land of Israel, and ultimately to any people or nation that is receptive. The whole world is Zion's intended hinterland.

However, justice is required for that conduction to occur. So wherever blessing is present in abundance, justice must be firmly in place. This necessary linkage is the theme of Psalm 72, a plea for royal justice offered "for Solomon" (v. 1 [title Eng.]), which gives the most comprehensive picture of the exchange of blessings operative on the horizontal plane. At the center of the exchange stands the king, through whom "all nations experience blessing" (v. 17), and upon whom blessing is prayed "the whole day" by the needy, the vulnerable, the poor whom he rescues from destitution (vv. 12–15). Blessing is secured for king and people, for royal acropolis and hinterland alike, when the grain grows tall "like the Lebanon" and the people in the city are thick "like grass in the field" (v. 16). There may well be an ironic edge to the association of this prayer with Solomon, since, according to one strand of the historical tradition, his empire building and the extravagance of his court placed an intolerable burden upon Israelite farmers (1 Kgs. 12:3–4).

Although the vision of blessing emanating from Zion consistently surpasses the political realities of Jerusalem, it is not utopian. On the contrary, as a true vision it exerts considerable pressure on those who hold political and economic power in the city, and certainly upon any who assert their own biblical faith. From the outset, the Bible makes it clear that the blessing conferred by the God of Abraham is given solely for the sake of dissemination.[32] Thus Zion, as the primary locus of blessing for the entire world, must be the radical antitype to Babylon, which stands throughout the Bible as the type of the proud, self-isolating city,

> the one who says in her heart,
> "*I* – and [there is] none besides me." (Isa. 47:8, cf. 10)

Beginning in Genesis 11, Babylon is repeatedly represented in the Hebrew Bible as a doomed city, the great Devastator who is herself marked for devastation.[33]

Her symbolic significance is such that in the New Testament, ancient "Baby-lon" (now a stand-in for imperial Rome) has one final collapse: "Fallen, fallen is Babylon the great!" an angel announces (Rev. 14:8), while the Lamb stands (appositely) on Mount Zion, surrounded by the company of the redeemed, 144,000 strong. At either end of the Christian canon, then, are matching frames, the twin collapses of Babylon, the archetypal city-gone-wrong.

The first of these several representations portends all the others. Tellingly for this study of the relationship between city and hinterland, the whole disastrous history of the empire unfolds from the etiological story of "Bavel/Babble,"[34] a city that is oblivious to anything outside its own walls. "Let us build a city, and a tower with its top in the sky . . . so we won't be scattered over the face of the whole land [or: earth]" (Gen. 11:4). As Frick observes, "The city concept which this story communicates has been obscured by commentators' preoccupation with seeing in it . . . a Mesopotamian temple-tower or ziggurat."[35] The nar-rator's jibe seems to aim not at the Babylonians' idolatrous worship or their impiety in storming heaven – things that are never mentioned – but rather at the city as the power center of empire. The "tower with its top in the sky" seems to be a citadel, not a temple; similar language appears elsewhere to describe the monumental fortifications of Babylon and Canaanite cities (Deut. 1:28; Jer. 51:53). "The city here is thus the prototype of all the cities which were the vis-ible centers of the centralized authority of the empire. . . . This story can thus be seen as an example of the recurring resistance against the concentration of resources in the claims of a central authority for the services of its subjects."[36]

Babylon is doomed as the arrogant city that claims all for itself and thus lives as a parasite on both its own soil and on distant vassal states. Babylon the Devastator is the diametric opposite of Zion, conceived as the source of blessing flowing to its hinterland. That image of Babylon stands in opposition also to the second and related icon, that of Zion as the nurturing mother-city, *mētro-polis* in the true sense. Though that coinage is Greek, the concept of mother-city was evidently well known in Israel (e.g., Josh. 15:45, 47; 17:11; 2 Sam. 20:19; Ezek. 26:6, 8), and it has strong antecedents in the religious and poetic traditions of the ancient Near East. Especially prominent in Israel's poetic traditions is the association of this image with Zion.[37] In a psalm celebrating God's beneficent presence in Jerusalem, which assures the safety of the city and her surrounding "daughter" villages, there is no need to translate or explain the familial metaphor:

> Your right hand is full of righteousness;
> Mount Zion is glad;
> the daughters of Judah rejoice
> on account of your judgments. (Ps. 48:12 [11 Eng.])

But Zion's sphere of influence and concern may extend far beyond "the daughters of Judah." One visionary poet sees that in God's registration of the nations, Egypt ("Rahab") and Babylon, Philistia and Tyre and Ethiopia – all are reckoned as having been born in Zion:

> And of Zion it shall be said,
> "Each and every one was born in her." (Ps. 87:5)

This psalmist, like the poet of Psalm 72, suggests that Zion's household, her hinterland, is finally coextensive with the world.

The icon of Zion as mother introduces into the relationship between city and hinterland the element of enduring responsibility, even lasting affection, which is distinct from and incompatible with sentimentality. "Sentimentality about nature denatures everything it touches,"[38] Jane Jacobs observes, for sentiment is cheap and easy; it thus entails disrespect for anything that is irreducibly complex, as are all natural systems. In an exposé of mid-twentieth-century America's "incompetence at city building,"[39] Jacobs decries the irony that we are "probably the world's champion sentimentalizers about nature" and "at one and the same time probably the world's most voracious and disrespectful destroyers of wild and rural countryside." We reduce natural systems to

> some insipid, standardized, suburbanized shadow of nature – apparently in sheer disbelief that we and our cities, just by virtue of being, are a legitimate part of nature too, and involved with it in much deeper and more inescapable ways than grass trimming, sunbathing, and contemplative uplift. And so, each day, several thousand more acres of our countryside are eaten by the bulldozers.... Our irreplaceable heritage of Grade I agricultural land (a rare treasure of nature on this earth) is sacrificed for highways or supermarket parking lots... in this great national effort to cozy up with a fictionalized nature and flee the "unnaturalness" of the city.[40]

"We and our cities... are a legitimate part of nature too." Even such a complex city as New York (where Jacobs wrote her classic work) may be capable of living well with its complex countryside, since each stands in need of the other. Big cities are necessary, "with all their diverse opportunities and productivity, so human beings can be in a position to appreciate the rest of the natural world instead of to curse it."[41] That lapidary statement reflects Jacobs's understanding that "vital cities" are compatible with natural systems precisely because they make it desirable to live and work and play in high-density environments, rather than in land-consumptive suburbs. One could add (although these are not necessarily Jacobs's own emphases) that a vital city is inevitably home to good schools and other institutions for research and education, to lively communities of worship, to places where the arts can be learned, practiced, and enjoyed. All of these are requisite if we humans, wherever we live, are to respect the world and bless it by our participation in its systems, rather than cursing it by our self-absorbed and shortsighted exploitation.

The New York City Water Protection Project, established in 1997, offers evidence that Jacobs's belief in the possibility of long-term responsibility and mutually beneficial interaction between the city and its hinterland can become a reality. Faced with a federal order to build a filtration plant for the city's drinking water, at an estimated cost of $8 billion, officials instead yielded to pressure from environmentalists to address the problem of pollutants upstream. The Land Acquisition Program now buys sensitive watershed land at market rates from willing sellers; no land is acquired by eminent domain, and property taxes are paid to local communities, which retain the right to limited development. The Watershed Agricultural Program works with both large and small farmers to protect stream buffers and thus to reduce or eliminate pollutants and flooding. The city's water supply is protected, and the ecological and economic health of the entire watershed region has improved – both at about 25 percent of the estimated cost of building a filtration plant.[42]

VISIONS OF *SHALOM*

In the icon of Zion (or Jerusalem) as mother, the biblical writers found the power to imagine the healing of city, land, and people as a whole. Notably, that icon received stronger definition in the wake of the Babylonian destruction of Judah and Jerusalem in the sixth century, and subsequently during their colonization by Persians and Greeks. The affective dimension of the image is drawn forth especially by an exilic prophet-poet working in the tradition of Isaiah:[43]

> Rejoice over Jerusalem and be glad in her,
> all [you] who love her.
> Share in her gladness,
> all [you] who are mourning over her,
> so you may suck and be satisfied
> from her comforting breast,
> so you may drink deep and take delight
> from her glorious bosom.
> For thus says YHWH:
> Here, I am extending to her
> *shalom* like a river,

> and like a flooding torrent,
> the glory of nations,
> and you shall suck.
> At [her] side you shall be carried,
> and on [her] knees you shall be dandled,
> as a boy-child whose mother comforts him –
> so I shall comfort you,
> and in Jerusalem you shall take comfort. (Isa. 66:10–13)

The *shalom* – prosperity, well-being, peace, wholeness – of Jerusalem was a focal point of Israel's prayer (Ps. 122:6). Here the prophet renders it with a vividness that is startling to a modern Western sensibility – not as an abstract concept but as a palpable condition of health that flows out from the city like milk from a breast, like the seasonal torrents that tumble down from the hill country and bring life to the Judean wilderness. Biblical poetry steadily resists the tendency that is common among us to isolate the physical from the spiritual, and further, to isolate the human body from the rest of the order of creation. For this poet, that order emphatically includes Jerusalem itself:

> Yes, here I am creating new heavens and a new earth. . . .
> Yes, here I am creating Jerusalem [as] a joy
> and her people, gladness. (Isa. 65:17–18)

The poetry of exilic Isaiah is addressed to the despairing, the "broken-hearted" (Isa. 61:1). The despair so prevalent in our own society Wendell Berry describes as "a wound that cannot be healed because it is encapsulated in loneliness, surrounded by speechlessness." He identifies the isolation of the body as "the fundamental damage of the specialist system," which brings the human body "into direct conflict with everything else in Creation." The result of our isolation is that our cultural products, including our cities and their operation, are typically "gigantic . . . past the scale of the human." And on that scale,

> our works do not liberate us – they confine us. They cut off access to the wilderness of Creation where we must go to be reborn – to receive the awareness, at once humbling and exhilarating, grievous and joyful, that we are part of Creation, one with all that we live from and all that, in turn, lives from us. They destroy the communal rites of passage that turn us toward the wilderness and bring us home again.[44]

There is in the Bible a second poetic evocation of Mother Jerusalem that resists the isolation of the body from other works of creation, even more energetically than does the Isaiah tradition. The Song of Songs is altogether the most complex and comprehensive biblical representation of Jerusalem, her people, and her hinterland, although it has received too little attention from that perspective. Elsewhere, I have argued that this dreamlike or iconographic text draws the reader's imagination back to the first garden of the Bible, imaging the healing of the three great ruptures that occurred in Eden: between man and woman, between human and nonhuman creation, and between humanity and God.[45] All of these have a bearing on the healing of the relationship between city and countryside, in the literary world of the Bible, in postexilic Israel, and in our contemporary world.

The city in the Song is a home that is not a haven, a "mother's house" (Song 3:4; 8:1–2; cf. 8:5) that is not secure for the lovers. The hostile "guards who patrol the city" (3:3) – likely the *peripoloi* of a Hellenistic city[46] – watch as the lovers go in and out to work; once they beat the woman and strip her of her wrap (5:7). The woman expresses her desire for security in terms that are strikingly similar to Isaiah's vision of Jerusalem as a nursing mother:

Would that you were [as] a brother to me,
the one who would once have sucked my mother's breasts.
I would find you in the street; I would kiss you –
yet they would not revile me.
I would lead you, bring you
to the house of my mother; she would teach me [or: you would teach me].
I would give you drink from spiced wine,
from the juice of my pomegranate. (8:1–2)

How could this poem, with its obvious sexual innuendoes, have anything to do with Jerusalem? Three observations must precede any attempt at an answer. First, the Song as a whole and any part of it are more than susceptible to multiple and widely divergent interpretations; they actively invite them. Second, no interpretation of the Song is definitive; one can only point to clues and suggest plausible inferences. Third, the Song is the most allusive book in the Hebrew Bible; the poet continually picks up recognizable phrases from earlier biblical texts and sets them in new contexts, thus adding new meanings to those already established.[47] Here the echoes of Isaiah's poem of Jerusalem the nursing mother are sufficiently pronounced to suggest that the "mother's house" into which the woman wants to bring her lover is that place of wholeness and holiness (ideally speaking) from which blessings pour out into the land. Thus her expression of longing has an affinity with the psalmist's injunction to "pray for the *shalom* of Jerusalem." It is noteworthy that Jerusalem or Zion figures in Israel's poetic iconography as both mother and daughter. Isaiah and others speak of Jerusalem and her people – and by extension the whole people Israel – as Bat Zion, "Daughter Zion" (Isa. 1:8; 37:22; 62:11; Jer. 4:31; Mic. 4:8; Zech. 9:9; Ps. 9:15; Lam. 2:1, etc.). I propose, then, that the young woman in the Song may be seen as the embodiment of Daughter Zion.[48] The element of personification latent in that designation is here for the first time fully exploited, with its implications of intimate belonging and also of vulnerability. This poet's designation for the young woman – "the Shulammite" (Song 7:1 [6:13 Eng.]) – likewise hints at her identification with the city. An apparent reference to her people and city, it can be derived from no known place name – except perhaps Shalem, an ancient name for Jerusalem, which to a poet's mind would surely imply the city's essential character of *shalom*.[49]

A second, more substantial clue to the woman's identity lies in her self-descriptions, which frame the Song on either side. She compares herself (incongruously, to modern taste) to elements of the built environment. In the first instance, when she addresses the "daughters of Jerusalem," she speaks as a farmworker, conscious of her social disadvantage. She compares her sun-darkened skin to nomads' tents, but also to the rich tapestries of the temple:

> I am black yet lovely, daughters of Jerusalem,
> like the tents of Kedar, like the curtains of Solomon.
> Do not see only that I am dark,
> that the sun has stared at me.
> My brothers were enraged with me;
> they made me a caretaker of the vineyards.
> My vineyard – my own – I have not kept. (1:5–6)

At the end of the Song, by contrast, the woman speaks confidently, imaging herself as a well-defended city:

> I am a wall, and my breasts are like towers.
> So I have become in his eyes like one who makes[50] peace. (8:10)

Similarly, the man's praise of the woman's beauty makes explicit her "physical" resemblance to Jerusalem:

> Like David's tower is your neck,
> erected in splendor.[51] (4:4)
> You are beautiful, my companion, as Tirza,
> lovely as Jerusalem. (6:4)

The significance of such metaphors is illumined by Edith Humphrey's study of four Jewish texts dating from the Greco-Roman period, probably a century or more after the Song, all of which employ what she calls "Woman-Building imagery." Of these texts, Humphrey says: "When such patently biblical pieces combine the image of a building (city or tower) with that of a woman, it should be clear to the reader that Zion or Jerusalem symbolism is in view." She notes that the woman-building-city imagery is consistently "linked with themes of suffering, persecution or sorrow.... In each case, the woman is transformed from weakness to strength through a remarkable event or series of events *reminiscent of Zion's triumph in the closing chapters of Isaiah*."[52] Because of its affinity with the imagery and pattern of transformation displayed in these works, the Song might be seen as an intermediate step in the development of the verbal iconography of Zion. Like the later works, it reflects the prophecy of exilic Isaiah, but the Song may itself be the model for the woman-building-city imagery that appears in the Hellenistic apocalypses and (later yet) in the book of Revelation.[53]

It seems evident that, in one of her facets, the woman in the Song evokes and represents Jerusalem. Yet it would be foolish and unconvincing to ignore the obvious sexuality of the poem's imagery, even if generations of ancient and medieval readers (some of them deeply insightful) were disposed to do so. Certainly the poem is about sex, *among other things*. That qualification is important, for in the Song, sexual love is located within a network of connections that is bewilderingly and maybe inexhaustibly complex. It is "located" in the strict sense; the lovers' dialogue shows throughout an intense awareness of place. As they describe one another, the lovers' geographically imbued imaginations range through the whole land of Israel, from north to south, and west and east of the Jordan. The woman speaks:

> A cluster of henna is my darling to me,
> in the vineyards of Ein Gedi. (1:14)

The man speaks:

> Your hair is like a flock of goats
> that wind down[54] from Gilead. (6:5, cf. 4:1)
> Your eyes are pools in Heshbon.... (7:5 [4 Eng.])[55]

If the woman is in some sense Jerusalem, then she is the city fully connected to its hinterland; the Song is "a paean to wholeness."[56] Her body incorporates the land in its legendary richness: "honey and milk are under your tongue" (4:11). In her own person, "the Shulammite" represents an integrated landscape, "the fertilisation of city by country":[57]

> Your limbs [or: channels] are a grove [*pardēs*] of pomegranates
> with choice fruits,
> henna with spikenard,
> spikenard and saffron,
> sweet cane and cinnamon,
> with all the woods of frankincense,
> myrrh and aloes,
> with all rarest spices –
> a garden spring, a well of fresh water,
> and flowing streams from Lebanon. (4:13–15)

Notably, this is a tended landscape, not a wilderness. Although the description is remarkably lush and exotic for a Levantine landscape, it is not entirely fantastic, with no basis in material reality. Rather, the poem seems to reflect, albeit with poetic license, the agricultural and horticultural innovations that began under the Persian Empire and advanced further in the early Hellenistic period, the probable range of dates for the Song. In those centuries (fifth to third B.C.E.), Judean agriculture was developed for the first time on private estates, alongside some highly profitable imperial plantations. Planters introduced to the region new crops, animals, and technologies, including artificial irrigation, and the lush descriptions of the land throughout the Song may show an awareness of the new agriculture. Use of the Persian loanword *pardēs* in this "spicy" passage may be a direct allusion to the *paradeisoi*, groves of precious balsam originally planted by the Persians at Jericho and Ein Gedi; these excited among Greek travelers an interest "not exceeded even by the accounts of the temple in Jerusalem."[58]

At the same time that agricultural intensification was taking place in the countryside, city life was becoming important in Judea as never before. Jerusalem, the only city reckoned by the Greeks as a *polis*, was not small even by their standards, and its economic domination of the countryside was complete. The correspondence of Zeno, steward of a large estate who made a thorough tour of Judea in 259 B.C.E., pictures "a very active, almost hectic commercial life, originated by that host of Greek officials, agents and merchants who . . . 'penetrated into the last village of the country.'"[59] A few Jews became hugely rich through commerce and speculation, including an active slave trade. Many others sank under the burden of taxes and duties imposed at multiple levels, and the social gulf grew wider. Zeno saw Jews, slave and free, working as domestics, vintners, and shepherds.[60] Moreover, cultural difference compounded economic division. Jerusalem was the only place where Hellenistic cultural influence was fully established, and "thus the old opposition between city and the people of the land (*'am hā-āreṣ*) reached a new climax"; it was to remain a decisive factor in the history of the region until the destruction of the temple in 70 c.e. This opposition could only have increased when population expansion forced many Jews to migrate from their ancestral homeland, the hill country, to non-Jewish parts of Judea and Egypt, where agricultural work and food were more abundant.[61]

Allusions to the social and economic divisions that existed not only between Greeks and Jews but also within the Jewish community may be seen in the contrast between the Song's "daughters of Jerusalem" – presumably the daughters of prosperous merchant or imperial agents – and the Shulammite (Song 1:5–6), who works in the field. Divisions among Jews may find further representation in the Song through the hostile city guards, the inaccessibility of the "mother's house," and the tension between the young woman and her brothers.[62] The woman's complaint to the daughters of Jerusalem, that her brothers forced her to neglect her own vineyard (1:6), recalls another biblical love song addressed to the "inhabitants of Jerusalem": namely Isaiah's famous "song to [the] beloved" about God's cherished "vineyard," the house of Israel, which proved disastrously wayward and was therefore consigned to destruction (Isa. 5:1–7).

At the end of this consummate Song of Songs, however, the love story of the vineyard that is Israel takes a more promising turn. Near its conclusion is this taunt directed at "Solomon," who now seems to instantiate the acquisitive imperial economy:

> There was a vineyard belonging to Solomon
> at Baal Hamon [Master of Plenty].
> He gave the vineyard over to caretakers;
> a man would bring in exchange for its fruit a thousand in silver.
> My vineyard, my own, is before me.
> The thousand is for you, Solomon.... (Song 8:11–12a)

The voice behind the taunt is not identified; as with several speeches in the Song, this one could belong to either lover. In the larger scriptural context of the Song and Isaiah, the repudiation of "Solomonic" viticulture and the vowed rededication to the care of "my vineyard" belong equally to Israel and to God. The Song speaks for both, against a greedy urban-dominated agriculture that is oblivious to rural or common people, their practices and their needs. Thus the Song shows an affinity with the Prophets, and equally with elements of the biblical Wisdom literature (e.g., Prov. 27:20–27; Eccl. 2:4–12; Sir. 7:15–31), a tradition that was consolidated and amplified in the Persian and Hellenistic periods, when the Song was composed.

If indeed the Song is a sexualized icon of Jerusalem and Israel, then its unique contribution to the canon is to stretch our religious imagination to see the larger dimensions of healthy sexual relationship. Although the lovers' devotion is total and sexually exclusive – "I am for my darling, and he is for me" (Song 6:3) – they are not isolated in "a sexual cul-de-sac."[63] Rather, their identity as a couple and their view of each other are informed by their place and everything in it. The lovers experience the city as a place of constraint and threat, but they imagine themselves into "a more generous enclosure," such as Wendell Berry describes:

> It is possible to imagine a marriage bond that would bind a woman and a man not only to each other, but . . . to all living things and to the fertility of the earth, and the sexual responsibility that joins them to the human past and the human future. It is possible to imagine marriage as a grievous, joyous human bond, endlessly renewable and renewing, again and again rejoining memory and passion and hope.[64]

That possibility of an enlarged fidelity is the obverse of a crucial impossibility, namely,

> to care for each other more or differently than we care for the earth. . . . There is an uncanny *resemblance* between our behavior toward each other and our behavior toward the earth. Between our relation to our own sexuality and our relation to the reproductivity of the earth, for instance, the resemblance is plain and strong and apparently inescapable. By some connection that we do not recognize, the willingness to exploit one becomes the willingness to exploit the other. The conditions and the means of exploitation are likewise similar.[65]

Writing thus, Berry is conscious of having entered into the realm of mystery, where it is possible to perceive correspondences accurately, and yet not be able to explain them fully – that is, in discursive language. The Song probes that same realm of mysterious analogy and connection between and within the orders of creation and culture, between a nonexploitative sexual relationship, on the one hand, and the flourishing of the earth, on the other. Berry is making a comprehensive statement about sexuality and ecology, about culture, agriculture, and economics. The Song likewise draws together all those facets of human fidelity in iconographic fashion, aiding us in the recognition that together they constitute the wholeness and holiness of human life lived consciously in the presence of God: "My vineyard, my own, is before me."

GROWING TOWARD WHOLENESS: DETROIT

The most important thing about the biblical icons of the city is just that: They are icons, inspired images that are firmly grounded in reality as viewed from the perspective of the divine. They are not merely fanciful, but neither are they limited to "the facts" as interpreted by the dominant culture. Like all icons, these are grounded by faithful memory – that is, by an imaginative appreciation of the past. Thus they may serve to guide us toward a future that honors the past yet differs from it substantially; they envision a new creation that God has yet to accomplish. These representations of Jerusalem express the biblical writers' understanding that a city is more like a person than an inert object. It has moral as well as physical character; its character grows and changes, for good or for ill. A city has a spirit, and a city with a future has a store of creative energy that enables it to respond to challenge, to turn away from a path leading toward death. Timothy Gorringe observes that "cities, by virtue of their tradition, or their activity, the way in which they 'gather' their regions, have a degree of *creative spirituality* which other places lack. It is this which constitutes their place in the economy of redemption, . . . indicated by the fact that they are often addressed as corporate personalities in Scripture."[66]

Detroit is one North American city that may be discovering (or rediscovering) its own creative spirit precisely by learning how to feed itself. Against many odds, Detroit is emerging as a "postindustrial green city." Once the fourth largest city in the country, the former Motor City has undergone a drastic depopulation, deindustrialization, and deurbanization at its center. The white population, almost in its entirety, has moved to the suburbs, and the overall population continues to decline at a rate of 10,000 per year. Since Ford and General Motors have dispatched their jobs to other places, Detroit has lost almost all commerce. The last train literally left the downtown station in January 1988. The resulting physical transformation of the city is dramatic; through abandonment, the countryside is gradually returning to the city. Rebecca Solnit reports:

> On so many streets in so many neighborhoods, you see a house, a little shabby but well built and beautiful. Then another house. Then a few houses are missing, so thoroughly missing that no trace of foundation remains. Grass grows lushly, as though nothing had ever disturbed the pastoral verdure. . . . Just about a third of Detroit, some forty square miles, has evolved past decrepitude into vacancy and prairie – an urban void nearly the size of San Francisco.[67]

What is emerging now out of that void is urban husbandry, of green space that has inadvertently become available and even affordable: The city owns 40,000 usable parcels, which it sells for as little as $100 to $200. One woman was left with her grandson on a nearly empty block; she bought the surrounding lots and now raises much of her food on them. Undergirding this venture in urban farming is a vision articulated by community activist Jimmy Boggs in 1988, the same year the last train left:

> We have to get rid of the myth that there is something sacred about large-scale production.... We have to begin thinking of creating small enterprises which produce food, goods, and services for the local market, that is, for our communities and for our city.... In order to create these new enterprises, we need a view of our city which takes into consideration both the natural resources of our area and the existing and potential skills and talents of Detroiters.[68]

With an unemployment rate in the mid-teens, many Detroiters have time on their hands and the need to develop new skills. The current situation and the response are remarkably similar to that which Detroit experienced following the severe depression of 1893, when Mayor Hazen Pingree proposed vacant-lot cultivation by the unemployed as an alternative to charity. After much ridicule and opposition by the wealthy, the mayor sold his prize horse at a public auction to initiate the program, which succeeded in reducing the city's poor roll by 60 percent, at a cost of $3.60 per family.[69] Both the economic and the noneconomic benefits were so great that the "Detroit Experiment" was emulated by many cities in the East around the turn of the nineteenth century. A hundred years after "Potato Patch Pingree," the Detroit Agriculture Network, founded in the mid-1990s, resumed work on vacant-lot gardening. It now includes in its Garden Resource Program two hundred family gardens, one hundred community gardens, and twenty school gardens. Seeds, plants, education, and technical assistance, such as tilling and soil testing, are available without cost.[70] More recently, the Food Security Coalition has formed to develop cooperative marketing and youth training programs, and also community health care. Among the most innovative of the educational programs is the Hay and Honey farm that students and faculty have built on the inner-city campus of Catherine Ferguson Academy, a public school for teenage mothers. The college-prep curriculum "teaches math and science through home repair, small animal husbandry and agriscience. Students landscape, raise vegetables and fruit trees, and plant, harvest and bale a two-acre alfalfa field in back of the school to feed the small animals that provide eggs, meat, milk and cheese for the school community."[71]

We do not yet know all the elements of cities that will in the long term prove to be "livable," in the strong sense of that word – for in a world with many more people, much less cheap energy, and no more virgin soil, the livability of cities is becoming a question of survival, not just desirability. However, if Detroit has become a focus of hope for many of its residents and others around the globe, that is because it demonstrates some of the features that will surely be essential for urban survival:

- The interpenetration of city and countryside through the revival of urban agricultural practices, some of which are ancient, that have only recently been suppressed in the industrialized world.
- Widespread community cooperation in developing networks for agricultural education; for sharing of technology, tools, and other resources; for distribution and marketing of food; and for connecting healthy food with other aspects of public health. Municipal governments and faith communities both have a role to play in creating and sustaining such networks.
- The initiative, inventiveness, and commitment of the most economically vulnerable members of the community, including women working on behalf of their young children and grandchildren. Worldwide, women play a key role in the revival of urban agriculture.[72] Janice Perlman, President of the Mega-Cities Project, observes that the exclusion of the urban poor, including women, from the public decision-making process is one of the greatest barriers to the growth of equitable cities: "The urban poor . . . are the greatest untapped source of ideas about improving their cities and lives."[73]

A new vision of the city emerges, now for Detroit as once it did for Jerusalem, by the grace of God and as a matter of sheer necessity. Strikingly apt are the words of exilic Isaiah, prophet to the desperate:

> You shall no longer be called "Abandoned,"
> nor shall your land be called "Devastated."
> For you shall be named *Hepṣî-bāh* [My Delight Is in Her],
> and your land *Bĕ'ûlâ* [Husbanded].
> For YHWH delights in you
> and your land shall be husbanded.
> For as a young man husbands a young woman,
> your children shall husband you,[74]
> and with the rejoicing of a bridegroom over a bride
> shall your God rejoice over you. (Isa. 62:4–5)

Postscript

The Agrarian Conversation

> Lately I have been thinking that the point must be reached when scientists, politicians, artists, philosophers, men of religion, and all those who work in the fields should gather here, gaze out over these fields, and talk things over together. I think this is the kind of thing that must happen if people are to see beyond their specialties.... An object seen in isolation from the whole is not the real thing.
>
> (Masanobu Fukuoka)[1]

Perhaps we have at last reached the point that Masanobu Fukuoka, a pioneer of sustainable agriculture in Japan, envisioned thirty years ago. That gathering of minds and perspectives is occurring now, in print and other media, and occasionally in person. It is the agrarian conversation, a broad-based exchange about the health of the whole earth and its communities, human and nonhuman, a conversation from which a renewed culture may evolve. The agrarian conversation thus has a kinship with what the Benedictine tradition calls *conversatio morum*, the transformation of an individual's practices and thinking in accordance with the wisdom and love that animates the larger community.

The immediate aim of any conversation that is not aimless is to see how one way of thinking intersects with another. In this volume, I have extended the agrarian conversation by integrating it fully with the work of the biblical writers, believing that may be the best way to bring numbers of Jews and Christians into the urgent conversation about how we secure our food. If that integration works – if it illumines the text and, at the same time, helps us assume and carry out our responsibility as citizens of the land community – the reason is that the Bible itself represents an ancient "conversation" not unlike the one Fukuoka hopes for in our own time. Through an agrarian reading of Israel's Scriptures, the different voices and perspectives can be heard as emerging from the place where Israelites gather (imaginatively speaking) to gaze at the land that God has entrusted to them – or frequently, to mourn its loss.

The biblical voices we have heard in this book belong to those whom Fukuoka calls (in translation) "men of religion"; certainly women's experience and perspectives are represented as well, especially in Proverbs and the Song of Songs. But these same people "of religion" belong also to several other categories he mentions. They are *artists*: poets especially, but also storytellers and practitioners of the liturgical arts; many of the texts treated here come from the so-called Priestly tradition (in Genesis, Exodus, and Leviticus), a tradition rich in metaphor, symbol, and ritual. They are *politicians*, in the sense that they have keen political awareness and, in the case of the prophets at least, speak directly and indirectly to people at the center of power. Some of them are *scientists* of a sort, knowledgeable about what we would call natural history and phenomena. Certainly Amos and probably others among them had worked in the fields of their home villages. All these biblical writers knew – as most contemporary heirs and proponents of "biblical faith" do not – how completely the health of human lives and cultures is bound up with care of the land and just distribution of its bounty.

Among the contemporary voices we have heard are those of poets from Kentucky (Wendell Berry – also a farmer) and New Hampshire (Donald Hall), and bards from Scotland. We have listened to soil scientists, especially those who are trying to learn not just *about* the land and its workings, but also *from* it. Students of modern economic and political systems have informed the conversation at multiple points as well – and that has been useful in making perspicuous the economic and political awareness of many biblical writers.

When people converse in a desperate situation, they are usually looking for hope. I believe that the Bible as a whole tends toward a tenacious but severely chastened hope. That finely balanced disposition rests on faith in God, but it reflects also the experience of land loss and the equally bitter experience of a people's self-recognition. In its character of hopefulness tempered by sad experience, the biblical conversation is a good match for our contemporary agrarian conversation, and a resource indispensable for enriching it.

Notes

INTRODUCTION

1. Raewynne J. Whiteley, "Empty Hands," in *Steeped in the Holy: Preaching as Spiritual Practice* (Lanham, Md.: Rowman & Littlefield, 2008), 22.
2. Because the agrarian history of the United States bears the taint and curse of slavery, contemporary agrarians are challenged to acknowledge that aspect of our history, to disavow its presuppositions about human worth, and also to recognize its current consequences, including the movement of large parts of Southern rural populations to Northern cities and the increase of suburbanism and urban poverty. Notably, Wendell Berry began his own reckoning with the bitter heritage of slavery early in his writing career, with the publication of *The Hidden Wound* (Boston: Houghton Mifflin, 1970). My final chapter in this volume treats the new urban agrarianism emerging in inner-city Detroit (among other U.S. cities). However, the North American agrarian conversation that this volume seeks to advance will remain incomplete without the active involvement of those who have historically been deprived of arable land on this continent.
3. Millennium Ecosystem Assessment, *Ecosystems and Human Well-Being*, vol. 1, *Current State and Trends* (Washington, D.C.: Island, 2005), 777.
4. James C. Scott, *Seeing Like a State* (New Haven: Yale University Press, 1998), 8.
5. See Carol Meyers, "The Family in Early Israel," in *Families in Ancient Israel*, ed. Leo Perdue et al. (Louisville: Westminster John Knox, 1997), 4.
6. Augustine, *De doctrina christiana* (*On Christian Teaching*) 3.10.14. Augustine's particular hermeneutical concern – when to read a text literally and when figuratively – is different from mine, yet his assertion that accurate exegesis is necessarily responsive to the claims of love is apt.
7. Wendell Berry, "Going to Work," in *The Essential Agrarian Reader: The Future of Culture, Community, and the Land*, ed. Norman Wirzba (Lexington: University Press of Kentucky, 2003), 264–65.
8. Norman Gottwald observes: "Once we recognize that the most basic questions about economic systems were entwined with biblical religion and fought over as an intrinsic aspect of living religiously, we gain leverage to criticize and evaluate economic systems today." Gottwald, *The Hebrew Bible in Its Social World and in Ours*, Semeia Studies (Atlanta: Scholars Press, 1993), 345.

9. Ibid., 364 (emphasis mine).

10. Richard B. Hays points out that the delay of Christ's return makes it necessary for Christians to offer "revisionist readings" of New Testament texts that look for the healing of creation exclusively through an imminent return; see Hays, *Echoes of Scripture in the Letters of Paul* (New Haven: Yale University Press, 1989), 185–86.

CHAPTER 1

1. Al Gore, Nobel Peace Prize acceptance speech, Oslo, Norway, December 10, 2007.

2. Wendell Berry's notion of "kindly use" of land being essential to securing a permanent food supply appears early and frequently in his writings. See, for example, *The Unsettling of America: Culture and Agriculture* (San Francisco: Sierra Club, 1977), 30–31, 37; *Home Economics* (San Francisco: North Point, 1987), 160.

3. Norman Wirzba, *The Paradise of God: Renewing Religion in an Ecological Age* (New York: Oxford University Press, 2003), 80–81 (emphasis mine).

4. Peter Vitousek, lecture at The Land Institute in Salina, Kansas, June 2003.

5. Throughout the essays, I follow the Hebrew convention of using four consonants (YHWH) to designate the "unpronounceable" name of God, revealed especially to Israel. Traditionally considered by Jews too sacred to be uttered, it is often rendered in English as "Lord."

6. Brevard Childs argues: "When we enter the Exilic and post-Exilic periods, the eschatological usage of *ra'aš* in connection with the final judgment through a returned chaos is everywhere evident. In fact, it is our contention that the term has become a *terminus technicus* within the language of the return of chaos." Childs, "The Enemy from the North and the Chaos Tradition," *Journal of Biblical Literature* 78 (1959): 189.

7. Robert Murray, *The Cosmic Covenant* (London: Sheed & Ward, 1991), 42.

8. The passage cited is from the "Postscript, July, 1968" to Wendell Berry's (1965) essay, "The Landscaping of Hell: Strip-Mine Morality in East Kentucky," in *The Long-Legged House* (New York: Harcourt, Brace & World, 1969), 28–29.

9. See Wes Jackson's description of Matfield Green, Kansas, in *Becoming Native to This Place* (Lexington: University Press of Kentucky, 1994), 87–103.

10. Richard Manning, *Against the Grain: How Agriculture Has Hijacked Civilization* (New York: North Point, 2004).

11. In 1978, the USDA estimated that since the prairie was first broken by the plow, "erosion in the Palouse River Basin in eastern Washington and northern Idaho had removed all of the original topsoil from 10% of the cropland, and one-fourth to three-fourths of the topsoil from another 60%"; see D. K. McCool et al., "Factors Affecting Agricultural Sustainability in the Pacific Northwest, USA: An Overview," in *Sustaining the Global Farm*, ed. D. E. Stott, R. H. Mohtar, and C. F. Steinhardt, selected papers from the 10th International Soil Conservation Organization meeting, May 24–29, 1999 (West Lafayette, Ind.: International Soil Conservation Organization, 2001), 256. Similarly, in the last 150 years of farming, fully half of Iowa's fertile topsoil has been lost. While new farming techniques have reduced erosion rates significantly since the late 1980s, the annual soil erosion rate for U.S. cropland is still many times the soil sustainability rate. See David Pimentel et al., "Environmental and Economic Costs of Soil Erosion and Conservation Benefits," *Science* 267 (February 24, 1995): 1117; Pierre Crosson (debating the complicated basis for

erosion estimates), "Soil Erosion Estimates and Costs," *Science* 269 (July 28, 1995): 461–63; and Pimentel et al., "Response," 464. Recent figures for wind and water erosion are available on the Web site of the National Resources Conservation Service, http://www.nrcs.usda.gov/technical/land/erosion.html.

12. In a frequently cited 1997 study, Anne-Marie Mayer published results indicating that in the period from 1936 to 1986, the mineral content of twenty fruits and twenty vegetables grown in the United Kingdom had declined substantially for six of the seven minerals analyzed (ranging from an average 14 percent for potassium to 81 percent for copper); see Mayer, "Historical Changes in the Mineral Content of Fruits and Vegetables," *British Food Journal* 99 (1997): 207–11. In a similar study of garden crops grown in the United States in 1950 and 1999, Donald R. Davis et al. found "apparent, statistically reliable declines" for six of the thirteen nutrients evaluated (ranging from 6 percent for protein to 38% for riboflavin). The study pointed most strongly to a genetically based "dilution effect," in which cultivars selected for traits such as rapid growth and high yield suffered limitations "in their abilities to extract soil minerals or transport them within the plant, or in their abilities to synthesize proteins, vitamins and other nutrients." See Donald R. Davis, Melvin D. Epp, and Hugh D. Riordan, "Changes in USDA Food Composition Data for 43 Garden Crops, 1950 to 1999," *Journal of the American College of Nutrition* 23 (2004): 669, 678.

13. George B. Caird, *The Language and Imagery of the Bible* (Grand Rapids: Eerdmans, 1997), 258. Similarly, Brevard Childs notes the "trans-historical, apocalyptic coloring" of Jer. 4:23–26. In his view, an early oracle of the prophet was expanded sometime after the fall of Jerusalem, and the language of chaos has been applied to that historical event ("Enemy from the North," 187–98).

14. Walter Brueggemann, *The Prophetic Imagination* (Minneapolis: Fortress, 1987), 45.

15. Abraham Joshua Heschel, *The Prophets* (New York: Harper & Row, 1962), xviii–xix.

16. Ibid., 24 (emphasis original).

17. Ibid., xiv–xv.

18. Ibid., xvi.

19. Tim Radford, "Two-thirds of World's Resources 'Used Up,'" *Guardian Unlimited* (UK), March 30, 2005, http://education.guardian.co.uk/higher/research/story/0,,1447996,00.html, discussing the release of the study's findings, *Ecosystems and Human Well-being* (Washington, D.C.: Island, 2005). The report comprises five technical volumes and six synthesis reports, capping four years of work by some 1,300 experts worldwide.

20. John Noble Wilford, "Ages-Old Icecap at North Pole Is Now Liquid, Scientists Find," *New York Times*, sec. A, August 19, 2000. Wilford published a second report ("Open Water at Pole Is Not Surprising, Experts Say," *New York Times*, sec. F, August 29, 2000), citing McCarthy's explanation that the "really unusual" phenomenon was not simply the open water at the Pole but the fact that "over a period of two weeks we never had a day of what would be considered normal ice." The article goes on to cite the findings of Drew Rothrock at the Applied Physics Laboratory of the University of Washington in Seattle indicating that average Arctic ice thickness, measured at 10.2 feet in the period between 1958 and 1976, decreased to 5.9 feet in the 1990s. Full data and an assessment are found in the *Arctic Climate Impact Assessment Scientific Report*, a comprehensive study produced by more than 300 authors (Cambridge: Cambridge University Press, 2005), available at http://www.acia.uaf.edu/pages/scientific.html.

21. Heschel, *Prophets*, xv.
22. The term *bat-'ammî* (literally, "my daughter-people") is in Jeremiah a common designation for Judah, Jerusalem, and their people (Jer. 4:11; 6:26; 8:11, 19, 21, 22, 23 [9:1 Eng.]; 9:6 [7 Eng.]); it implies Jeremiah's (and God's) intimate connection with them, as well as the "pathos" occasioned by their destruction.
23. Garrett Green, *Imagining God: Theology and the Religious Imagination* (San Francisco: Harper & Row, 1989), 109–10.
24. Wendell Berry, "Writer and Region," in *What Are People For?* (New York: North Point, 1990), 78.
25. David Orr, "The Uses of Prophecy," in *The Essential Agrarian Reader: The Future of Culture, Community, and the Land*, ed. Norman Wirzba (Lexington: University Press of Kentucky, 2003), 184.
26. John Robert McNeill, *The Mountains of the Mediterranean World: An Environmental History* (Cambridge: Cambridge University Press, 1992); J. R. McNeill and Verena Winiwarter, eds., *Soils and Societies: Perspectives from Environmental History* (Cambridge: White Horse, 2006).
27. Daniel Hillel, *Out of the Earth: Civilization and the Life of the Soil* (New York: Free Press, 1991); *The Natural History of the Bible: An Environmental Exploration of the Hebrew Scriptures* (New York: Columbia University Press, 2006).
28. Jared Diamond, *Collapse: How Societies Choose to Fail or Succeed* (New York: Viking Penguin, 2005).
29. Orr, "Uses of Prophecy," 184.
30. See Ellen F. Davis, *Getting Involved with God* (Boston: Cowley, 2001), 195–208, and also Chapter 7 in this volume.
31. Orr, "Uses of Prophecy," 176.
32. Wendell Berry, "The Responsibility of a Poet," in *What Are People For?* 88–89.
33. Brian Doyle has caught the alliteration here nicely; see Doyle, *The Apocalypse of Isaiah Metaphorically Speaking: A Study of the Use, Function and Significance of Metaphors in Isaiah 24–27* (Leuven: Leuven University Press, 2000), 161.
34. Here the meaning of the verb *ḥārû* is uncertain. Joseph Blenkinsopp offers evidence that might support another reading: "dwindle"; see Blenkinsopp, *Isaiah 1–39*, Anchor Bible 19 (New York: Doubleday, 2000), 350.
35. Robert Murray sees the intervening phrase in this verse, "on the host of the height in the height," as referring to an old myth of a breach of the "cosmic covenant" by an alliance of heavenly and earthly rebels (*Cosmic Covenant*, 16–22). To avoid multiplying literary entities without necessity, I tend toward J. Richard Middleton's less speculative suggestion that creation and covenant are analogous works of God; see Middleton, *The Liberating Image: The Imago Dei in Genesis 1* (Grand Rapids: Brazos, 2005), 67ff. Although Brian Doyle sees echoes of both Sinai and Noah in Isaiah 24–27, he views the metaphor underlying the whole as "a marriage between YHWH, earth and its inhabitants" (*Apocalypse of Isaiah*, 214–16). For my own treatment of the "eternal covenant" in Isaiah, the origin of the metaphor is less important than the fact that Murray and Doyle (and now numerous others) treat the whole chapter as a single poem. On the question of literary unity, see Doyle, *Apocalypse of Isaiah*, 23–24.
36. Specifically, the phrase *běrît 'ôlām* ("everlasting covenant") is used variously with reference to the Sabbath (Exod. 31:16; cf. Lev. 24:8), to the Abrahamic (Gen. 17:7; Ps. 105:10//1 Chron. 16:17) and Davidic (2 Sam. 23:5; Isa. 55:3) covenants, or more generally to God's covenant with Israel (Jer. 32:40; 50:5; Ezek. 16:60; 37:26).

37. Cf. Michael Welker, *Creation and Reality* (Minneapolis: Fortress, 1999), 37–38. Michael S. Northcott offers a thorough survey of the scientific data and current political responses in his theological study of climate change: *A Moral Climate: The Ethics of Global Warming* (London: Darton, Longman & Todd, 2007). Northcott considers the evidence for climate change and environmental degradation in ancient Mesopotamia and the Levant as the background for some biblical passages, especially in Genesis and Jeremiah.

38. Doyle, *Apocalypse of Isaiah*, 169–70.

39. Wendell Berry, *The Gift of Good Land: Further Essays Cultural and Agricultural* (New York: North Point, 1981), 273.

40. Anne Porter, "A Short Testament," in *Living Things: Collected Poems* (Hanover, N.H.: Zoland, 2006), 94.

CHAPTER 2

1. *The Fathers According to Rabbi Nathan*, trans. Judah Goldin (New Haven: Yale University Press, 1955), 125.

2. Leviticus Rabbah 25.3, cited in *Hammer on the Rock: A Short Midrash Reader*, ed. Nahum N. Glatzer (New York: Schocken, 1962), 21.

3. Rainer Maria Rilke, Sonnet 12, *The Sonnets to Orpheus: First Series*, trans. A. Poulin Jr., *Duino Elegies and the Sonnets to Orpheus* (New York: Mariner, 2005), 107 (emphasis original).

4. Maurice Telleen, "The Mind-Set of Agrarianism . . . New and Old," in *The Essential Agrarian Reader: The Future of Culture, Community, and the Land*, ed. Norman Wirzba (Lexington: University Press of Kentucky, 2003), 53.

5. Robert L. Zimdahl, *Agriculture's Ethical Horizon* (Amsterdam/Boston: Elsevier, 2006), 193–94. Zimdahl's may be the first book-length study of agricultural ethics in nearly a century – since Liberty Hyde Bailey's agricultural classic, *The Holy Earth* (1915) – to be written by a "mainstream" plant or crop scientist.

6. See Zimdahl, *Agriculture's Ethical Horizon*, 183–87.

7. Aldo Leopold, "The Land Ethic," in *A Sand County Almanac* (New York: Oxford University Press, 1966), 240.

8. Ibid., 262.

9. Ibid., 263–64.

10. Barry Lopez, "The Naturalist," *Orion*, (Autumn 2001), available online at http://orionmagazine.org/index.php/articles/article/91/.

11. "Abraham knew exactly what the land was for: it was to drip milk and honey into Abraham's mouth." Leopold, "Land Ethic," 240.

12. Lopez, "Naturalist."

13. Scott Russell Sanders, "Letter to a Reader," in *Writing from the Center* (Bloomington: Indiana University Press, 1995), 178.

14. Sanders, "Imagining the Midwest," in *Writing from the Center*, 51.

15. Richard B. Hays, *The Moral Vision of the New Testament: Community, Cross, New Creation: A Contemporary Introduction to New Testament Ethics* (New York: HarperSanFrancisco, 1996), 3–7.

16. The phrase "active apprehension" appears in George Steiner's definition of hermeneutics, which involves acting out our understanding of a text. See Steiner, *Real Presences* (Chicago: University of Chicago Press, 1989), 7.

17. Steven C. Blank, "The End of the American Farm?" *The Futurist*, April 1999, 22–27; quotations, 25, 27. Blank is also the author of a book entitled *The End of Agriculture in the American Portfolio* (Westport, Conn.: Quorum, 1998).

18. Blank, "End of the American Farm," 25.

19. Writing about the possible use of biomass rather than fossil fuels by farmers, Amory Lovins et al. observe: "The land comes first. All operations must be based on a concern for soil fertility and long-term environmental compatibility." Amory B. Lovins, L. Hunter Lovins, and Marty Bender, "Energy and Agriculture," in *Meeting the Expectations of the Land*, ed. Wes Jackson, Wendell Berry, and Bruce Colman (San Francisco: North Point, 1984), 80.

20. Theodore Hiebert, *The Yahwist's Landscape: Nature and Religion in Early Israel* (New York: Oxford University Press, 1996), 157.

21. Ibid., 66.

22. Prayers of the People, Form IV, *Book of Common Prayer* (1979), 388.

23. A near parallel is Isa. 27:3, where God's protection of the "vineyard" Israel is twice denoted by the synonymous verb *n-ṣ-r*.

24. Contemporary biblical scholars generally acknowledge the existence of two major components of the (editorially integrated) creation story: the Yahwistic account (Gen. 2:4b–3:24 and the Priestly account (1:1–2:4a). The second of these is the focus of Chapter 3 in this volume.

25. On the precision of the terms here, see Hiebert, *Yahwist's Landscape*, 37–38.

26. A creation text from Ur in Mesopotamia focuses on the phenomenon of irrigation, recalling a (primeval) time when " . . . no canals were opened, / No dredging was done at dikes and ditches." "The Eridu Genesis," trans. Thorkild Jacobsen, cited in Hiebert, *Yahwist's Narrative*, 36.

27. Wendell Berry, "It Wasn't Me," in *The Wild Birds* (San Francisco: North Point, 1986), 68.

28. On the syntax of the verbs in Gen. 9:20, see Frank Spina, "The 'Ground' for Cain's Rejection (Gen 4): '*a damah*' in the Context of Gen 1–11," *Zeitschrift für die alttestamentliche Wissenschaft* 104 (1992): 329–30.

29. Norman Wirzba, *The Paradise of God: Renewing Religion in an Ecological Age* (New York: Oxford University Press, 2003), 34. For other treatments of the Noah story that are sensitive to its "agrarian ethos" (*Paradise of God*, 31), see Hiebert, *Yahwist's Landscape*, 44–51; and William P. Brown, *The Ethos of the Cosmos: The Genesis of Moral Imagination in the Bible* (Grand Rapids: Eerdmans, 1999), 177–81.

30. Evan Eisenberg, *The Ecology of Eden* (New York: Knopf, 1998), 288–89.

31. Biologist Janine M. Benyus highlights the concept of nature as model, measure, and mentor in her study *Biomimicry: Innovation Inspired by Nature* (New York: Harper-Collins, 1997). Of the six areas of research treated in the book, she regards "farming in nature's image," as practiced at The Land Institute, as "the most radical . . . , and perhaps the most important" (13; see her lengthy treatment, 11–58).

32. Jerry D. Glover, Cindy M. Cox, and John P. Reganold, "Future Farming: A Return to Roots?" *Scientific American*, August 2007, 84.

33. Wes Jackson, introduction to *The Virtues of Ignorance: Complexity, Sustainability, and the Limits of Knowledge*, by Bill Vitek and Wes Jackson (Lexington: The University, Press of Kentucky, 2008), 1.

34. Wes Jackson, *Becoming Native to This Place* (Lexington: University Press of Kentucky, 1994), 23.

35. Zimdahl, *Agriculture's Ethical Horizon*, 209.

36. Ibid., 201.

37. John Calvin calls on himself and his readers to show the qualities of a disciple: "poor, empty, and void of self-wisdom: eager to learn but knowing nothing, and even wishing to know nothing but what He has taught." Calvin, preface to *Psychopannychia*, trans. Henry Beveridge, *Tracts and Treatises in Defense of the Reformed Faith*, vol. 3 (Grand Rapids: Eerdmans, 1958), 418.

38. David F. Ford and Graham Stanton, *Reading Texts, Seeking Wisdom: Scripture and Theology* (Grand Rapids/Cambridge, U.K.: Eerdmans, 2003), 2–3 (emphasis mine).

39. On the antithesis between sloth and wisdom, see Chapter 8 in this volume.

40. The readings for the words translated "rows" and "strips" are uncertain; the first may refer also to another grain (sorghum?). Both NJPS and NRSV treat them as designations for planting practices.

41. Wendell Berry, "The Way of Ignorance" in *The Way of Ignorance and Other Essays* (Emeryville, Calif.: Shoemaker & Hoard, 2005), 54.

42. Wendell Berry, "Enriching the Earth," in *Collected Poems, 1957–1982* (San Francisco: North Point, 1985), 110.

43. See, for example, Craig Holdrege, "Can We See with Fresh Eyes? Beyond a Culture of Abstraction," *Land Report*, no. 85, (Summer 2006): 8–12.

44. Wendell Berry, "Going to Work," in Wirzba, *Essential Agrarian Reader*, 266.

45. E. F. Schumacher, *Good Work* (New York: Harper & Row, 1979), 122–23.

46. Ibid., 98.

47. Cf. Berry's comments on the "religification and evangelizing of science," in Berry, *Life Is a Miracle: An Essay Against Modern Superstition* (Washington, D.C.: Counterpoint, 2000), 19–21. Berry goes on to speak of "militant" materialism, which is intolerant of any sort of mystery (25–29).

48. Barbara Kingsolver, foreword to Wirzba, *Essential Agrarian Reader*, xiii.

49. Leopold, "Land Ethic," 257.

50. Daniel J. Hillel, *Out of the Earth: Civilization and the Life of the Soil* (New York: Free Press, 1991), 78–87. See also Thorkild Jacobsen, *Salinity and Irrigation Agriculture in Antiquity: Diyala Basin Archaeological Projects; Report on Essential Results, 1957–58*, Bibliotheca Mesopotamica 14 (Malibu, Calif.: Undena, 1982). Jacobsen's general discussion of ancient agricultural practices and their ecological consequences is followed by detailed discussion of a region in northeastern Babylonia; no similar information for Southern Babylonia was available at that time.

51. Wendell Berry, "Renewing Husbandry," in *The Way of Ignorance*, 100.

52. Wendell Berry, " "It Wasn't Me," in *The Wild Birds*, 68.

53. See Christopher J. H. Wright, *God's People in God's Land: Family, Land, and Property in the Old Testament* (Grand Rapids: Eerdmans, 1990), 56–57.

54. On arable land as a multigenerational trust held within a family, see chapter 6 below.

55. Wendell Berry, "The Agrarian Standard," in Wirzba, *Essential Agrarian Reader*, 28–29.

56. Although the participle *zābat* is normally translated "flowing [with]," the verb most commonly refers to genital emissions, and the rate of flow is therefore moderate.

57. Wright, *God's People in God's Land*, 104–5.

58. Ibid., 23.

CHAPTER 3

1. Dietrich Bonhoeffer, *Creation and Fall* (New York: Macmillan, 1959), 25.
2. Wendell Berry, "Notes: Unspecializing Poetry," in *Standing by Words* (Emeryville, Calif.: Shoemaker & Hoard, 2005), 90–91.
3. Daniel Hillel, *The Natural History of the Bible: An Environmental Exploration of the Hebrew Scriptures* (New York: Columbia University Press, 2006), 245.
4. Theodore Hiebert, *The Yahwist's Landscape: Nature and Religion in Early Israel* (New York: Oxford University Press, 1996), 157. Likewise, William P. Brown sees a "stark difference" between J's "landlings" and P's "landlords"; yet unlike Hiebert, who assigns no positive function to the Priestly tradition in Genesis, Brown gives much attention to the way in which it may have stimulated and educated ancient Israel's "moral imagination." See Brown, *The Ethos of the Cosmos: The Genesis of Moral Imagination in the Bible* (Grand Rapids: Eerdmans, 1999), 44.
5. Norman Habel, "Geophany: The Earth Story in Genesis 1," in *The Earth Story in Genesis*, ed. Norman Habel and Shirley Wurst (Sheffield/Cleveland: Sheffield Academic/Pilgrim, 2000), 47. For a statement of Habel's principles and assumptions, see "Introducing the Earth Bible," in *Readings from the Perspective of Earth*, ed. Habel (Sheffield/Cleveland: Sheffield Academic/Pilgrim, 2000), 25–37.
6. Norman Wirzba, *The Paradise of God: Renewing Religion in an Ecological Age* (New York: Oxford University Press, 2003), 27–34. Wirzba follows Hiebert in seeing an agrarian ethos only in the Yahwist account, suggesting that the Priestly account stresses separation from the rest of creation, a view that I counter here.

   Among contemporary scholars who accept the composite character of the creation account, several emphasize strong elements of continuity between Genesis 1 and 2. A generation ago, Michael Fishbane's work was unusual in this regard; see Fishbane, *Text and Texture: Close Readings of Selected Biblical Texts* (New York: Schocken, 1979), 18. More recently, see Terence Fretheim, *God and World in the Old Testament: A Relational Theology of Creation* (Nashville: Abingdon, 2005), 29–67; and (on the theological integrity of Genesis 1–11 as a unit) J. Richard Middleton, *The Liberating Image: The Imago Dei in Genesis 1* (Grand Rapids: Brazos, 2005), 185–231. See p. 56 in this volume.
7. Genesis 1 employs neither "the language of 'scientific history' nor the language of 'mythology and rationalism'"; rather, "[a]s liturgy, this poetry invites the congregation to *confess and celebrate* the world as God has intended it." Walter Brueggemann, *Genesis*, Interpretation: A Bible Commentary for Teaching and Preaching (Atlanta: John Knox, 1982), 26, 30 (emphasis original).
8. Carol A. Newsom, *The Book of Job: A Contest of Moral Imaginations* (New York: Oxford University Press, 2003), 82, citing the work of Pavel Medvedev and Mikhail Bakhtin (emphasis original).
9. Among recent treatments of Gen. 1:1–2:4a, those of Fishbane and Brueggemann are noteworthy for paying particular attention to the aesthetics of the text. Fishbane treats Gen. 1:1–2:4a as a unified and "highly stylized" narrative. He describes it as "nonpoetic in formulation" (*Text and Texture*, 15), by which he seems to mean that it does not employ epic imagery of the sort found in Psalm 89, Job 26, etc. Nonetheless, it is suggestive that Fishbane sets his own translation in breath units—one might say, as free verse.

10. Gerhard von Rad, *Genesis: A Commentary* (Philadelphia: Westminster, 1973), 27 (emphasis original).

11. Wendell Berry, "The Responsibility of the Poet," in *What Are People For?* (New York: North Point, 1990), 89.

12. Ibid., 89.

13. Of particular value for theologians and biblical scholars is Wendell Berry's essay "Poetry and Place," in *Standing by Words*, 106–213, in which he offers an insightful exploration of the connection between traditional literature that speaks to the imagination (including the religious imagination) and the places that inform such literature. See pp. 57–58 in this volume.

14. Scott Russell Sanders, "Letter to a Reader," in *Writing from the Center* (Bloomington: Indiana University Press, 1995), 169.

15. See Paul Ricoeur, *Interpretation Theory: Discourse and the Surplus of Meaning* (Fort Worth: Texas Christian University Press, 1976).

16. Norman Habel observes: "God does not pronounce light and Earth 'good,' thereby imprinting them with integrity from a position of authority . . . 'Good' is God's response to what is seen, experienced in the moment of creation" (*Earth Story in Genesis*, 42).

17. The story exists as a fragment, but its significance is suggested by its placement immediatcly before the flood narrative, and also by the consequent imposition of a limit on the human lifespan (Gen. 6:3). Both suggest that intermarriage between the divine and human realms constitutes a trespass, like the eating of the fruit. The stories in Genesis 3 and Genesis 6 are further linked by the (otherwise unparalleled) constellation of three words or phrases: "saw," "how good," "took."

18. Erazim Kohák, "Perceiving the Good," in *The Wilderness Condition: Essays on Environment and Civilization*, ed. Max Oelschlaeger (San Francisco: Sierra Club, 1992), 173 (emphasis original).

19. Ibid., 182.

20. Ibid., 183. The instance he cites is Heidegger's failure to adopt, even retrospectively, a critical view of Nazism.

21. Anestis G. Keselopoulos, *Man and the Environment: A Study of St. Symeon the New Theologian* (Crestwood, N.Y.: St. Vladimir's Seminary Press, 2001), 104.

22. Maximus the Confessor, *To Thalassius*, Patrologia graeca 90.296A; translation from Keselopoulos, *Man and the Environment*, 110.

23. Keselopoulos, *Man and the Environment*, 108. The importance of repentance and "the baptism of tears" as the means of entry into knowledge of the inner principles of created things was emphasized especially by St. Symeon the New Theologian in the tenth century C.E.

24. St. Basil the Great, in *The Westminster Collection of Christian Prayers*, ed. Dorothy M. Stewart (Louisville: Westminster John Knox, 2002), 6. I have set the prayer in poetic lines, to represent breath units.

25. Wendell Berry, "Going to Work," in *The Essential Agrarian Reader: The Future of Culture, Community, and the Land*, ed. Norman Wirzba (Lexington: University Press of Kentucky, 2003), 263.

26. Von Rad notes that the expression "is meant to be prosaic and degrading," so as to discourage worship of sun and moon (*Genesis*, 55). If the phrasing is quotidian, it may also imply the earth's "hominess."

27. The root *d-š-'* occurs in a verb only here. Claus Westermann notes that it is "probably a formation of P"; see Westermann, *Genesis 1–11: A Commentary* (Minneapolis: Augsburg, 1984), 124.

28. Ibid.

29. Ibid., 125.

30. Evan Eisenberg, *The Ecology of Eden* (New York: Knopf, 1998), 76.

31. See Daniel Hillel, *Out of the Earth: Civilization and the Life of the Soil* (New York: Free Press, 1991), 72–73; also Oded Borowski, *Agriculture in Iron Age Israel* (Winona Lake, Ind.: Eisenbrauns, 1987), 87; C. Wayne Smith, *Crop Production: Evolution, History, and Technology* (New York: John Wiley, 1995), 60.

32. Westermann, *Genesis 1–11*, 124.

33. Wirzba, *Paradise of God*, 182–83 (emphasis mine).

34. On the connection between Mesopotamian creation accounts, irrigation agriculture, and the temple cult, see Middleton, *Liberating Image*, 147–84.

35. Thomas S. Cox et al., "Prospects for Developing Perennial Grain Crops," *BioScience* 56 (2006): 649–50.

36. Andrew Kimbrell, ed., *Fatal Harvest: The Tragedy of Industrial Agriculture* (Washington, D.C.: Island, 2002), 102.

37. Eisenberg, *Ecology of Eden*, 50–51.

38. Kimbrell, *Fatal Harvest*, 102.

39. John Seabrook, "Sowing for Apocalypse: The Quest for a Global Seed Bank," *The New Yorker*, August 27, 2007, 69.

40. Robert Schubert, "Farming's New Feudalism," *World Watch*, May/June 2005, 15.

41. Physicist and activist Vandana Shiva, a leader in South Asia's efforts to protect biodiversity and free local farmers from corporate control, articulates a strong and widely respected critique of seed patenting, Terminator technology, and other industrial practices that threaten or damage food security; see her *Stolen Harvest: The Hijacking of the Global Food Supply* (Cambridge, Mass.: South End, 2000).

42. From 1998 to 2004, the European Union observed an informal "moratorium" on the authorization of genetically modified crops or plants for commercial use. In May 2003, the United States, with Canada and Argentina, initiated a case through the World Trade Organization (WTO) arguing that there was unfair discrimination against their products. Since 2004, the European Commission has begun to clarify the conditions for possible authorization of GM crops; see Sarah Lieberman and Tim Gray, "The So-called 'Moratorium' on the Licensing of New Genetically Modified (GM) Products by the European Union 1998–2004: A Study in Ambiguity," *Environmental Politics* 15 (2006): 592–609. Canada reintroduced the issue at the WTO meeting in February 2005 in Bangkok; intergovernmental debate seems likely to continue.

43. See Tony Szumigalski, "Literature Review on Genetic Use Restriction Technologies" (April 2006), endorsed by the Canadian Foodgrains Bank, available at http://www.foodgrainsbank.ca/admin/docs/GURT%20review%20-%20final%20rev2.pdf. Szumigalski cites T. Goeschl and T. Swanson, "The Development Impact of Genetic Use Restriction Technologies: A Forecast Based on the Hybrid Crop Experience," *Environment and Development Economics* 8 (2003): 149–65. Szumigalski concludes: "It is very difficult to assess the environmental, social, economic and political ramifications of GURTs because there is a lack of peer-reviewed publications with

novel research addressing these issues"; until such research is publicly available, "it is recommended that a precautionary approach . . . be followed" (12).

44. "Seedless in Seattle: Terminator Tech Trumps Trade Talks," news release, Rural Advancement Foundation International, December 1, 1999, available at http://www. etcgroup.org/upload/publication/351/01/news_trait.pdf. See also Mooney, *The ETC Century: Erosion, Technological Transformation, and Corporate Concentration in the 21st Century* (Uppsala/Winnipeg: Dag Hammerskjöld/Rural Advancement Foundation International, 1999/2001), available at http://www.ratical.org/co-globalize/ETCcent.pdf.

45. See the Web sites for CGIAR (http://www.cgiar.org/impact/agribiotech.html) and its affiliate CIMMYT International Maize and Wheat Improvement Center (http://www.cimmyt.org; see especially the Guiding Principles for Developing and Deploying Genetically Engineered Maize and Wheat).

46. In June 2003, the Independent Science Panel, an international group of twenty-four scientists in a variety of disciplines, published an extensive 136-page report, *The Case for a GM-Free Sustainable World* (London: Institute of Science in Society, 2003), available at http://www.indsp.org. Its primary conclusion regarding GM is that "GM crops have failed to deliver the promised benefits and are posing escalating problems on the farm. Transgenic contamination is now widely acknowledged to be unavoidable, and hence there can be no co-existence of GM and non-GM agriculture. Most important of all, GM crops have not been proven safe. On the contrary, sufficient evidence has emerged to raise serious safety concerns, that if ignored could result in irreversible damage to health and the environment. GM crops should be firmly rejected now" (ix). The report goes on to make a positive assessment of sustainable and organic agricultural practices.

47. Middleton suggests that the preposition in this phrase might be read as a *beth essentiae* (*Liberating Image*, 88 n. 116).

48. Peter Vitousek and Harold A. Mooney, "Human Domination of Earth's Ecosystems," *Science* 277 (July 25, 1997): 494; cf. James Gustave Speth, *Red Sky at Morning: America and the Crisis of the Global Environment* (New Haven/London: Yale University Press, 2004), 20.

49. See P. M. Vitousek, P. R. Ehrlich, A. H. Ehrlich, and P. A. Matson, "Human Appropriation of the Products of Photosynthesis," *Bioscience* 36 (1986): 368–73. The same figure was reached through independent research by Stuart L. Pimm; see *The World According to Pimm: A Scientist Audits the Earth* (New York: McGraw-Hill, 2001). In the 1997 study cited above, Vitousek says that "the fraction of the land's biological production that is used or dominated" falls in the range of 39 to 50 percent. "These numbers have large uncertainties, but the fact that they are large is not at all uncertain." Vitousek and Mooney, "Human Domination," 495.

50. Jonathan A. Foley et al., "Global Consequences of Land Use," *Science* 309 (July 22, 2005): 570; see also L. R. Oldeman, R. T. A. Hakkeling, and W. G. Sombroek, *World Map of the Status of Human-Induced Soil Degradation: An Explanatory Note*, 2nd ed. (Wageningen/Nairobi: International Soil Reference and Information Centre/United Nations Environment Programme, 1991), 28. According to Speth (citing The U.N. Environment Programme's *Global Environment Outlook*), "about three-fourths of the world's drylands are degraded, and about a fourth of all land is degraded to a degree sufficient to reduce its productivity" (*Red Sky at Morning*, 31).

51. Pimm, *World According to Pimm*, 228. See Norman Myers, Russell A. Mittermeier, and Cristina G. Mittermeier, "Biodiversity Hotspots for Conservation Priorities," *Nature* 403 (February, 24, 2000): 853–58.

52. Vitousek and Mooney, "Human Domination," 498.

53. Alistair McIntosh, *Soil and Soul* (London: Aurum, 2004), 38.

54. Speth, *Red Sky at Morning*, 15, citing the *2000 IUCN Red List of Threatened Species* from the International Union for Conservation of Nature and Natural Resources, available at http://www.redlist.org.

55. Vitousek and Mooney, "Human Domination," 499.

56. Ludwig Koehler and Walter Baumgartner, *The Hebrew and Aramaic Lexicon of the Old Testament*, vol. 2 (Leiden: Brill, 2001), 1190.

57. Middleton, *Liberating Image*, 52 (emphasis mine).

58. For a review of the history of interpretation of *imago Dei*, with an emphasis on Christian doctrine, see Westermann, *Genesis 1–11*, 147–58.

59. See also Gen. 9:6 ("image") and 5:1 ("likeness").

60. Middleton, *Liberating Image*, 291. Drawing on the structure of Mesopotamian mythology, Jeffrey Tigay argues: "In light of the *Atrahasis Epic*, covering the history of humanity from creation through the aftermath of the flood, Genesis 1:1–9:17 may likewise be understood as a single literary unit"; see Tigay, "The Image of God and the Flood," in *Studies in Jewish Education and Judaica in Honor of Louis Newman*, ed. A. M. Shapiro and B. I. Cohen (New York: Ktav, 1984), 177.

61. This chapter focuses on reading the metaphor within the several contexts of Hebrew Scripture. The most important New Testament passage pointing to the possibility that the image may be realized in humankind as a whole is probably Rom. 8:19: "The creation is waiting on tenterhooks for the revealing of the children of God." Genesis 5:3 shows that the word ("image") can denote a child's resemblance to the parent.

62. The works most frequently cited in connection with the ancient Near Eastern background of the divine image are those of H. Wildberger, "Das Abbild Gottes: Gen. 1,26–30," *Theologische Zeitschrift* 21 (1965): 245–59, 481–501; and W. H. Schmidt, *Die Schöpfungsgeschichte der Priesterschrift* (Neukirchen-Vluyn: Neukirchener Verlag, 1967), 127–49. In *The Liberating Image*, Middleton offers a fresh and insightful study of the metaphor in the context of Genesis and against the background of Mesopotamian literature and culture.

63. Middleton, *Liberating Image*, 60. Jon D. Levenson discusses "the extension of the royal status of the image of God to all humanity" in *Creation and the Persistence of Evil: The Jewish Drama of Divine Omnipotence* (San Francisco: HarperSanFrancisco, 1988), 114–16. Nathan MacDonald (following Phyllis Bird) argues for connecting the divine image in Genesis 1 with the notion of Israel's election rather than with royal status, asserting that "the verbal allusions are far less persuasive than that with the people of Israel as a whole"; see MacDonald, "The *Imago Dei* and Election: Reading Genesis 1:26–28 and Old Testament Scholarship with Karl Barth," *International Journal of Systematic Theology* (2007): 24. As my discussion implies, even if the Priestly understanding of humanity's status does include a regal element, that is seen as realized only (if at all) through the election of Israel.

64. On the Priestly understanding of Israel's holiness, see Chapter 5 in this volume.

65. See Aldo Leopold, "Natural History," in *A Sand County Almanac* (New York: Oxford University Press, 1966), 210.

66. Leopold, "The Land Ethic," in *Sand County Almanac*, 253.
67. Bonhoeffer, *Creation and Fall*, 33. In addition to Habel (n. 5 in this chapter), others that focus on the agency of the nonhuman creatures, including the earth, are Michael Welker, "What Is Creation? Rereading Genesis 1 and 2," in *Creation and Reality* (Minneapolis: Fortress, 1999), 6–20; and Bernhard W. Anderson, "The Priestly Creation Story: A Stylistic Study," in *From Creation to New Creation: Old Testament Perspectives*, Overtures to Biblical Theology (Minneapolis: Fortress, 1994), 42–55.
68. Berry, "Poetry and Place," 144 (emphasis original).
69. Habel, "Geophany," 47.
70. Berry, "Responsibility of the Poet," 89.
71. Berry, "Poetry and Place," 125.
72. My argument here gives substance to Middleton's suggestion that the fundamental human task is understood in Gen. 1:26–28 as "the exercise of significant power over the earth and its nonhuman creatures (*likely including the agricultural cultivation of land and the domestication of animals* – which together constitute the minimal historical requirements for organizing human society or culture)" (*Liberating Image*, 60; emphasis mine).
73. On the prominence of the number seven in the structuring of Gen. 1:1–2:3, see Jon Levenson's discussion of the work of Umberto Cassuto in *Creation and the Persistence of Evil*, 66–68.
74. H. W. F. Saggs, *The Encounter with the Divine in Mesopotamia and Israel* (London: Athlone, 1978), 168.
75. Edward O. Wilson, *The Future of Life* (New York: Knopf, 2002), 23.
76. So NRSV; Everett Fox, *The Five Books of Moses* (New York: Schocken, 1995), 17; Richard Elliot Friedman, *Commentary on the Torah* (San Francisco: HarperSanFrancisco, 2001), 13. Robert Alter, *The Five Books of Moses* (New York: Norton, 2004), 19, uses "conquer," but without comment.
77. James Barr, "Man and Nature – The Ecological Controversy and the Old Testament," *Bulletin of the John Rylands University Library of Manchester* 55 (1972/73): 22; similarly, see Middleton, *Liberating Image*, 52.
78. Norbert Lohfink, *Theology of the Pentateuch: Themes of the Priestly Narrative and Deuteronomy* (Minneapolis: Fortress, 1994), 10, cf. 126–28. Following Lohfink, William P. Brown says that the word's sharp edge "is blunted by the irenic tenor conveyed in the Priestly account" (*Ethos of the Cosmos*, 46).
79. Walter Brueggemann, "The Kerygma of the Priestly Writers," in *The Vitality of Old Testament Traditions*, by Walter Brueggemann and Hans Walter Wolff (Atlanta: John Knox, 1982), 109 (emphasis original).
80. The notion of the "original" form of the Priestly account of creation is highly plastic. A. Graeme Auld also considers that the verb *k-b-š* is not easily "tamed," but he regards it as a late editorial addition to the "original blessing" in Genesis 1, designed to make it conform to the events described in Joshua and 1 Chron. 22:18–19; see Auld, "Creation and Land: Sources and Exegesis," in *Joshua Retold: Synoptic Perspectives* (Edinburgh: T. & T. Clark, 1998), 63–68. Auld does not, however, take up the larger question of its meaning. The possibility that some form of the Priestly poem predates the exile is suggested by the echo of it found in Jer. 4:19–27 (if that passage comes from the prophet himself). The Priestly poem may well have taken multiple generations to reach its final form, as liturgical poetry often does. My reference to "the Priestly

poet" in this essay is to some degree a literary conceit; I am trying to make sense of a compositional intelligence that informs the whole.

81. Brueggemann, "Kerygma of the Priestly Writers," 110.

82. It is instructive that Wendell Berry, in an essay that "attempt[s] a Biblical argument for ecological and agricultural responsibility," instinctively moves from the command in Gen. 1:28 to the story of the giving of the land to the Israelites. While he does not read the first directly in light of the second, he perceives that the larger story is the necessary context for working out "the definition of an ecological discipline," precisely because "the Promised Land is a divine gift to a *fallen* people. For that reason the giving is more problematical, and the receiving is more conditional and more difficult." Berry, "The Gift of Good Land," in *The Gift of Good Land: Further Essays Cultural and Agricultural* (San Francisco: North Point, 1981), 267, 269 (emphasis original).

83. I follow Richard Elliot Friedman in setting these lines as poetry; see his *Commentary on the Torah* (New York: HarperSanFrancisco, 2001), 408–9.

84. Wendell Berry, "1982/VII: The clearing rests in song and shade," in *A Timbered Choir: The Sabbath Poems 1979–1997* (Washington, D.C.: Counterpoint, 1998), 49.

85. Oral communication.

86. Mark G. Brett, *Genesis: Procreation and the Politics of Identity* (London: Routledge, 2000) treats a number of instances of narrative irony in Genesis. Although Brett does not view Gen. 1:28 as ironic, his study is generally pertinent to my argument here.

87. Linda Hutcheon, *Irony's Edge: The Theory and Politics of Irony* (New York: Routledge, 1995), 37.

88. Ibid., 60.

89. Mark Brett argues that the command to the humans to conquer is itself ironized by the snake in Genesis 3: "the one that creeps upon the earth wins out" (*Genesis*, 33).

90. Middleton, *Liberating Image*, 212. Similarly, Michael Fishbane observes that the seventh day marks "the end of divine creation and the transfer of the earthly dominion to mankind" (*Text and Texture*, 9).

91. Middleton, *Liberating Image*, 292.

92. Middleton agrees that Genesis 1 should be read in conjunction with what follows, and he acknowledges that "humans as *imago Dei* exercise their God-given power, but not in the manner that God intended" (ibid., 220).

93. Wendell Berry, "1979/III: To sit and look at light-filled leaves," in *Timbered Choir*, 8.

CHAPTER 4

1. Wendell Berry, foreword to *Living the Sabbath: Discovering the Rhythms of Rest and Delight*, by Norman Wirzba (Grand Rapids: Brazos, 2006), 11.

2. The agrarian prophets Amos and Hosea are treated in Chapter 7 in this volume. and Micah in Chapter 9.

3. Hesiod, *Works and Days*, lines 248, 250–51, trans. Richmond Lattimore, *Hesiod* (Ann Arbor: University of Michigan Press, 1959), 49. On the social situation underlying Hesiod's challenge to the aristocracy, see Victor Davis Hanson's highly informative study *The Other Greeks: The Family Farm and the Agrarian Roots of Western Civilization* (New York: Free Press, 1995).

4. Brian Donahue, "The Resettling of America," in *The Essential Agrarian Reader: The Future of Culture, Community, and the Land*, ed. Norman Wirzba (Lexington: University Press of Kentucky, 2003), 38.

5. Ibid., 35. Cf. Leo Marx, *The Machine in the Garden: Technology and the Pastoral Ideal in America* (New York: Oxford University Press, 1964).

6. Wendell Berry, "The Agrarian Standard," in Wirzba, *Essential Agrarian Reader*, 24.

7. Donald B. Redford, *Egypt, Canaan, and Israel in Ancient Times* (Princeton: Princeton University Press, 1992), 258.

8. For the two sides of the debate, see Mark Smith, *The Early History of God* (Grand Rapids: Eerdmans, 2002), who argues that Israel originated through a process of internal differentiation within Canaan; and Stephen Cook, *The Social Roots of Biblical Yahwism* (Atlanta: Society of Biblical Literature, 2004), who believes that the Israelites were distinct in origin.

9. Redford, *Egypt, Canaan, and Israel*, 209.

10. See Carol Redmount, "Bitter Lives: Israel in and out of Egypt," in *The Oxford History of the Biblical World*, ed. Michael D. Coogan (Oxford: Oxford University Press, 1998), 79–80. On the royal economy of the Canaanite city-state, see Marvin L. Chaney, "You Shall Not Covet Your Neighbor's House," *Pacific Theological Review* 15 (Winter 1982): 7.

11. See Lionel Casson, *Everyday Life in Ancient Egypt*, rev. ed. (Baltimore: Johns Hopkins University Press, 2001), 42–49.

12. Nahum Sarna, *Exodus*, JPS Torah Commentary (Philadelphia: Jewish Publication Society, 1991), 86.

13. See Jacquetta Hawkes, *The First Great Civilizations: Life in Mesopotamia, the Indus Valley, and Egypt* (New York: Knopf, 1973), 396.

14. Bob Brier and Hoyt Hobbs, *Daily Life of the Ancient Egyptians* (Westport, Conn.: Greenwood, 1999), 99–115; Hawkes, *First Great Civilizations*, 325–42, 395.

15. See, for instance, Wendell Berry, *The Unsettling of America: Culture and Agriculture* (San Francisco: Sierra Club, 1977), 30, 43; and Norman Wirzba, *Living the Sabbath: Discovering the Rhythms of Rest and Delight* (Grand Rapids: Brazos, 2006), 25.

16. Norbert Lohfink, "'I am Yahweh, your Physician' (Exodus 15:26): God, Society and Human Health in a Postexilic Revision of the Pentateuch (Exod.15:2b, 26)," in *Theology of the Pentateuch: Themes of the Priestly Narrative and Deuteronomy*, trans. Linda M. Maloney (Minneapolis: Fortress, 1994), 93.

17. Hawkes, *First Great Civilizations*, 380.

18. Ibid., 393.

19. Casson, *Everyday Life in Ancient Egypt*, 37. See also Pierre Montet, *Everyday Life in Egypt in the Days of Ramesses the Great*, trans. A. R. Maxwell-Hyslop and Margaret S. Drower (Philadelphia: University of Pennsylvania Press, 1998), 116.

20. Contemporary scholars generally agree that the primary source for Exodus 16 is the Priestly tradition, with interpolations from JE. See the recent discussion by William H. C. Propp, *Exodus 1–18*, Anchor Bible 2 (New York: Doubleday, 1999), 588–92.

21. Norbert Lohfink refers to the manna story and the account of the tabernacle construction as "counter-narrative[s] to the work world of Egyptian slaves"; see Lohfink, "God the Creator and the Stability of Heaven and Earth," in *Theology of the Pentateuch*, 132. On the concept of the moral economy of food production, see Michael

Northcott, "Eucharistic Eating: The Moral Economy of Food," in *The Eucharist and Creation Spirituality*, ed. Lukas Vischer (Geneva: Centre International Réformé John Knox, 2007), 89–138.

22. See, for example, the instruction concerning the Israelite debt slave: "You shall not exercise mastery *ruthlessly* [*běpārek*] with respect to him" (Lev. 25:43, 46, cf. 53). Of the three other occurrences of the phrase, two refer to the harsh Egyptian rule over the Israelites (Exod. 1:13, 14).

23. Personal communication, November 2006, Cambridge, U.K. I treat the phenomenon of royal dominance (by Israel's kings) over agricultural production in Chapter 7 in this volume.

24. Montet, *Everyday Life in Egypt*, 113–14 and plate II.

25. Hawkes, *First Great Civilizations*, 340.

26. Ibid., 371.

27. Wendell Berry cites Richard E. Bell, assistant secretary of agriculture for international affairs and commodity programs (speech, fall convention of the National Farm Broadcasters Association, Kansas City, Kans., November 15, 1975). See Berry, *Unsettling of America*, 34–35.

28. The comment was made at a World Food Conference in Rome and reported in "What to Do: Costly Choices," *Time* (November 11, 1974): 80. On Butz's food policies and their consequences, see Christopher D. Cook, *Diet for a Dead Planet: How the Food Industry Is Killing Us* (New York/London: New Press, 2004), 79–85.

29. Sarna, *Exodus*, 38.

30. I am indebted to Robert Hayward for pointing out this echo (personal communication, November 2006, University of Durham, U.K.).

31. See Lev. 16:1, cf. Ps. 119:169.

32. The story of the plagues and the crossing of the sea is punctuated with the recognition formula; see Exod. 7:5, 17; 8:10, 22; 14:4, 18, etc.

33. Similarly Deut. 24:19–21, although the verb that is characteristic of this injunction in the Priestly source does not appear here.

34. Wirzba, *Living the Sabbath*, 35.

35. Montet, *Everyday Life in Egypt*, 119.

36. On the contrast between "rational-instrumental thinking" and the Priestly writer's "analogical thinking," see Mary Douglas, *Leviticus as Literature* (Oxford: Oxford University Press, 1999), 13–40. See Chapter 5 in this volume for further discussion of the analogical thinking of the Priestly writer.

37. Montet, *Everyday Life in Egypt*, 119.

38. "Resource Demand Is Called Threat to Environment," *Washington Post* (April 17, 2000): A2, cf. James Gustave Speth, *Red Sky at Morning: America and the Crisis of the Global Environment* (New Haven/London: Yale University Press, 2004), 30–31.

39. The statistic for water use comes from Fred Kirschenmann of the Leopold Center for Sustainable Agriculture at Iowa State University (http://www.leopold.iastate.edu), cited by Scott Bontz, "Weather Report," *Land Report*, no. 89 (Fall 2007): 14.

40. Speth, *Red Sky at Morning*, 33. See the discussion of threats to biodiversity and ecosystems, 30–36.

41. See Cook, *Diet for a Dead Planet*, 217–42.

42. Douglas H. Boucher, *The Paradox of Plenty: Hunger in a Bountiful World* (Oakland: Food First, 1999), xii.

43. Wendell Berry, "Two Economies," in *Home Economics* (New York: North Point, 1987), 58–59.
44. Ibid., 57.
45. The infinitive *lĕhaśkîl* may mean both "to give understanding" and "to look at"; I have followed Everett Fox's translation here. See Fox, *The Five Books of Moses* (New York: Schocken, 1995), 21.
46. In addressing the accusing question to the man, God makes no distinction between man and woman with respect to their violation of the divine prohibition (although commentators have often ascribed to the woman the primary guilt). The fact that it is the woman who "serves" the food may well reflect the ordinary social role of women in ancient Israel.
47. Jürgen Moltmann, *God in Creation: A New Theology of Creation and the Spirit of God*, Gifford Lectures 1984–1985 (Minneapolis: Fortress, 1993), 6.
48. Wirzba, *Living the Sabbath*, 23.
49. Ibid., 37.
50. Brevard Childs likewise argues that "there is a theological point which caused the writer to override the chronological sequence," although he sees a different point than the one I identify here. See Childs, *The Book of Exodus* (Philadelphia: Westminster, 1974), 291–92.

CHAPTER 5

1. This chapter (like the Hulsean Lecture on which it is based) is dedicated to my teacher Jacob Milgrom. His published work on Leviticus now extends over more than forty years, the biblical span representing the fullest possible accomplishment of an adult life.
2. Wendell Berry, "The Law That Marries All Things," in *Collected Poems 1957–1982* (San Francisco: North Point, 1985), 247.
3. Masanobu Fukuoka, *The One-Straw Revolution: An Introduction to Natural Farming*, ed. Larry Korn (Emmaus, Pa.: Rodale, 1978), 119.
4. E. F. Schumacher, *Small Is Beautiful: Economics as if People Mattered* (New York: HarperCollins, 1989), 146–59.
5. Ibid., 155.
6. Ibid., 154–59; *The Home-comers* was Schumacher's original title for the book. More recently, Wes Jackson has focused on the notion of homecoming in his *Becoming Native to This Place* (Lexington: University Press of Kentucky, 1994).
7. Carl Sagan, *Pale Blue Dot: A Vision of the Human Future in Space* (New York: Random House, 1994), 49, 403, 405.
8. Ibid., 385.
9. Ibid., 398: "By the time we're ready to settle even the nearest other planetary systems, we will have changed. The simple passage of so many generations will have changed us. The different circumstances we will be living under will have changed us. Prostheses and genetic engineering will have changed us. Necessity will have changed us. We're an adaptable species."
10. Ibid., 405.
11. Cf. the comment of Brevard S. Childs: "The problem of relating the church's eschatological hope to the faith of the Old Testament [arose] from the side of those within the

church who sought to dissolve the Old Testament tension between the new and the old by rejecting the first creation." Childs, *Biblical Theology in Crisis* (Philadelphia: Westminster, 1970), 213–14.

12. Wendell Berry, "The Gift of Good Land," in *The Gift of Good Land* (San Francisco: North Point, 1981), 276, 278–79.

13. There is an obvious contrast between the mandate to honor the trees of Canaan in Deut. 20:19 and the command to exterminate Canaanites in 20:17. On the way the Deuteronomistic tradition problematizes the latter command, see my essays "Critical Traditioning," in *The Art of Reading Scripture*, ed. Ellen F. Davis and Richard B. Hays (Grand Rapids: Eerdmans, 2003), 170–73; and "The Poetics of Generosity," in *The Word Leaps the Gap: Essays on Scripture and Theology in Honor of Richard B. Hays*, ed. J. Ross Wagner, C. Kavin Rowe, and A. Katherine Grieb (Grand Rapids: Eerdmans, 2008).

14. Jackson, *Becoming Native to This Place*, 3.

15. Aldo Leopold, "The Land Ethic," in *A Sand County Almanac* (New York: Oxford University Press, 1966), 239. Scattered references within the essay (pp. 238, 240) indicate that Leopold thought he was departing from the ethical sensibility of Torah; I believe he is unfolding its implications. Leopold's interest in the Bible is expressed more positively in an early essay, "The Forestry of the Prophets," reprinted in *Judaism and Environmental Ethics: A Reader*, ed. Martin Yaffe (Lanham, Md.: Lexington, 2001), 105–11.

16. H. H. Schmid, "Creation, Righteousness, and Salvation: 'Creation Theology' as the Broad Horizon of Biblical Theology" (orig. German, 1973), in *Creation in the Old Testament*, ed. Bernhard W. Anderson (Philadelphia/London: Fortress/SPCK, 1984), 103.

17. Ibid., 105.

18. Julius Wellhausen, *Prolegomena to the History of Ancient Israel* (German, 1978; Gloucester, Mass.: Peter Smith, 1983), 102, 104.

19. Wendell Berry, "Two Economies," in *Home Economics* (New York: North Point, 1987), 72–73.

20. While there are at least two major traditions preserved within the book, Priestly Torah and the Holiness Code (Leviticus 17–26), there is a strong family resemblance between them, and broadly speaking, the term "Priestly tradition" applies to both. I distinguish between them where necessary.

21. Mary Douglas, *Leviticus as Literature* (New York: Oxford University Press, 1999), 18.

22. Ibid., 45.

23. Wendell Berry, "Solving for Pattern," in *The Gift of Good Land*, 138.

24. Ibid., 137 (emphasis original).

25. Mary Douglas identifies Leviticus 19 as the most important chapter in the whole book, "the chapter on the meaning of righteousness" (*Leviticus as Literature*, 239). Jacob Milgrom treats the chapter as the central instruction in "ethics"; see Milgrom, *Leviticus: A Book of Ritual and Ethics*, Continental Commentary (Minneapolis: Fortress, 2004), 212–45.

26. J. Joosten, *People and Land in the Holiness Code: An Exegetical Study of the Ideational Framework of the Law in Leviticus 17–26* (Leiden: Brill, 1996), 197.

27. Ibid., 176–77. See also Milgrom's observation (on the use of the word *miškān* in 26:11) that for the Holiness writer (in contrast to the larger Priestly tradition), "YHWH is

not confined to a sanctuary but is present everywhere in the land." Jacob Milgrom, *Leviticus 23–27*, Anchor Bible 3B (New York: Doubleday, 2001), 2301.

28. In addition to the two uses in this chapter (cf. Lev. 19:34), Abraham Malamat cites two further occurrences of the verbal phrase: 2 Chron. 19:2 and 1 Kgs. 5:15 [1 Eng.]. See Malamat, "'Love Your Neighbor as Yourself': What It Really Means," *Biblical Archaeology Review* 16 (July/August 1990): 50–51. Everett Fox translates "be-loving to your neighbor"; see Fox, *The Five Books of Moses* (New York: Schocken, 1995), 603.

29. Milgrom, *Leviticus*, 236–38; also *Leviticus 17–22*, Anchor Bible 3A (New York: Doubleday, 2000), 1660–65. The correctness of this interpretation (in contrast to the common idea that the prohibition is a metaphor for disorder or intermarriage) appears to be confirmed by the similar prohibition in Deuteronomy: "You shall not seed your vineyard with two kinds, *lest the whole*, the seed that you sow and the vineyard's produce, *become holy*" (22:9). It is noteworthy also that the only other place in the Bible that seems to imply that different seed species should be kept apart is the parable of the farmer in Isaiah (28:24–29), a prophetic tradition that is throughout keenly attuned to God's radical holiness; Isaiah's farmer "places" spelt (and evidently each crop) "in its own section" (*gĕbūlātô*, Isa. 28:25). See Oded Borowski, *Agriculture in Iron Age Israel* (Winona Lake, Ind.: Eisenbrauns, 1987), 151. For more on mixtures, see the use of *tebel*, "confusion," not "perversion," in Lev. 18:23. On this usage, see *The Brown-Driver-Briggs Hebrew and English Lexicon* (Peabody, Mass.: Hendrickson, 1999), 117d; cf. the note by Baruch Levine in *Leviticus*, JPS Torah Commentary (Philadelphia: Jewish Publication Society, 1989), 123.

30. As Richard Elliott Friedman points out, linen does not take dye easily, and so the colored elements of the priest's clothing are likely to have been of wool, as is confirmed by fabric excavated at Kuntillat 'Ajrud (New York: HarperSanFrancisco, 2001).

31. My own view on the practice of polycropping in ancient Israel contrasts with that of Oded Borowski, who assumes (based on this prohibition and Isaiah's parable of the farmer) that "the biblical farmer" would have avoided the practice (*Agriculture in Iron Age Israel*, 150–51). On the widespread practice of polycropping as part of the traditional "craft" of farming, see James C. Scott, *Seeing Like a State: How Certain Schemes to Improve the Human Condition Have Failed* (New Haven/London: Yale University Press, 1998), 273–82. On cultivation as craft, see Scott, 301; also Colin Tudge, *So Shall We Reap* (London: Penguin, 2003), 185–278.

32. Joosten suggests that the Holiness Code (in contrast to the Priestly Torah of Leviticus 1–16) "is the product of a priestly school located in the countryside," and further, that "H is addressed to a provincial audience, called 'people of the land,' far removed from the realities of the capital and its preoccupations; the political organization of the state does not touch it directly" (*People and Land in the Holiness Code*, 163–64). This may be overstated; the people of the land were likely affected by decisions made in Jerusalem, even if they did not participate in them. Milgrom takes the opposite view of the Holiness school, suggesting that the writer(s) may have been "[s]equestered in the Jerusalem temple or, at best, [had] on occasion visited regional sanctuaries and the surrounding countryside" (*Leviticus*, 227).

33. Borowski supposes that "each farmer left a seventh of his land fallow each year" and that grains and legumes were rotated in the six years of planting (*Agriculture in Iron Age Israel*, 145, 151). However, David C. Hopkins argues that such land usage would

be much too intensive for the thin soil of the highlands; he posits a biennial fallow practice on each farmer's holding, as well as a community-wide fallow in the seventh year. See Hopkins, *The Highlands of Canaan: Agricultural Life in the Early Iron Age* (Decatur, Ga.: Almond, 1985), 191–210.

34. Edward O. Wilson, *The Future of Life* (New York: Knopf, 2002), 116.

35. Claire Hope Cummings, "Trespass," *World Watch* (January/February 2005): 34.

36. M. W. Eubanks, "Tapping Ancestral Genes in Plant Breeding: An Alternative to GMO Crops," in *Ethnobiology and Biocultural Diversity*, ed. John R. Stepp et al. (Athens, Ga.: International Society of Ethnobiology, 2002), 226.

37. Margaret Mellon and Jane Rissler, *Gone to Seed: Transgenic Contaminants in the Traditional Seed Supply* (Cambridge, Mass.: Union of Concerned Scientists, 2004), 1. The full report is available at http://www.ucsusa.org.

38. Jules Pretty, *Agri-Culture: Reconnecting People, Land and Nature* (London/Sterling, Va.: Earthscan, 2002), 132.

39. See Noah Zerbe, "Feeding the Famine? American Food Aid and the GMO Debate in Southern Africa," *Food Policy* 29 (2004): 593–608. Rather than "dumping" North American grain in famine-ravaged areas, the United States could help advance a region's capacity to feed itself. Most donor nations purchase and distribute surplus food grown in Africa, which is available even in a famine year. On the involvement of the seed industry in the promotion of GM technology, see Jeffrey M. Smith, *Seeds of Deception* (Fairfield, Iowa: Yes, 2003). A comprehensive scientific assessment of the risks associated with genetic modification was published by the Independent Science Panel in 2003; see *The Case for a GM-Free Sustainable World* (London: Institute of Science in Society, 2003), available at http://www.indsp.org (see further, in the present volume, n. 46 in Chapter 3).

40. Wilson, *Future of Life*, 116.

41. Cf. Pretty, *Agri-Culture*, 142.

42. M. W. Eubanks, "A Genetic Bridge to Utilize *Tripsacum* Germplasm in Maize Improvement," *Maydica* 51 (2006): 315.

43. Jerry D. Glover, Cindy M. Cox, and John P. Reganold, "Future Farming: A Return to Roots?" *Scientific American* (August 2007): 88.

44. Leopold identifies ecology as the "science of relationships"; see Leopold, "Natural History," in *Sand County Almanac*, 210. Cf. Jacob Milgrom's observation that the priestly tradition teaches that "nature maintains a balance between the forces of life and death. . . . With P, therefore, we can detect the earliest [gropings] toward an ecological position" (*Leviticus*, 13).

45. The reference to *sha'atnez* was evidently obscure even to an ancient audience; Deuteronomy defines it as a blend of wool and linen (22:11).

46. Wendell Berry, *The Unsettling of America: Culture and Agriculture* (San Francisco: Sierra Club, 1977), 43.

47. Wendell Berry, "Prayers and Sayings of the Mad Farmer," *Collected Poems, 1957–1982*, 130.

48. Milgrom, *Leviticus 17–22*, 1679.

49. Berry, *Unsettling of America*, 47–48.

50. These figures are drawn from publications of the U.S. Department of State: "Distinctions between Human Smuggling and Human Trafficking" (January 1, 2005);

"The Link between Prostitution and Sex Trafficking" (November 24, 2004); "Citizen Action: How Can I Help End Modern-Day Slavery?" (August 9, 2004).

51. Scyller J. Borglum, unpublished paper, October 2002.

52. Milgrom asserts that "[the Holiness writer's] term *'ăḥuzzâ* is only theologically different from [the Priestly writer's] word *naḥălâ* – to forestall the belief that Israel's land is an unconditional endowment – but juridically, it is exactly equivalent" (*Leviticus 23–27*, 2201). The term *naḥălâ* occurs widely throughout Hebrew Scripture and always in the Deuteronomic tradition; on the ideology and culture associated with it, see my Chapter 6 in this volume. On the distinction and overlap between the two terms and their distribution in Torah, see Milgrom, *Leviticus 23–27*, 2171–73.

53. Ibid., 2190.

54. Ibid., 2234.

55. Ibid., 2193.

56. Ibid., 2208–10.

57. Ibid., 2216.

58. Milgrom argues that "the jubilee and, indeed, most of [the Holiness writer's] laws were motivated by the economic stress of the eighth century, as forcefully punctuated by the prophets" (ibid., 2245). Although the dates of the Priestly and Holiness traditions are widely debated by scholars, the pressures on small farmers to which the prophets drew attention continued until the exile and thereafter, under both Israelite and foreign rulers. See my Chapters 6, 7, and 8 in this volume.

59. For an early statement by Wendell Berry on eating and farming as cultural acts, see *Unsettling of America*, 27–48.

60. Ibid., 38.

61. Douglas cites, for example, an interpretation of the dietary rules from the first-century Alexandrian Philo: "Fish with fins and scales, admitted by the law, symbolize endurance and self-control, whilst the forbidden ones are swept away by the current, unable to resist the force of the stream." Mary Douglas, *Purity and Danger: An Analysis of the Concepts of Pollution and Taboo* (London/New York: Routledge, 1966), 47.

62. Ibid., 57.

63. Milgrom, *Leviticus*, 12; cf. Milgrom, *Leviticus 1–16*, Anchor Bible 3 (New York: Doubleday, 1991), 735.

64. Milgrom, *Leviticus*, 103; cf. Milgrom, *Leviticus 1–16*, 704–42.

65. In her first treatment of Leviticus, Douglas dismissed I. Epstein's view that the real purpose of the dietary law "is to train the Israelite in self-control" in favor of the symbolic reading (*Purity and Danger*, 44). Apparently, she was unaware of Milgrom's then-recent (1963) article on Leviticus 11 "The Biblical Diet Laws as as Ethical System," *Intepretation* 17: 288–301.

66. Douglas, *Leviticus as Literature*, 44.

67. Mary Douglas's treatment of Leviticus emphasizes that the careful structuring and phrasing characteristic of the book bespeak a delight in literary craft; see, for example, ibid., 46.

68. Jacob Milgrom presents a strong argument for the development of the chapter in several stages, and he identifies vv. 24–40 as "the intrusive purification bloc" (*Leviticus 1–16*, 694). The fact that the two patterns of seven that appear in this chapter may

not have been present in the first stage of composition does not argue against their significance.

69. On this translation, see ibid., 680.

70. Here I am following canonical order without prejudicing the vexed question of dating various strands within the Priestly tradition.

71. Milgrom, *Leviticus*, 114–15.

72. Mary Douglas, "Food as a System of Communication," in *In the Active Voice* (London: Routledge & Kegan Paul, 1982), 123.

73. This formula, with variations, is a favorite expression of the Holiness writer; the short formulation occurs in 18:5, 6, 21; 19:12, 14, 16, 18, 28, 30, 32, 37; 21:12; 22:2, 3, 8, 30, 31, 33; 26:2, 45. The longer formulation, "I am YHWH your God," appears in Lev. 18:2, 4, 30; 19:2, 3, 4, 10, 25, 31, 34, 36; 20:7, 24, etc.

74. Gary Rendsburg, "The Inclusio in Leviticus XI," *Vetus Testamentum* 43 (1991): 418–19.

75. Douglas, *Leviticus as Literature*, 49.

76. Milgrom likewise criticizes Douglas's use of the category of holiness with respect to the animals (*Leviticus 1–16*, 721).

77. For a recent survey of the poultry and meatpacking industries, "the sweatshops that produce our food," see Christopher D. Cook, *Diet for a Dead Planet: How the Food Industry Is Killing Us* (New York/London: New Press, 2004), 187–216.

78. Cited by William Greider, "The Last Farm Crisis," *The Nation* (November 20, 2000): 16.

79. Matthew Scully, *Dominion: The Power of Man, the Suffering of Animals, and the Call to Mercy* (New York: St. Martin's, 2002), ix–x.

80. Tudge, *So Shall We Reap*, 181.

81. Scully, *Dominion*, 29.

82. Ibid., 263–69.

83. Ibid., 282.

84. *Animal Waste Pollution in America: An Emerging National Problem; Environmental Risks of Livestock and Poultry Production*, Minority Staff of the U.S. Senate Committee on Agriculture, Nutrition, and Forestry, December 1997, cited by Cook, *Diet for a Dead Planet*, 179–80.

85. Cook, *Diet for a Dead Planet*, 182.

86. Most translations eliminate the metaphor. Friedman, *Commentary on the Torah*, 409, for example, renders the line "My soul will not scorn you"; Milgrom, *Leviticus 23–27*, 2301, adopts a middle course, "I will not expel you," although he acknowledges that the phrase literally conveys the sense of nausea.

87. Wendell Berry, "We Who Prayed and Wept," in *Collected Poems, 1957–1982*, 211.

CHAPTER 6

1. Joseph Sittler, "The Care of the Earth," in *Evocations of Grace*, ed. Steven Bouma-Prediger and Peter Bakken (Grand Rapids: Eerdmans, 2000), 58.

2. Wendell Berry, "The Whole Horse," in *The Art of the Commonplace*, ed. Norman Wirzba (Washington, D.C.: Counterpoint, 2002), 240.

3. John Hagee, from an address to 3,500 evangelical Christians at a gathering sponsored by Christians United for Israel in July 2006. "You" seems to be an inclusive address to Christians as well as Jews, with an implicit supersessionist agenda. See Andrew

Higgins, "A Texas Preacher Leads Campaign to Let Israel Fight," *Wall Street Journal*, sec. A (July 27, 2006).

4. For a recent report on the devastating profit-driven land wars in Brazil – where an estimated 40% of the Amazon rain forest will have been cleared within the next twenty years – see Scott Wallace, "Last of the Amazon," *National Geographic*, (January 2007) 40–71.

5. Christopher J. H. Wright, *God's People in God's Land: Family, Land, and Property in the Old Testament* (Grand Rapids: Eerdmans, 1990), 63.

6. Ibid., 88.

7. Carol Meyers argues that through the tenth century, subsistence farmers – virtually all Israelites – felt no negative pressure from the state, since foreign conquests met its economic and labor demands. See Meyers, "Kinship and Kingship: The Early Monarchy," in *The Oxford History of the Biblical World*, ed. Michael D. Coogan (New York: Oxford University Press, 1998), 201–3. Marvin Chaney, however, argues that the flow of booty was insufficient for Solomon's ambitions, and he "pressed his agrarian economic base to the breaking point"; see Chaney, "Systemic Study of the Israelite Monarchy," *Semeia* 37 (1986): 69. For a similar view, see Norman Gottwald, "The Participation of Free Agrarians in the Introduction of Monarchy to Ancient Israel," *Semeia* 37 (1986): 84–86.

8. J. Joosten suggests that the Shunammite woman's response indicates indifference to the state; see Joosten, *People and Land in the Holiness Code* (Leiden: Brill, 1996), 92. Others see a sharper political edge to the story: She is part of a rural upper class that was increasingly dissatisfied with Ahab's policies regarding land ownership and lived "according to a cultural reality that implicitly or explicitly challenged the dominant hegemony . . . "; see Tamis Hoover Rentería, "The Elijah/Elisha Stories: A Socio-cultural Analysis of Prophets and People in Ninth-Century B.C.E. Israel," in *Elijah and Elisha in Socioliterary Perspective*, ed. Robert B. Coote (Atlanta: Scholars Press, 1992), 113; see also, in the same volume, Judith A. Todd, "The Pre-Deuteronomistic Elijah Cycle."

9. The slogan comes from Ezra Taft Benson, secretary of agriculture under Dwight Eisenhower; see Wendell Berry, *The Way of Ignorance* (Emeryville, Calif.: Shoemaker & Hoard, 2005), 117.

10. David W. Orr noted in 2002 that 4.5 million farms had disappeared in the previous 60 years; see Orr, *The Nature of Design: Ecology, Culture, and Human Intention* (New York: Oxford University Press, 2002), 47. For the most recent census of the United States Department of Agriculture, see *2002 Census of Agriculture*, available at http://www.nass.usda.gov/census/census02/volume1/us/index1.htm.

11. Wendell Berry, *The Unsettling of America: Culture and Agriculture* (San Francisco: Sierra Club, 1977), 32.

12. The statistics on the farming population come from Fred Kirschenmann of the Leopold Center for Sustainable Agriculture, Iowa State University (http://www.leopold.iastate.edu), cited by Scott Bontz, "Weather Report," *Land Report*, no. 89 (Fall 2007): 14. See also Brian Halweil, "Where Have All the Farmers Gone?" *World Watch* (September/October 2000): 12–28.

13. Berry, *Unsettling of America*, 33.

14. John Tuxill, "The Biodiversity That People Made," *World Watch* (May/June 2000): 27.

15. Peter Rosset, *The Multiple Functions and Benefits of Small Farm Agriculture in the Context of Global Trade Negotiations*, Food First Policy Brief no. 4 (Oakland, Calif.: Institute for Food and Development Policy, 1999), available at http://www.foodfirst.org/pubs/policybs/pb4.html.

16. The Movimento dos Trabalhadores Rurais Sem Terra (MST) is the largest social movement in Latin America, with an estimated 1.5 million members. See http://www.mstbrazil.org.

17. Michael Pollan dates the turning point in the industrialization of North American agriculture "with some precision to the day in 1947 when the huge munitions plant at Muscle Shoals, Alabama, switched over to making chemical fertilizer." Pollan, *The Omnivore's Dilemma: A Natural HIstory of Four Meals* (New York: Penguin, 2006), 41.

18. Wendell Berry, "The Idea of a Local Economy," in *In the Presence of Fear: Three Essays for a Changed World* (Great Barrington, Mass.: Orion Society, 2001), 27.

19. Among others, Wendell Berry observes that "rural America . . . is in many ways a colony of what the government and the corporations think of as the nation"; see Berry, "The Work of Local Culture," in *What Are People For?* (New York: North Point, 1990), 167.

20. See David Morris, "Local Self-Reliance: Inevitable Food Fight," *Co-op America Quarterly* (Spring 2000): 11. Morris is vice president of the Institute for Local Self-Reliance (http://www.ilsr.org), based in Minneapolis and Washington, D.C.

21. Jane Goodall, *Harvest for Hope: A Guide to Mindful Eating* (New York: Warner, 2005), 39. In 2007, as Australia endured the worst drought in a century, it was reported that on average, one farmer committed suicide every four days; see World Watch Updates, "Depression Down Under," *World Watch* (January/February 2007): 7. The Indian government reports that between 1993 and 2003, over 100,000 bankrupt farmers committed suicide. "In recent years India has averaged 16,000 farmer suicides a year – usually by drinking Green Revolution pesticides. It's not that these farmers missed out on the Green Revolution. On the contrary, their destitution and desperation are the *result* of the Green Revolution." See "The Gates-Rockefeller Green Revolution for Africa," *Food First News and Views*, (Fall 2006): 2; similarly, see John Elliott, "Field of Greens," *Fortune* (October 2, 2006): 55.

22. Gail Toff Bergman, ed., "Mental Health Services in Rural America," *State Health Reports* 58 (June 1990): 1.

23. Joel Dyer, *Harvest of Rage: Why Oklahoma City Is Only the Beginning* (Boulder: Westview, 1997), 71. On violence and the growth of hate groups in rural regions, see also Osha Gray Davidson, *Broken Heartland: The Rise of America's Rural Ghetto* (Iowa City: University of Iowa Press, 1996).

24. See Douglas H. Boucher, ed., *The Paradox of Plenty: Hunger in a Bountiful World* (Oakland: Food First, 1999).

25. See Stephen C. Smith, *Ending Global Poverty: A Guide to What Works* (New York: Palgrave Macmillan, 2005); Amartya Sen, *Poverty and Famines: An Essay on Entitlement and Deprivation* (Oxford/New York: Oxford University Press, 1984); Jeffrey D. Sachs, *The End of Poverty: Economic Possibilities for Our Time* (New York: Penguin, 2005); and the various publications of the Institute for Food and Development Policy (aka Food First), a "people's" nonprofit think tank and education-for-action center, especially Boucher's *Paradox of Plenty*.

26. See Berry, "Idea of a Local Economy," 11–33.

27. Norman Habel, *The Land Is Mine: Six Biblical Land Ideologies* (Minneapolis: Fortress, 1995), 76.

28. Ibid., 101 n. 14.

29. See Norman Habel, *Yahweh Versus Baal* (New York: Bookman, 1964).

30. Eric Freyfogle, "Private Property Rights in Land: An Agrarian View," in *The Essential Agrarian Reader: The Future of Culture, Community, and the Land*, ed. Norman Wirzba (Lexington: University Press of Kentucky, 2003), 237. See also Freyfogle's extended study *The Land We Share: Private Property and the Common Good* (Washington, D.C.: Island, 2003).

31. Herman E. Daly, "Policies for Sustainable Development," in *Agrarian Studies: Synthetic Work at the Cutting Edge*, ed. James C. Scott and Nina Bhatt (New Haven: Yale University Press, 2001), 277.

32. T. J. Gorringe, *A Theology of the Built Environment: Justice, Empowerment, Redemption* (Cambridge: Cambridge University Press, 2002), 22, 243–44.

33. Carol Meyers, *Discovering Eve: Ancient Israelite Women in Context* (New York/Oxford: Oxford University Press, 1988), 40–41.

34. See Henry M. Caudill, *Night Comes to the Cumberlands: A Biography of a Depressed Area* (Boston: Little, Brown, 1963); also Wendell Berry, "Harry Caudill in the Cumberlands," in *What Are People For?* 30–35.

35. Deut. 11:29; 27:12–13; see Daniel Hillel, *The Natural History of the Bible: An Environmental Exploration of the Hebrew Scriptures* (New York: Columbia University Press, 2006), 149.

36. Berry, *Unsettling of America*, 31.

37. E. F. Schumacher, *Small Is Beautiful: Economics as if People Mattered* (New York: HarperCollins, 1989), 33–34.

38. On the theology of the Holiness Code, see Chapter 5 in this volume (84–87, 90–94, 99–100).

39. William P. Brown, *The Ethos of the Cosmos: The Genesis of Moral Imagination in the Bible* (Grand Rapids: Eerdmans, 1999), 118.

40. Joosten, *People and Land in the Holiness Code*, 189–90. Similarly, Norman Habel says that the Israelites "are designated something like 'immigrant tenants' who hold their land by the authority and goodness of YHWH, the landowner" (*The Land Is Mine*, 107). The term used by the Priestly tradition to designate land as the property of a family is *'aḥuzzâ* (Lev. 25:10, 24, etc.). It is generally analogous to the more common term *naḥălâ* and is sometimes conjoined with it (Num. 27:7; 35:2, etc.).

41. Habel, *The Land Is Mine*, 114, 110.

42. Allan Savory is cofounder of Holistic Management International (http://www.holisticmanagement.org). For an extended description of the workings of a similar program of holistic management (Polyface Farm, a family-owned, local-market farm in Virginia's Shenandoah Valley), see Pollan, *The Omnivore's Dilemma* (New York: Penguin, 2006), 185–273.

43. See Edward F. Campbell, "A Land Divided," in Coogan, *Oxford History of the Biblical World*, 229.

44. David usurps the entitlement of Meribaal (Mephiboshet), son of Saul, and gives it to Tsiba (2 Sam. 16:4; cf. 19:30–31 [29–30 Eng.]). See Norman Habel's treatment of the royal land ideology in *The Land Is Mine*, 17–32.

45. David E. Klemm, "Material Grace: The Paradox of Property and Possession," in *Having: Property and Possession in Religious and Social Life*, ed. William Schweiker and Charles Mathewes (Grand Rapids: Eerdmans, 2004), 222. As far as I can tell, Klemm does not have this story in mind.

46. I am indebted to Loren Johns for this suggestion (personal communication, March 2008). Nathan MacDonald notes that Ahab's desire for a vegetable garden recalls Israel's culpable longing in the wilderness for the vegetables of Egypt, in place of the manna that they have come to find contemptible (Num. 11:5; personal communication, October 2007).

47. See Philip J. King and Lawrence E. Stager, *Life in Biblical Israel* (Louisville: Westminster John Knox, 2001), 98–101.

48. Nathan MacDonald, *Not Bread Alone: The Uses of Food in the Old Testament* (Oxford: Oxford University Press, 2008), in press.

49. Ibid.

50. Rentería, "Elijah/Elisha Stories," 95.

51. Ibid., 89–91.

52. Todd, "Pre-Deuteronomistic Elijah Cycle," 8. Norman K. Gottwald argues at length that the verb *y-š-b* appears frequently in participial form to designate various functions as a specialized sense denoting "sitting in judgment" and various other modes of exercising communal leadership; see Gottwald, *The Tribes of Yahweh: A Sociology of the Religion of Liberated Israel 1250–1050 B.C.E.* (Maryknoll: Orbis, 1979), 512–32.

53. Berry, "Work of Local Culture," 166.

54. See the Deuteronomic description of the proper action of a king (Deut. 17:14–20) and Samuel's warning of how the king will inevitably compromise the people's freedom (1 Sam. 8:11 17).

55. Here and in Deut. 28:68, the *hitpa'el* form of *m-k-r* denotes a voluntary "sale," literal or metaphorical, which either constitutes or results from disobedience to Israel's God. On the contrast in usage between the *nip'al* and *hitpa'el* forms of the verb, see Jacob Milgrom, *Leviticus 23–27*, Anchor Bible 3B (Garden City: Doubleday, 2001), 2219–20.

56. For example, Artur Weiser, *The Psalms*, Old Testament Library (Philadelphia: Westminster, 1962), 314–15, views it as a collection of proverbs. Similarly Walter Brueggemann, *The Message of the Psalms* (Minneapolis: Augsburg, 1984), 42; Brueggemann does, however, suggest some thematic coherence: "If we seek to find a more substantive concern in this psalm, we may find it in a series of reflections on *how to keep land and how to lose it*" (43; emphasis original).

57. Brueggemann, *Message of the Psalms*, 43.

58. Wendell Berry, "The Responsibility of the Poet," in *What Are People For?* 89.

59. Emanuel Katongole, personal communication, summer 2007.

60. With my translation "landowner" for Hebrew *gĕbĕr*, I am adopting the suggestion of Hans Walter Wolff (followed by many others) that in Mic. 2:2 the word denotes a male who is eligible for military service specifically because he is a fully enfranchised citizen, in possession of an ancestral allotment of land. See Wolff, *Micah: A Commentary*, trans. G. Stansell (Minneapolis: Augsburg, 1990), 78.

61. Jacqueline Osherow, "Psalm 37 at Auschwitz," in *Dead Men's Praise* (New York: Grove, 1999), 60–64.

62. The translation "citizen" for *'îš* reflects Wolff's understanding of the word as denoting one possessed (or, in Mic. 2:2, deprived) of the full legal rights and obligations associated with hereditary land tenure; see Wolff, *Micah*, 78.

63. Freyfogle, "Private Property Rights in Land," 238.

64. Eric T. Freyfogle, *Agrarianism and the Good Society: Land, Culture, Conflict, and Hope* (Lexington: University Press of Kentucky, 2007), 93–94.

65. Ibid., 97, 102.

66. Chapter 9 in this volume explores in depth the way the biblical writers represent the relationship between a city and its hinterland.

67. Thus David Ehrenfeld characterizes our present age; see Ehrenfeld, *Beginning Again: People and Nature in the New Millennium* (New York: Oxford University Press, 1993), 194.

68. Brian Donahue, "The Resettling of America," in Wirzba, *Essential Agrarian Reader*, 46–47.

69. Marian Burros, "Preserving Fossil Fuels and Nearby Farmland by Eating Locally," *New York Times* (April 25, 2007): F 10.

70. Bill McKibben, *Deep Economy: The Wealth of Communities and the Durable Future* (New York: Henry Holt, 2007), 81.

71. On this understanding of *naḥălâ*, see Hans-Joachim Kraus, *Psalms 1–59*, trans. H. C. Oswald (Minneapolis: Fortress, 1993), 238.

CHAPTER 7

1. Kathleen Raine, "Triad," in *The Hollow Hill* (London: Hamish Hamilton, 1965), 53.

2. See also my *Getting Involved with God* (Cambridge, Mass.: Cowley, 2001), 196–200; and David W. Orr, "The Uses of Prophecy," in *The Essential Agrarian Reader: The Future of Culture, Community, and the Land*, ed. Norman Wirzba (Louisville: University Press of Kentucky, 2003), 171–87.

3. Victor Davis Hanson, *The Other Greeks: The Family Farm and the Agrarian Roots of Western Civilization* (New York: Free Press, 1995), 45. Hanson himself does not show any awareness of Israelite agrarianism.

4. In comparison to Amos, Hosea, and Micah, Isaiah's allusions to rural life and land appropriation are brief; nonetheless, he is aware of the exploitation of the rural populace (Isa. 3:14) and the systematic annexation of their land (5:8). Note also the extended plowing metaphor in Isa. 28:24–28. The explicit overlap between the books of Isaiah and Micah (Isa. 2:2–4// Mic. 4:1–3) indicates that both traditions were preserved within a single religious circle or subculture.

5. Robert Gordis, following the Targum and Ibn Ezra, renders the line: "The advantage of land is paramount; even a king is subject to the soil"; see Gordis, *Koheleth – The Man and His World*, 3rd ed. (New York: Schocken, 1968), 166, cf. 250. Similarly, Alfredo Tepox Varela reads: "The king is the servant of the land"; see Varela, "A New Approach to Ecclesiastes 5.8–9," *The Bible Translator* 27 (1976): 240–41. I am indebted to Prof. John Jackson for drawing to my attention this possible interpretation; he notes, however, that with every other occurrence of the *nip'al* form of the verb *'-b-d*, tilled land is its grammatical subject.

6. Edward F. Campbell estimates the size of the farming population at 85% Paula M. McNutt suggests that it may have been as high as 95%. See Campbell, "A Land Divided: Judah and Israel from the Death of Solomon to the Fall of Samaria," in *The Oxford History of the Biblical World*, ed. Michael D. Coogan (Oxford/New York: Oxford University Press, 1998), 229; McNutt, *Reconstructing the Society of Ancient Israel* (London/Louisville: SPCK/Westminster John Knox, 1999), 152.

7. John Andrew Dearman argues that in contrast to the "general prosperity" in the Omride kingdom of the ninth century B.C.E., Israelite wealth of the eighth century B.C.E. was confined to the royal court and its officials; see Dearman, *Property Rights in the Eighth-Century Prophets: The Conflict and Its Background*, SBL Dissertation Series 106 (Atlanta: Scholars Press, 1988), 139–40, 147. Nathan MacDonald demonstrates that feasting was an important means of displaying and maintaining political power and therefore an incentive for control of food distribution by the elite; see MacDonald, *Not Bread Alone: The Uses of Food in the Old Testament* (Oxford: Oxford University Press, 2008), in press.

8. On the competition between farmers and the state for the limited quantities of metals, see Marvin Chaney, "Systemic Study of the Israelite Monarchy," *Semeia* 37 (1986): 69.

9. See David Hopkins, "Dynamics of Agriculture in Monarchical Israel," in *Society of Biblical Literature 1983 Seminar Papers*, ed. Kent Harold Richards (Chico, Calif.: Scholars Press), 195–96. Hopkins cites Gerhard Lenski's judgment that it has been the norm in advanced agrarian societies (such as ancient Israel's) to tax peasants to the limit of their ability to pay; see Lenski, *Human Societies: A Macrolevel Introduction to Sociology* (New York: McGraw-Hill, 1970), 268.

10. "Fields which produced as little as a ten to fifteenfold harvest in good years typically failed altogether in three years out of ten.... Either there was not enough rain to plant or there was too much rain after the crops were planted." Victor H. Matthews and Don C. Benjamin, *Social World of Ancient Israel 1250–587 BCE* (Peabody, Mass.: Hendrickson, 1993), 38, 44.

11. The only other usage of the term *nōqēd* is with reference to King Mesha of Moab, as an owner of flocks (2 Kgs. 3:4).

12. Campbell, "Land Divided," 234. Each of the ostraca lists a commodity (wine or oil), a place of origin, a personal name, and a date (according to the king's regnal years); the ostraca date to the first part of Jeroboam's reign (ca. 770 B.C.E.).

13. See Stephen L. Cook, *The Social Roots of Biblical Yahwism* (Atlanta: Society of Biblical Literature, 2004), 151. A household at Tell Beit Mirsim in Judah may have controlled as many as thirty-four silos, each with a storage capacity of one metric ton of grain; see Philip J. King and Lawrence E. Stager, *Life in Biblical Israel* (Louisville: Westminster John Knox, 2001), 91.

14. Indeed, the same technology and probably some of the same terraces are still in use today. See Gershon Edelstein and Shimon Gibson, "Ancient Jerusalem's Rural Food Basket," *Biblical Archaeology Review* 8 (July/August 1982): 46–54; Gershon Edelstein and Mordechai Kislev, "Mevasseret Yerushalayim: The Ancient Settlement and Its Agricultural Terraces," *Biblical Archeologist* 44 (Winter 1981): 53–56.

15. Dearman, *Property Rights*, 123–26.

16. My translation is adapted from that of Marvin Chaney, who argues that many translations fail to construe the text "in conformity with the known facts of either Hebrew syntax or the economic history and geography of ancient Judah.... There is

no warrant in this text for placing large herds in the Shephelah and the plains . . . or plowmen in the uplands" ("Systemic Study," 73–74). Anson Rainey, in his discussion of the passage, suggests that "the Carmel" refers to districts in the southern hill country where the altitude was lower and the soil less productive than in the hills north of Hebron; see Rainey, "Wine from the Royal Vineyards," *Bulletin of the American Schools of Oriental Research* 245 (1982): 58.

17. Amos's village of Tekoa was in the Judean hill country, five miles south of Bethlehem. Stephen Cook makes a strong argument that Hosea was a rural priest of Levitical lineage (*Social Roots*, 233, 244–64).

18. The *ephah* is a dry measure (of perhaps about 23 liters) for grain and the *shekel* a weight. The merchants are dispensing the grain for sale with a deceptively small measure, but they are using too heavy a weight when they buy grain from farmers, thus getting more for their money.

19. The concept of land as a "biotic community," including the soil and all the creatures, human and nonhuman, whose well-being depends upon the health of the whole system, is set forth in Aldo Leopold's classic essay "The Land Ethic," in *A Sand County Almanac* (New York: Oxford University Press, 1966), 237–64.

20. The ambiguous verb *yē'āsēpû*, "gathered in," suggests both harvesting and death.

21. Kathleen Raine, "Eileann Chanaidh: The Ancient Speech," in *Hollow Hill*, 29.

22. Cook, *Social Roots*, 271.

23. T. J. Gorringe, *A Theology of the Built Environment: Justice, Empowerment, Redemption* (Cambridge: Cambridge University Press, 2002), 51. For a detailed critical study of land ownership patterns in Scotland at the end of the twentieth century, with a proposal for new patterns that could be economically viable and socially responsible, see Andy Wightman, *Who Owns Scotland?* (Edinburgh: Canongate, 1996); and Robin Callander, *How Scotland Is Owned* (Edinburgh: Canongate, 1998). Auslan Cramb offers a more anecdotal account of land use on large private estates in *Who Owns Scotland Now? The Use and Abuse of Private Land* (Edinburgh/London: Mainstream, 1996).

24. On the buyouts, and the ecological restoration that has followed upon them, see Michael S. Northcott, "Wilderness, Religion, and Ecological Restoration in the Scottish Highlands," *Ecotheology* 10 (2005): 382–99. The Land Reform Act, one of the first major pieces of legislation considered by the recently restored Scottish Parliament, became law in 2004; it grants tenants the right to buy (at rates determined by the government) when the land is put up for sale, regardless of whether the laird wishes to sell to them.

25. Alastair McIntosh, *Soil and Soul: People versus Corporate Power* (London: Aurum, 2004), 177.

26. Ibid., 256.

27. See Chapter 6 in this volume.

28. Klaus Koch observes that "every saying of Amos' returns explicitly or implicitly to *hā'āreṣ)*, the fruitful land given by [YHWH]." Koch, *The Prophets*, vol. 1, *The Assyrian Period*, trans. M. Kohl (Philadelphia: Fortress, 1982), 74–75.

29. The ten occurrences of the word *'ădāmâ* in Amos constitute the greatest density of its appearance (in proportion to the total number of words) in any book of the Bible; second in this respect is Deuteronomy, where the density is only half of that in Amos.

The word appears frequently also in the books of Ezekiel (28×), Jeremiah (18×), and Isaiah (16×).

30. The fact that every legal code in the Bible gives prominent attention to the situation of the landless – indentured service or enslavement of Israelites (Exod. 21:1–11; Deut. 15:12–18; cf. Exod. 21:37–22:3[22:1–4 Eng.]), debt slavery and land loss (Leviticus 25) – attests to the persistence of the problem throughout the monarchic period.

31. Koch, *Prophets*, 49–50 (emphasis original).

32. Ibid., 62.

33. See Chapters 3, 4, and 5 above, and the discussion of the tabernacle construction in Chapter 8 in this volume.

34. Dearman uses the terms "redistribution system" and " redistributing economy," in preference to the frequently used term "rent capitalism" (*Rentenkapitalismus*). The former are more reflective of the social realities of ancient societies, where the prime economic movers were not private entrepreneurs or corporations but monarchs and the tiny social elite created by the crown. "The crucial role of the state in redistributing substantial segments of the economy's production is important for understanding the place of land grants, taxation privileges, and patronage in the conflict over property rights." Dearman, *Property Rights*, 134; see also Dearman, "Prophecy, Property, and Politics," in *Society of Biblical Literature 1984 Seminar Papers*, ed. Kent Harold Richards (Chico, Calif.: Scholars Press, 1984), 392–93.

35. Dearman distinguishes between the royal acropolis of Samaria ("her") and the surrounding "mountains" (plural), where the former oppressors are to gather. The focus is particularly on the residents of the royal and administrative precinct, those officially responsible for economic oppression and the misappropriation of property. See Dearman, *Property Rights*, 26 27.

36. Ibid., 27; cf. n. 12 above.

37. "Rosen und Lavendel statt Blut und Eisen." Wellhausen, *Die kleinen Propheten übersetzt und erklärt* (1898; reprint, Berlin: De Gruyter, 1963), 96.

38. Robert B. Coote, *Amos among the Prophets: Composition and Theology* (Philadelphia: Fortress, 1981), 122.

39. McIntosh, *Soil and Soul*, 140–41.

40. The verb *h-p-k* recurs in 4:11; 5:8; 6:12; and 8:10.

41. An alternative reading is, "With you I have a case, O priest."

42. Cook, *Social Roots*, 81.

43. J. David Pleins observes that Hosea's strong sense of social justice "has reverberated down through the later prophetic tradition." Further, because this book is placed at the head of the Book of the Twelve (Minor Prophets), it "helps to place the social critique of the rest of the Twelve within a wider theological and philosophic framework." Pleins, *The Social Visions of the Hebrew Bible: A Theological Introduction* (Louisville: Westminster John Knox, 2001), 355.

44. George Steiner, *After Babel* (London: Oxford University Press, 1975), 233.

45. Laurie J. Braaten argues that Hos. 1:2, appearing at the head of the Book of the Twelve, highlights land as an important theme throughout the Minor Prophets; see Braaten, "God Sows the Land: Hosea's Place in the Book of the Twelve," in *Society of Biblical Literature 2000 Seminar Papers* (Atlanta: Society of Biblical Literature, 2000), 219.

46. Typical is Hans Walter Wolff's suggestion that the image of the fornicating land stands for "a profusion of Canaanite fertility cults in whose theology 'the land' appears in the form of a Mother Goddess" who is inseminated by the storm god Baal; see Wolff, *Hosea*, trans. G. Stansell, Hermeneia (Philadelphia: Fortress, 1974), 15.

47. Alice A. Keefe, "The Female Body, the Body Politic, and the Land," in *A Feminist Companion to the Latter Prophets*, ed. Athalya Brenner (Sheffield: Sheffield Academic, 1995), 83. See Jo Ann Hackett, "Can a Sexist Model Liberate Us? Ancient Near Eastern 'Fertility' Goddesses," *Journal of Feminist Studies in Religion* 5 (1989): 65–76. Their argument against the standard scholarly representation of Canaanite fertility religion does not negate fertility as a cultural and religious concern for Canaanites and Israelites alike. Israel (as represented unapologetically by the biblical writers) appealed to YHWH as the one who conferred "blessings of breasts and womb" (Gen. 49:25). Indeed, concern for fertility in all spheres – human, animal, and agricultural – would seem to be both natural and essential for any viable religion in any culture with a future. Hackett comments aptly: "Anyone who has ever prayed for a baby, or 'thanked God' when the rain came and the crops did not die, is practicing a form of fertility religion" ("Can a Sexist Model Liberate Us?" 68).

48. Alice A. Keefe, *Woman's Body and the Social Body in Hosea*, JSOT Supplement Series 338 (New York: Sheffield Academic, 2001), 199.

49. The phrase "symbolic alibi" is taken from Gale Yee's study of Hosea 1–2, which generally follows the line of Keefe's argument; see Yee, *Poor Banished Children of Eve: Woman as Evil in the Hebrew Bible* (Minneapolis: Fortress, 2003), 100.

50. Keefe, *Woman's Body and the Social Body in Hosea*, 216.

51. Keefe, "Female Body, Body Politic, and Land," 89.

52. James Luther Mays observes: "Heart in Hosea is the mind, the responsible intelligence." Mays, *Hosea*, Old Testament Library (Philadelphia: Westminster, 1969), 111. The translation "new wine" for *tîrôš* is standard but probably not accurate; Oded Borowski, *Agriculture in Iron Age Israel* (Winona Lake, Ind.: Eisenbrauns, 1987), 113, argues well that it is a simple synonym for *yayin*. Since English does not have such a synonym, I adopt the standard translation, with reservation.

53. The NJPS translation associates *yitgôrārû* (7:14) with Aramaic *gar/yegur*, "to commit adultery."

54. Wolff, *Hosea*, 128.

55. Compare the standard translation: "They shall fornicate, but not increase" (ibid., 72; similarly Mays, *Hosea*, 66). See NJPS for the rendering of *hiznû* as "swill"; if this is correct, then Hosea is exploiting the coincidence with the root *z-n-h*, "fornicate." Support for my rendering (which differs in the second verb from NJPS, "not be satisfied") comes from Prov. 3:10, where the verb *p-r-ṣ*, "burst," is used, as here, in parallel with the root *ś-b-'*, "be full to satiety," for vats bursting with wine.

56. See Matthews and Benjamin, *Social World of Ancient Israel*, 187. Similarly, G. W. Ahlström argues that priests and Levites were "soldiers for god and king" and that the very term "Levite" indicates that they were "attached to" (*l-w-h*) the central government as employees; see Ahlström, *Royal Administration and National Religion in Ancient Palestine* (Leiden: Brill, 1982), 48–49. Further, he suggests that the Levites, called a tribe and yet lacking a *naḥălâ*, or ancestral portion, in the land, lived on lands associated with the state sanctuaries. Like temple lands in Egypt, these would have

been exempt from tax revenues and confiscation, at least until Josiah's administrative reorganization in the late seventh century (50–51).

57. Matthews and Benjamin, *Social World of Ancient Israel*, 192.

58. Ephraim's father, Joseph, whose name is likewise eponymous for the northern kingdom of Israel, is described as *bēn pōrāt*, "a wild ass" (Gen. 49:22).

59. Commentaries generally treat these chapters as discrete units, thus obscuring the thematic connections between them. The image of fruit, once plentiful and now destroyed, links this poem also with the oracle that begins in Hos. 10:1.

60. Harold Fisch, "Hosea: A Poetics of Violence," in *Poetry with a Purpose: Biblical Poetics and Interpretation* (Bloomington/Indianapolis: Indiana University Press, 1988), 146. Fisch notes also the wordplay between *'eprayim* and *rop'î*, "my [God's] healing," in Hos. 7:1 (145).

61. Wendell Berry, "Sex, Economy, Freedom, and Community," in *Sex, Economy, Freedom, and Community* (New York/San Francisco: Pantheon, 1993), 133.

62. Wendell Berry, *The Unsettling of America: Culture and Agriculture* (San Francisco: Sierra Club, 1977), 124.

63. Ibid., 127.

64. Ibid., 124 (emphasis original).

65. As a designation for a trader, the term *kĕna'an* (=Canaan) appears first here and in Isa. 23:8. Evidently in the eighth century, Israelites were beginning to conform to the negative stereotype of the Canaanite in their mercantile activities. See Keefe, *Woman's Body and the Social Body in Hosea*, 206.

66. Berry, *Unsettling of America*, 136.

67. Wolff, *Hosea*, 53.

68. See Mark S. Smith's discussion of this passage in relation to Hosea in *The Early History of God: Yahweh and the Other Deities in Ancient Israel*, 2nd ed. (Grand Rapids/Dearborn: Eerdmans/Dove, 2002), 73–75; quotation/translation, 74. His fuller discussion of the passage appears in Smith, *The Ugaritic Baal Cycle*, vol. 1, Supplements to Vetus Testamentum 55 (Leiden: Brill, 1994), 173–81.

69. Israelite religious poetry is literarily conservative; it preserves various elements from Canaanite poetry: stylistic devices, stereotyped phrasing and word pairs, similes, divine epithets, and also, as in Hosea 2, larger image structures and themes. See Jonas C. Greenfield, "The Hebrew Bible and Canaanite Literature," in *The Literary Guide to the Bible*, ed. Robert Alter and Frank Kermode (Cambridge, Mass.: Belknap/Harvard University Press, 1987), 545–60.

70. It is possible to speak of Berry's work as participating in the same tradition as do Hosea and the Baal epic without assuming that Berry knows Ugaritic poetry or even consciously draws upon Hosea. Their unity stems from the existence of a poetic tradition, stretching across multiple cultures and places and times, that observes and celebrates what is often called the Great Chain of Being. See Chapter 3 in this volume, and further, Wendell Berry, "Poetry and Place," in *Standing by Words* (Emeryville, Calif.: Shoemaker & Hoard, 2005), 106–213. A complementary treatment of the Great Chain of Being as a source of wisdom and challenge to contemporary culture is found in E. F. Schumacher, *A Guide for the Perplexed* (New York: Harper & Row, 1977). Specifically on the theme of "converse" as it emanates in the fertility of the land, see Berry's remarks on agriculture using nature "in the manner of a conversationalist," by asking questions about what nature would do, and waiting for a response, in

Berry, "Nature as Measure," in *What Are People For?* (New York: North Point, 1990), 208–9.

71. Wendell Berry, *Remembering*, in *Three Short Novels* (Washington, D.C.: Counterpoint, 2002), 220.

72. Norman Wirzba, "An Economy of Gratitude," in *Wendell Berry: Life and Work*, ed. Jason Peters (Lexington: University Press of Kentucky, 2007), 143.

CHAPTER 8

1. Wendell Berry, "Healing," in *What Are People For?* (New York: North Point, 1990), 10.

2. In a detailed study of the history and effects of the industrial fixation of nitrogen for fertilizer (the "Haber-Bosch" process), Vaclav Smil asserts: "Without this synthesis about 2/5 of the wworld's population would not be around." Smil, *Enriching the Earth: Fritz Haber, Carl Bosch, and the Transformation of World Food Production* (Cambridge/London: MIT Press, 2001), xv.

3. James Gustave Speth identifies land-use conversion as the most serious of "nine principal threats to biodiversity and to healthy ecosystems," noting that "in this category the principal problem is the conversion of tropical forests to agricultural uses and tree plantations." Speth, *Red Sky at Morning: America and the Crisis of the Global Environment* (New Haven/London: Yale University Press, 2004), 30.

4. Donald Hall, *Life Work* (Boston: Beacon, 1993), 96.

5. Wendy Wasserstein, *Sloth* (New York: Oxford University Press, 2005).

6. Siegfried Wenzel traces the development of the concept of *acedia* from the fourth century onward, highlighting especially the contributions of Cassian (d. 435 C.E.) and Aquinas (d. 1274 C.E.); see Wenzel, *The Sin of Sloth: Acedia in Medieval Thought and Literature* (Chapel Hill: University of North Carolina Press, 1967).

7. Karl Barth, *Church Dogmatics* IV/2, trans. G. W. Bromiley (Edinburgh: T. & T. Clark, 1958), 412. Subsequent page references for this volume will be placed in parentheses within the text.

8. Speth, *Red Sky at Morning*, 139.

9. Ibid., 16.

10. On the risks associated with GMOs, see M. W. Eubanks, "Tapping Ancestral Genes in Plant Breeding: An Alternative to GMO Crops," in *Ethnobiology and Biocultural Diversity*, ed. John R. Stepp, Felice S. Wyndham, and Rebecca K. Zarger (Athens, Ga.: International Society of Ethnobiology,University of Georgia Press, 2002), 225–38; and Jeffrey M. Smith, *Seeds of Deception* (Fairfield, Ohio: Yes, 2003).

11. While the cause of the die-offs is not determined at the time of writing, it appears to be an unidentified virus compounded by other factors, such as drought and resulting undernutrition, and the practices of industrialized beekeeping. See Andrew C. Revkin, "Virus Is Seen as Prime Suspect in Death of Honeybees," *New York Times*, sec. A (September 7, 2007), citing a study published in the journal *Science*, online edition (September 6, 2007; with related bibliography at eurekalert.org/bees); print edition, *Science* 318 (October 12, 2007): 283–87.

12. See Wenzel, *Sin of Sloth*, 48–49.

13. For this insight I am indebted to my student Ailsa Guardiola Gonzalez (unpublished paper, February 24, 2005).

14. T. J. Gorringe, *A Theology of the Built Environment: Justice, Empowerment, Redemption* (Cambridge: Cambridge University Press, 2002), 48.

15. On the verbal correspondences between the Priestly creation story, the tabernacle account, and other parts of the Priestly narrative, see Joseph Blenkinsopp, *Prophecy and Canon* (Notre Dame/London: University of Notre Dame Press, 1977), 59–69. See also Jon D. Levenson, *Sinai and Zion* (San Francisco: Harper & Row, 1985), 142–45; and his further development of the correspondence in *Creation and the Persistence of Evil* (San Francisco: Harper & Row, 1988), 66–99.

16. *ʿăbōdâ kāšâ*, "hard labor," appears elsewhere, always with negative connotations, in Exod. 6:9; Deut. 26:6; 1 Kgs. 12:4 (see v. 13); 2 Chron. 10:4; Isa. 14:3. See John Robert Jackson's wide-ranging and valuable study, "Enjoying the Fruit of One's Labor: Attitudes toward Male Work and Workers in the Hebrew Bible" (PhD diss., Duke University, 2005; University Microfilms), 393.

17. Sabbath and its violation, along with good work and bad work, all serve as structuring elements in the book of Exodus. See my essay "Slaves or Sabbath-Keepers? A Biblical Perspective on Human Work," *Anglican Theological Review* 83 (Winter 2001): 25–40.

18. Contrast NRSV and NJPS, which employ "skill" throughout this passage.

19. Susanne Langer, *Philosophy in a New Key: A Study in the Symbolism of Reason, Rite, and Art* (New York: New American Library, 1942), 237–38.

20. E. F. Schumacher, *Small Is Beautiful: Economics as if People Mattered* (New York: HarperCollins, 1989), 33–34.

21. Ibid., 34.

22. E. F. Schumacher, "The Party's Over," in *Good Work* (New York: Harper & Row, 1979), 126–27, cf. 140.

23. On the formation of individuals and communities by the buildings in which they worship, see my essay "The Tabernacle Is Not a Storehouse: Building Sacred Space," *Sewanee Theological Review* 49 (Pentecost 2006): 305–19.

24. The statistics and the quotation are from David W. Orr, "A Meditation on Building," *The Chronicle of Higher Education* (October 20, 2006): B6–8; see also Orr, *Design on the Edge: The Making of a High-Performance Building* (Cambridge/London: MIT Press, 2006), ch. 1.

25. Claudia V. Camp, building upon Patrick Skehan's proposal about earlier and later redactions of Proverbs, argues that 31:1–9 once was the conclusion of the book. Now, however, "one social ideal has replaced another"; specifically, the royal figure (and a foreigner) has been displaced by "the ideal Israelite housewife–the mainstay of society in the post-exilic period." See Camp, *Wisdom and the Feminine in the Book of Proverbs* (Decatur, Ga.: Almond, 1985), 252–53.

26. On the echoes between this poem and the psalmists' representation of God, see Ellen F. Davis, *Proverbs, Ecclesiastes, and the Song of Songs* (Louisville: Westminster John Knox, 2000), 152–53.

27. Joseph Blenkinsopp, "The Family in First Temple Israel," in *Families in Ancient Israel*, ed. Leo Perdue et al. (Louisville: Westminster John Knox, 1997), 84.

28. On the aptness of the poem as a representation of women's work in the Iron Age, see Carol Meyers, "Material Remains and Social Relations: Women's Culture in Agrarian Households of the Iron Age," in *Symbiosis, Symbolism, and the Power of the Past*, ed. William Dever and Seymour Gitin (Winona Lake, Ind.: Eisenbrauns, 2003), 435. Meyers does not take a position on the poem's date of composition. Katharine J.

Dell observes that the poem "may... have had an earlier life" before being placed at the end of Proverbs; see Dell, *The Book of Proverbs in Social and Theological Context* (Cambridge: Cambridge University Press, 2006), 87.

29. See Charles E. Carter, *The Emergence of Yehud in the Persian Period: A Social and Demographic Study*, JSOT Supplement Series 294 (Sheffield: Sheffield Academic, 1999), 259.

30. Diana Edelman, *The Origins of the 'Second' Temple: Persian Imperial Policy and the Rebuilding of Jerusalem* (London/Oakville, Conn.: Equinox, 2005), 326–28, 340–51. Edelman argues that the temple was part of the master plan for the rebuilding of Jerusalem, carried out during the governorship of Nehemiah. See also Pierre Briant's magisterial study of the Persian Empire, *From Cyrus to Alexander: A History of the Persian Empire* (Winona Lake, Ind.: Eisenbrauns, 2002). Although Briant makes little specific reference to Yehud, he provides useful background on the empire's governmental structure and the enormous economic burden imposed on its subjects, both individually and corporately (see esp. 388–421).

31. Industrial-scale weaving shops dating to Persian-period Yehud have recently been identified (on the basis of loom-weights) in Jerusalem and other sites; Carter supposes they "would have functioned primarily to produce goods to support the conscripts stationed in the fortresses" (*Emergence of Yehud*, 252).

32. Two different Hebrew words (*yād* and *kap*, "palm") are used to denote the woman's hands. The number seven (and its multiples) is often used by the biblical writers to connote completeness.

33. Victor Davis Hanson highlights the strong agrarian elements in the portrait of Odysseus's father in his illumining study of Greek agrarianism starting with the eighth century, *The Other Greeks: The Family Farm and the Agrarian Roots of Western Civilization* (New York: Free Press, 1995).

34. James C. Scott, *Seeing Like a State: How Certain Schemes to Improve the Human Condition Have Failed* (New Haven/London: Yale University Press, 1998), 313.

35. The phrase "art de la localité" derives from Henri Mendras, *The Vanishing Peasant: Innovation and Change in French Agriculture*, trans. Jean Lerner (Cambridge: Cambridge University Press, 1970); see also Jan Douwe van der Ploeg's study of localized, craft-based agriculture in the Andean highlands, "Potatoes and Knowledge," in *An Anthropological Critique of Development: The Growth of Ignorance*, ed. Mark Hobart (London/New York: Routledge, 1993), 209–27.

36. Scott, *Seeing Like a State*, 318.

37. Ibid., 340 (emphasis original).

38. The fact that local knowledge cannot be appropriated from without accounts for the fact that, as Scott observes, "the destruction of mētis and its replacement by standardized formulas legible only from the center is virtually inscribed in the activities of both the state and large-scale bureaucratic capitalism.... The reduction or... the elimination of mētis and *the local control it entails* are preconditions, in the case of the state, of administrative order and fiscal appropriation and, in the case of the large capitalist firm, of worker discipline and profit." Ibid., 335–36 (emphasis mine).

39. Ibid., 319.

40. van der Ploeg, "Potatoes and Knowledge," 211–12.

41. Wendell Berry, in "Hunting for Reasons to Hope: A Conversation with Wendell Berry," by Harold K. Bush Jr., *Christianity and Literature* 56 (Winter 2007): 234.

42. The word *ḥōq* could also be rendered "prescribed portion."
43. Christopher J. H. Wright, *God's People in God's Land: Family, Land, and Property in the Old Testament* (Grand Rapids/Exeter: Eerdmans/Paternoster, 1990), 1.
44. Camp, *Wisdom and the Feminine*, 263.
45. See Prov. 1:8 (cf. 6:20).
46. The religious significance of the valorous woman's daily work is clarified by the memorable portrayal of her antitype, the "strange woman" (*'iššâ zārâ*, Prov. 7:5); see my commentary, *Proverbs, Ecclesiastes, and the Song of Songs*, 58–62, 153–54. Interestingly, although the "strange woman" is called a "foreigner" (7:5), there is no indication that she is a non-Israelite. Rather, it is as an adulteress, a "whore" (7:10), that she stands outside the community and threatens it (see Wright, *God's People in God's Land*, 92–97.) She is utterly deadly; "*her* house is the way to Sheol" (7:27). The most serious threat, from the perspective of the community, is that households will be destroyed and children not properly brought up in the covenant. A related instruction sums up the dangerous character of such a "foreign woman" in distinctly religious terms, as "the one who abandons the companion of her youth / [and] forgets the covenant of her God" (Prov. 2:17).
47. Wendell Berry, "The Farm," in *A Timbered Choir: The Sabbath Poems, 1979–1997* (Washington, D.C.: Counterpoint, 1998), 141.

CHAPTER 9

1. Wendell Berry, in "Rendering Us Again in Affection: An Interview with Wendell Berry," by Katherine Dalton, *Chronicles* (July 2006): 36.
2. Tom Daniels has aptly described the United States at the beginning of the twenty-first century as a "metropolitan nation," with 80% of its population living in 273 metropolitan regions, each with a city of 50,000 or more, suburbs, "edge cities" that have grown out of the suburbs, and a rural fringe; see Daniels, *When City and Country Collide: Managing Growth in the Metropolitan Fringe* (Washington, D.C./Covelo, Calif.: Island, 1999), 4.
3. Jacques Ellul's assertion of what he supposes to be the wholly negative biblical estimation of the city has been influential; see Ellul, *The Meaning of the City*, trans. Dennis Pardee (Grand Rapids: Eerdmans, 1970). Herbert N. Schneidau cites the destruction of Jericho as a key instance of the Bible's "devaluation of cultural attainments"; see Schneidau, *Sacred Discontent: The Bible and Western Tradition* (Baton Rouge: Louisiana State University Press, 1976), 5. In a similar vein, Isaac M. Kikawada and Arthur Quinn, *Before Abraham Was: The Unity of Genesis 1–11* (Nashville: Abingdon, 1985) perceive an antiurban bias in Genesis.
4. Philip J. King and Lawrence E. Stager note the "floruit of monumental construction" in the form of palaces, temples, and other public buildings that began to appear in the tenth century in Jerusalem, as well as the northern cities of Beth-Shemesh, Gezer, Megiddo, Ta'anach, Beth-Shean, Yokneam, and Hazor – evidence that all these cities served an administrative or military function in the reigns of David and especially Solomon. See King and Stager, *Life in Biblical Israel* (Louisville: Westminster John Knox, 2001), 202.
5. Stephen L. Cook supposes that Micah was a landed aristocrat and clan head. See Cook, *The Social Roots of Biblical Yahwism* (Atlanta: Society of Biblical Literature, 2004), 270–71.

6. The *ephah* is a dry measure, used for grain.
7. Bruce K. Waltke offers a good discussion of the linguistic difficulties of the passage in his *Commentary on Micah* (Grand Rapids/Cambridge: Eerdmans, 2007), 394–406. See also the brief notes to the NJPS.
8. See Chapter 6 of this volume.
9. The definitive feature that distinguished an Israelite city from a village was the wall that provided protection from attack. Volkmar Fritz calls the small nonroyal urban communities "residential cities" and notes that they begin to appear in the same period as the royal cities. He supposes that the former, which lack a formal plan and public buildings, may have been places of relocation for many families previously living in villages. See Fritz, *The City in Ancient Israel* (Sheffield: Sheffield Academic, 1995), 76–120.
10. Frank S. Frick, *The City in Ancient Israel*, SBL Dissertation Series 36 (Missoula, Mont.: Scholars Press, 1977), 114. That the Deuteronomic tradition (at least) might include Israelites among those classified as *gērîm* is supported by the several occurrences of the verb *gûr* to denote the residence of a Levite, who was "by definition" landless, in an Israelite town or district (Deut. 18:6; Judg. 17:7; 19:1).
11. Because the capital cities of Jerusalem and Samaria could command tribute throughout their kingdoms, they could sustain a larger population than other cities (see Frick, *City in Ancient Israel*, 185). Magen Broshi and Israel Finkelstein estimate the population of Samaria in the mid-eighth century to be 15,000, and of Jerusalem, 7,500; see Broshi and Finkelstein, "The Population of Palestine in Iron Age II," *Bulletin of the American Schools of Oriental Research* 287 (August 1992): 54. After the fall of Samaria in 722 B.C.E., Jerusalem grew substantially to accommodate the refugees. Later, during the Persian period, Jerusalem may have had a population of only 1,500, according to Charles Carter; Broshi, using different calculation criteria, puts the figure at 4,500. See Carter, *The Emergence of Yehud in the Persian Period: A Social and Demographic Study*, JSOT Supplement Series 294 (Sheffield: Sheffield Academic, 1999), 195–202, citing Broshi, "Estimating the Population of Ancient Jerusalem," *Biblical Archaeology Review* 4 (1978): 12.
12. Kai N. Lee projects that 88% of the net human population growth in the first third of the twenty-first century will be in the cities of low- and medium-income countries; see Lee, "An Urbanizing World," in *2007 State of the World: Our Urban Future*, ed. Linda Starke (New York/London: Norton, 2007), 7.
13. Ibid., 21.
14. One important partnership between city planners and ecologists is the Green Communities project, jointly sponsored by the Natural Resources Defense Council and Enterprise Community Partners; see http://www.greencommunitiesonline.com/projects.asp.
15. Wendell Berry, "Out of Your Car, Off Your Horse," in *Sex, Economy, Freedom, and Community* (New York/San Francisco: Pantheon, 1993), 21 (emphasis original).
16. An excellent survey of gardening in American cities is found in Laura J. Lawson, *City Bountiful: A Century of Community Gardening in America* (Berkeley: University of California Press, 2005). The Urban Agriculture Network (http://www.cityfarmer.org/TUAN.html) is a good source of information and bibliography.
17. Brian Halweil and Danielle Nierenberg, "Farming the Cities," in Starke, *2007 State of the World*, 49.

18. Michael Balter, *The Goddess and the Bull: Çatalhöyük: An Archaeological Journey to the Dawn of Civilization* (New York: Free Press, 2004), 314–15.

19. Halweil and Nierenberg, "Farming the Cities," 49.

20. For these and other examples of using urban agriculture for wastewater treatment and bioremediation, see ibid., 55; and Toni Nelson, "Closing the Nutrient Loop," *World Watch* (November/December 1996): 11–15.

21. An initial 20% of the waste stream is diverted by curbside recycling. The entire Department of Sanitation study, "Composting in New York City: A Complete Program History," is available online at http://www.nyc.gov/html/nycwasteless/html/recycling/waste_reports.shtml.

22. Jac Smit, Annu Ratta, and Joe Nasr, *Urban Agriculture: Food, Jobs, and Sustainable Cities* (New York: UNDP, 1996), 26.

23. Halweil and Nierenberg, "Farming the Cities," 49–55.

24. Ibid., 60.

25. Daniels, *When City and Country Collide*, 9.

26. American Farmland Trust, "Farming on the Edge Report," http://www.farmland.org/resources/fote/default.asp.

27. Laura Lawson reports on urban garden programs currently operative in such intensely developed sites as Battery Park City, New York, and Watts, Los Angeles (*City Bountiful*, 7, 238–86).

28. Randall Arendt, "Saving Agricultural Lands through Cluster Development," in *Charter of the New Urbanism*, ed. Michael Leccese and Kathleen McCormick (New York: McGraw-Hill, 2000), 34. The Congress for the New Urbanism is a broad-based advocacy group whose aim is to reestablish "the relationship between the art of building and the making of community, through citizen-based participatory planning and design" (vi). The Congress views "disinvestment in central cities, the spread of placeless sprawl, increasing separation by race and income, environmental deterioration, loss of agricultural lands and wilderness, and the erosion of society's built heritage as one interrelated community-building challenge" (v).

29. Aidan Hart, "Christianity and Sacred Art Today," lecture given at Hillsdale College, Hillsdale, Minn., October 6, 2005.

30. Daniel W. Hardy and David F. Ford, *Praising and Knowing God* (Philadelphia: Westminster, 1985), 81–82.

31. Jon D. Levenson, "The Jerusalem Temple in Devotional and Visionary Experience," in *Jewish Spirituality from the Bible through the Middle Ages*, ed. Arthur Green (New York: Crossroad, 1986), 38.

32. When the blessing is first conferred upon Abraham, YHWH charges him, "And be a blessing!" (12:2).

33. See Jeremiah 51–52, esp. 51:53, 55; Ps. 137:8–9; cf. Isa. 33:1, where the doomed "devastator" is not identified with any one nation.

34. This rendering of the Hebrew *bābel* is taken from Everett Fox, *The Five Books of Moses* (New York: Schocken, 1995), 46, 49; cf. the NEB.

35. Frick, *City in Ancient Israel*, 207.

36. Ibid., 208–9.

37. The image of Zion as mother-city may be in part a monotheistic adaptation of the Mesopotamian tradition of goddesses as the protectors of cities. The close association between a goddess and her city is indicated by the motif of the "turreted crown";

the goddess wears on her own person the wall that is its defensive architecture. The association finds further expression in the lament tradition, where the goddess weeps over a city damaged or destroyed by an enemy. In these laments, the deity often bears the title *ama*, "Mother," and sometimes the citizens are identified as her children. See F. W. Dobbs-Allsopp, *Weep, O Daughter of Zion: A Study of the City-Lament Genre in the Hebrew Bible* (Rome: Pontificio Istituto Biblico, 1993), 75–90. John J. Schmitt takes a different view, arguing that the biblical poets took the image of Zion's motherhood from Canaanite culture, in which cities were regularly imaged as feminine; see Schmitt, "The Motherhood of God and Zion as Mother," *Révue Biblique* 92 (1985): 557–69.

38. Jane Jacobs, *The Death and Life of Great American Cities* (New York: Random House, 1961), 447.

39. Ibid., 7.

40. Ibid., 445.

41. Ibid., 447.

42. Updated reports can be found at the U.S. Environmental Protection Agency's Web site, http://www.epa.gov/Region2/water/nycshed/protprs.htm. See also the site for the New York City Watershed Protection Project 1997, http://www.nypirg. org/enviro/water/watershed_agreement.html. Cost figures are from Richard Manning, "We Need and Owe Rural People," *Land Report*, no. 86 (Fall 2006): 26. Endorsement of the program can be found on the Web site of the Earth Institute at Columbia University, http://www.earthinstitute.columbia.edu.

43. The image of Jerusalem as mother (and wife of God) is developed in Isa. 49:20–21; 50:1; 54:1–8; 66:7–14; it is thus one element (among many) of continuity between the two sections conventionally designated Second Isaiah (Isaiah 40–55) and Third Isaiah (56–66). Benjamin D. Sommer has argued that both sections derive from the same prophet-poet in *A Prophet Reads Scripture: Allusion in Isaiah 40–66* (Stanford: Stanford University Press, 1998). A final determination on this matter is not essential to my argument.

44. Wendell Berry, *The Unsettling of America: Culture and Agriculture* (San Francisco: Sierra Club, 1977), 104.

45. See Ellen F. Davis, *Proverbs, Ecclesiastes, and the Song of Songs* (Louisville: Westminster John Knox, 2000); and "Reading the Song Iconographically," in *Scrolls of Love: Ruth and the Song of Songs*, ed. Peter S. Hawkins and Lesleigh Cushing Stahlberg (New York: Fordham University Press, 2006), 172–84.

46. See André LaCocque, who argues plausibly for a Hellenistic date for the Song in *Romance, She Wrote: A Hermeneutical Essay on Song of Songs* (Harrisburg, Pa.: Trinity Press International, 1998), 194.

47. The importance of recognizing scriptural allusion within the Song is central to my own commentary and also to that of André LaCocque, although we differ fundamentally on the *meaning* of the allusions for a general interpretation of the Song and of any given passage. For LaCocque, the Song is a declaration of purely personal devotion, and moreover, "a critique of the [sexual] mores of conformist societies" (ibid., 7).

48. In focusing on the woman's identity in this essay, I bracket here the question of the man's identity, a complex issue to which I give some attention in my commentary. Likely the identities of both man and woman are multifaceted in the Song, and their

love points to the "ecology of blessing" (Hardy and Ford, *Praising and Knowing God*, 82) operating at many levels, including the mutual devotion that obtains between God and Israel. So the man may, at moments, speak for and image God, Jerusalem's passionate divine Lover (see especially Isaiah 54). Nonetheless, since his physical and emotional identity with the woman is so close, he may also participate in her identification with Jerusalem.

49. The intended *shalom* of Jerusalem is instantiated in the person of Melchizedek, king of Salem, who, in the first act of peacemaking reported in the Bible, pronounces blessing upon Abraham (Gen. 14:18–24).

50. As J. Cheryl Exum notes, the participle *môṣ'ēt* may be taken as either a *qal* form of the root *m-ṣ-'*, "find," or a *hip'il* form of the root *y-ṣ-'*, "bring forth"; see Exum, *Song of Songs: A Commentary* (Louisville: Westminster John Knox, 2005), 258–59. My translation, "makes", allows for either possibility, although it inclines toward the latter, more proactive sense.

51. Although the hapax *lĕtalpîyôt* remains enigmatic, Ariel Bloch raises serious objections to the common rendering, "in courses"; he suggests an adverbial sense, "in perfection." See Ariel Bloch and Chana Bloch, *The Song of Songs* (New York: Random House, 1995), 170–72. While David is said to have fortified Jerusalem (2 Sam. 5:9), no specific "tower of David" is known from the Iron Age or the postexilic period; the present structure known by that name was constructed by Herod the Great.

52. Edith McEwan Humphrey, *The Ladies and the Cities: Transformation and Apocalyptic Identity in Joseph and Aseneth, 4 Ezra, the Apocalypse, and The Shepherd of Hermas* (Sheffield: Sheffield Academic, 1995), 20–21 (emphasis mine).

53. On the use of this imagery in Revelation, see Barbara Rossing, *The Choice Between Two Cities: Whore, Bride, and Empire in the Apocalypse*, Harvard Theological Studies 48 (Harrisburg, Pa.: Trinity Press International, 1999).

54. Exum connects the root *g-l-š* with Ugaritic *g-l-ṯ*, "to flow in waves" (*Song of Songs*, 153); similarly, see Bloch and Bloch, *Song of Songs*, 169.

55. Heshbon figures in biblical history as the capital city of the Amorites (Num. 21:25–30). Similarly, Tirza (Song 6:4) is the predynastic capital of the northern kingdom of Israel.

56. Ellen Bernstein, "The Natural Intelligence of the Song of Songs" (MA thesis, Hebrew College, 2006), 41.

57. Francis Landy, *Paradoxes of Paradise: Identity and Difference in the Song of Songs* (Sheffield: Almond, 1983), 27.

58. Martin Hengel, *Judaism and Hellenism: Studies in their Encounter in Palestine during the Early Hellenistic Period*, vol. 1 (Philadelphia: Fortress, 1974), 45. Hengel sees references to Jericho's balsam plantations in Song 5:13; 6:2; and 8:14. On the privatization of Judean agriculture in the fifth century, see also Choon-Leong Seow, "The Social World of Ecclesiastes," in *Scribes, Sages, and Seers: The Sages in the Eastern Mediterranean World*, ed. Leo G. Perdue (Göttingen: Vandenhoeck & Ruprecht, in press).

59. Hengel, *Judaism and Hellenism*, 43.

60. Ibid., 41, 50.

61. Ibid., 53.

62. Although her focus is on "nature imagery" in the Song rather than on agrarian concerns, Carole R. Fontaine observes: "We cannot think of the 'family farm' in the

Song without noting the somewhat hostile acquisitiveness with which the royals of the city seem to eye it and those who keep it." Fontaine, "'Go Forth into the Fields': An Earth-Centered Reading of the Song of Songs," in *The Earth Story in Wisdom Traditions*, ed. Norman C. Habel and Shirley Wurst (Sheffield/Cleveland: Sheffield Academic/Pilgrim, 2001), 129.

63. Berry, *Unsettling of America*, 119.

64. Ibid., 120.

65. Ibid., 123–24 (emphasis original).

66. T. J. Gorringe, *A Theology of the Built Environment* (Cambridge: Cambridge University Press, 2002), 140 (emphasis original).

67. Rebecca Solnit, "Detroit Arcadia," *Harper's Magazine* (July 2007) 66–67.

68. Cited by Solnit, "Detroit Arcadia," 72.

69. Lawson, *City Bountiful*, 23–26.

70. Information on these and other programs is available at http://www.detroitagriculture.org.

71. Grace Lee Boggs, "One Thing Leads to Another: Cooperative Developments in Urban Communities," address to the Michigan Alliance of Cooperatives, October 20, 2000; http://www.uvm.edu/giee/ESDA/gbspeech.html.

72. George Matovu, regional director of the Municipal Development Partnership in Tanzania, observes: "Once national and municipal leaders understood the on-the-ground reality of urban agriculture, they were convinced of its economic value – especially for poor families and women" (Halweil and Nierenberg, "Farming the Cities," 63). Tanzanian women who farm may make two to three times the income of their husbands. Halweil and Nierenberg note that in Villa María del Triunfo in Peru, 83% of urban farmers are women; the municipality has established a program to create and support community and family farming on formerly vacant lots (61).

73. Janice E. Perlman with Molly O'Meara Sheehan, "Fighting Poverty and Environmental Injustice in Cities," in Starke, *2007 State of the World*, 174.

74. Many emend the text to read, "Your builder(s) shall rejoice over you" (cf. Ps. 147:2), presumably because the idea of children "husbanding" the land seems incestuous. Yet the foregoing discussion of the analogy between farming and marriage suggests that the received Hebrew text makes good (agrarian) sense.

POSTSCRIPT

1. Masanobu Fukuoka, *The One-Straw Revolution: An Introduction to Natural Farming*, ed. Larry Korn (Emmaus, Pa.: Rodale, 1978), 25–26.

Scripture Index

Brackets indicate English references where English versification differs from the Hebrew (Masoretic Text).

Index